MW01474141

Why Feminism Matters

Also by Kath Woodward

EMBODIED SPORTING PRACTICES
SOCIAL SCIENCES: The Big Issues
BOXING, IDENTITY AND MASCULINITY: The 'I' of the Tiger
UNDERSTANDING IDENTITY
QUESTIONS OF IDENTITY (*edited*)
THE NATURAL AND THE SOCIAL: Uncertainty, Risk and Change (*co-edited*)
IDENTITY AND DIFFERENCE (*edited*)
THE GENDERED CYBORG (*co-edited*)

Also by Sophie Woodward

WHY WOMEN WEAR WHAT THEY WEAR

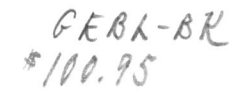

Why Feminism Matters
Feminism Lost and Found

Kath Woodward
Open University, UK

and

Sophie Woodward
University of Manchester, UK

palgrave
macmillan

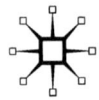

© Kath Woodward and Sophie Woodward 2009

All rights reserved. No reproduction, copy or transmission of this publication may be made without written permission.

No portion of this publication may be reproduced, copied or transmitted save with written permission or in accordance with the provisions of the Copyright, Designs and Patents Act 1988, or under the terms of any licence permitting limited copying issued by the Copyright Licensing Agency, Saffron House, 6-10 Kirby Street, London EC1N 8TS.

Any person who does any unauthorized act in relation to this publication may be liable to criminal prosecution and civil claims for damages.

The authors have asserted their rights to be identified as the authors of this work in accordance with the Copyright, Designs and Patents Act 1988.

First published 2009 by
PALGRAVE MACMILLAN

Palgrave Macmillan in the UK is an imprint of Macmillan Publishers Limited, registered in England, company number 785998, of Houndmills, Basingstoke, Hampshire RG21 6XS.

Palgrave Macmillan in the US is a division of St Martin's Press LLC, 175 Fifth Avenue, New York, NY 10010.

Palgrave Macmillan is the global academic imprint of the above companies and has companies and representatives throughout the world.

Palgrave® and Macmillan® are registered trademarks in the United States, the United Kingdom, Europe and other countries.

ISBN-13: 978–0–230–21619–8 hardback

This book is printed on paper suitable for recycling and made from fully managed and sustained forest sources. Logging, pulping and manufacturing processes are expected to conform to the environmental regulations of the country of origin.

A catalogue record for this book is available from the British Library.

A catalog record for this book is available from the Library of Congress.

10 9 8 7 6 5 4 3 2 1
18 17 16 15 14 13 12 11 10 09

Transferred to Digital Printing in 2010

To mothers and daughters

Kath would like to thank Sophie for the experience and all her support in writing this book as well as her technical help; I may have given birth to a cyborg.

Sophie would like to thank Kath for the conversations, sharing great ideas and the fine lunches, and Simeon for his support and patience during the at times frantic writing.

To our family Steve, Richard, Tamsin and Jack, and Kath's sister Sarah

Contents

Introduction: Opening up the Debate 1
1 Contemporary Voices: Starting Out 12
2 I Said, She Said, We Said 35
3 The Promise of Technoscience 58
4 A Grown-up Politics of Difference 85
5 Visibility and Invisibility, Silence, Absences 111
6 Material Bodies: Bodies as Situations 136
7 Conclusion 161

Appendix 173
References 175
Index 189

Introduction: Opening up the Debate

We are two people but related, as mother and daughter – Sophie is the youngest of Kath's four children – and through our involvement and interest in feminism. We come from different generational positions and life experiences from which we seek to engage in a cross-generational dialogue about feminism and acknowledge and draw on our own situated experiences. We are not only related to each other, but each of us has a relationship with feminist ideas and the women's movement, which we aim to bring together in this book, a project that arises from conversations between us. This book is a continuation of this engagement. Our aim is to open up and continue the debates started by others (e.g. Henry, 2004; Gillis, Mumford and Howie, 2007). In doing so, we are attempting to buck the trend of much writing that can be categorised as 'third wave', which would entail positioning Kath's experiences in opposition to Sophie's. In contrast, through a series of conversations, we aim to chart both the commonalities and the divergences in different historical moments of feminism. We are not attempting to elide the differences between us, and this is evidenced in how the book is written. Where the example or experience arises from one of us individually we write as I-Sophie or I-Kath; when it is something we both argue and write together, we write as 'we'. We are therefore attempting to situate the 'we' and to explore the possibilities of cross-generational authorship. Thus our co-authorship is constitutive of the dialogue in which we are engaged, and the points of convergence as well as difference, ambiguities and contradictions which are part of the genealogy of feminist ideas and practices.

We both currently work in UK universities and share some disciplinary concerns. Kath is a sociologist and Sophie trained as an anthropologist and previously works in a fashion and design department. What we have found through writing this book is that our strongest area of interest and commonality, apart from our tie of kinship, is a commitment to exploring the relevance of feminism today. We both feel that this is a timely intervention in a field characterised by linear narratives of waves and alternatives and the constant reiteration of 'post-'. 'Post-' implies that something has been replaced, or even lost, and it is our intention to revisit what can be found, reclaimed and reconstituted while still retaining all the creativities of postmodernist and poststructuralist feminism.

Informal discussions between us have crystallised around particular experiences, including instances of unequal gender differences and even misogyny as represented in the media and popular culture and often expressed routinely in everyday life, as well as more academic examples of reading particular feminist texts. The contemporary status and relevance of feminism has often underpinned these conversations. Our participation in teaching and research has frequently been the trigger for such reflections. One such moment occurred when I-Sophie was carrying out an ethnographic research project into how women choose their clothing from their wardrobe in order to interrogate the construction of the self though material culture. In a research seminar where the methodology was being presented, the question 'what is a woman?' was posed. Following on from this was, perhaps unsurprisingly, a discussion informed by the concerns of poststructuralists, especially in the wake of Judith Butler's critiques of the early 1990s, over whether the use of the word 'woman' is problematic in terms of those it excludes, and indeed whether the category woman is meaningful or politically useful at all. This discussion occurred prior to the fieldwork; however, when the fieldwork did take place, none of the participants ever questioned their identity as women. They may have found their femininity problematic, but their existence as women was unquestioned. There is a clear disconnect between questioning the meaningfulness of the category woman in academic poststructuralist feminism and what is experienced by many women on an everyday basis.

This discrepancy was also marked in another question that I-Sophie encountered in the initial seminar when the methodology was presented and in subsequent presentations of the work: 'Why are you looking at women?' No one else had to justify their research topic. This may in part be due to the anthropological focus on the unusual or exotic, yet it also raises the ways in which looking at women is somehow seen as archaic, out of date or unnecessary. This example is one that we have discussed together on numerous occasions and it raises many of the core issues of this book. It highlights the problematic separation between academia and the everyday experiences of women, and the dissatisfaction that each of us has felt at conferences or in reading academic texts, where the languages of feminism often do not resonate with findings from our own empirical work.

In many ways the experience of feminism in the academy, although problematic, was very different in the 1980s and early 1990s. On the one hand, there was a marginalisation of the burgeoning discipline of what was then called women's studies and some resistance from established hierarchies of higher education, but, on the other hand, especially among students encountering feminist ideas for the first time, there was an enormous exhilaration at being permitted both to speak as a woman and to hear other women's voices detailing women's contributions historically and valuing women's experience in public and private life, as well as accessing explanatory frameworks and theories through which they could make sense of these experiences. I-Kath recalls one pedagogic strategy at the time, which attempted to link the personal and the political, whereby teachers who called themselves feminists recounted the moment at which they made this identification. In a kind of feminist moment of interpellation (Althusser, 1971), these narratives were used to link personal experience to feminism as a set of diverse political positions, each of which included a recognition (not misrecognition) of women as a collective category. In what was then called women's education and in women's studies in the academy, as well as in feminist activism, the second wave, although sometimes characterised by oversimplification and over-enthusiasm, was marked by engagement with inextricable links between the personal and the political, a key element in feminism which might get lost in the further deconstruction of woman as a speaking subject and women as political agents.

This book is about feminist theories and as such much of our focus is on education and the academy, which have been important in our own experience. I-Sophie teaches as a feminist, but not a course in feminism, which raises questions about the ways in which young women are able to change their minds. As hooks (2003) notes about teaching more widely, it is a means of consciousness-raising. In I-Sophie's experience in the twenty-first century, numerous young women in higher education do end up writing their dissertations on topics related to feminism, and as such it is evident that they start to change their minds and become aware of the gendering of difference and are critical of the world around them.

Whether to use the 'f' word is still contentious and many women say, 'I'm not a feminist but...'. It has long been troubling, but now that it has been made possible through the women's movement, it seems particularly worrying that so many young women avoid it and that even the identification with woman might be lost. I-Kath's mother (I-Sophie's grandmother) would not have called herself a feminist but was committed to women's rights and women's education, having studied science at university in the 1930s and subsequently been committed to her daughters achieving the best they could in higher education. Although she did not use the label, she was someone from a working-class family of five children, who had managed to gain access to higher education at a time when this was impossible for the vast majority of women (and men).

I-Kath taught 'return to learn' courses for women and fledgling women's studies in the late 1970s and early 1980s in what were then called extramural or continuing education departments, when it was possible to run university-level courses in the liberal educational tradition of an interest in the subject and in ideas and not necessarily measurable in terms of qualifications. In the 1980s, 1990s and through to 2005 I-Kath taught women's studies courses at undergraduate and postgraduate levels. By 2005, a UK university which had led the way in the early 1980s decided that women's studies had been mainstreamed and student recruitment would not warrant the continuance of such courses even at masters' level. Women's studies in the 1980s were new, innovative and challenging. Such courses might have been seen as threatening to what was called the malestream (Daly, 1979) patriarchal establishment, but for the (mainly) women who studied them and for those who taught them, they were often life-transforming through their validation of women's experiences and intimate and private social worlds. The first undergraduate course I-Kath taught in women's studies was a second-year module called 'The Changing Experience of Women', which did indeed focus on change and its possibilities for women, by putting 'herstories' into history. There may have been a naivety about some of the debates, especially those which reflected the wider sphere of feminist political action about men's inclusion in or exclusion from women's studies course, suggesting a gender-simplified binary, but this was a particular strategic strength. Putting gender on the agenda made some gender inequalities apparent and provided women with a vocabulary in which they could express their own situated view of the world as well as exposing the limitations of the so-called gender neutrality of both the academy and of everyday life. Students of women's studies began to realise that much of what passed for objective knowledge was indeed gender-specific and heavily weighted in favour of a patriarchal social system. Many students in the 1980s would not have called themselves feminists, but they were receptive to feminist contributions to knowledge and ways of understanding the world. Feminism, like left-wing politics in Europe in the late 1960s, was marked by factions and sectarian disagreements (latterly taught as 'different strands of feminism'), but the major contribution of women's studies was to put women's lives and experiences on the map and in the public arena of debate, thus suggesting that gender matters, there are unequal gender weightings and that change is possible. The impact of women's studies and the link between pedagogy, research, the academy and activism are also illustrative of the politicising nature of education, but have become more utilitarian and functional in times of economic recession, and have been marginalised and underplayed. However, our aim is to explore the impact, not only of markets but of feminist theoretical developments on what could be seen as the disarticulation of feminism and the dissociation of theory, form, practice and lived experience (McRobbie, 2008).

These issues have been raised in many third-wave texts (Baumgardner and Richards, 2000), which discuss the separation between activism and academic feminism (often expressing hostility towards the latter, as the former is seen as more 'real'). What is interesting is that, often, within these third-wave texts, in promoting activist feminism, hostility towards the second wave of feminism can still be found. Third-wave feminism often defines itself as encouraging feminist activism (Dicker and Piepmeier, 2003) or as considering the very personal stories and experiences of the women (Tzintzun, 2002) as they problematise the category of woman and of what it means to be a feminist. This is often defined in opposition to poststructuralist feminism, which has come to dominate academic feminism, especially the development of theoretical positions. Despite the opacity of the language of poststructuralist feminism and the apparent contrast to accounts within the third wave which are written often as a personal narrative, they are unified, in many instances, in their relation to second-wave feminism. Both pit themselves against the supposed simplicity of second-wave feminism and see themselves as more 'knowing'.

The conversations in this book present an exchange between different feminist moments and theoretical positions, rather than a linear narrative. The story of feminist writers has been constructed as a conventional history, which is told as a series of events in a linear chronology, whether this is in the form of edited collections of key texts (Jackson and Scott, 2001; Letherby and Marchbank 2007; Richardson and Robinson, 2008), or as a personalised narrative (Oakley, 2006; Segal

2007). Each event becomes explicable only when seen in the context of what precedes it, and its significance is seen through what comes after. The feminist chronology has been subdivided into the first-wave movement of the political activism of the suffragettes, the post-second world war second wave, itself divided into liberal, radical, socialist and black feminisms, and, in recent years, what is controversially discussed as 'post-feminism'. This trajectory is punctuated by a series of defining moments and texts, from Simone de Beauvoir's *Second Sex* to Betty Friedan's *Feminine Mystique* and Germaine Greer's *Female Eunuch*, Shulamith Firestone's *Dialectic of Sex*, Mary Daly's *Gyn/ecology*, Adrienne Rich's *Of Woman Born* to Judith Butler's *Gender Trouble* and *Bodies that Matter*, among so many others. This book argues that these represent multiplicities of interrelated feminist perspectives which are constitutive of contemporary feminist theorising. By interrogating the links between popular cultural representations, political activism and feminist theorising, this book aims to reclaim what has been lost, and in doing so offer a new perspective on the type of feminism that is needed now, to engage with the current 'post-feminist' climate. We therefore intend to build on writers such as Gillis, Howie and Munford (2007), who point towards the need for cross-generational discussions.

This is not just an intellectual conceit, but arises from a sense that this is what is needed in order to address the issues that matter to feminism today. What has emerged from conversations between the two of us is that many of the concerns or ideas of second-wave feminism are still very relevant and pertinent to today. The debates of the second wave were closely imbricated with political activism and campaigns, which frequently centred on women's rights – the right to equal pay, participation in public and political life, recognition of women's unpaid labour, the right to determine our own sexuality, reproductive rights, sometimes to control fertility through contraception and abortion, and in other instances the right to access fertility treatment. Many of these rights focused on control over our bodies and they were contentious. In the 1980s there was already considerable debate about the ethnocentrism of earlier feminism and the need to encompass diversity and the experience of women across the globe (Anthias and Yuval Davis, 1989). Some feminist scholars saw diversity as a strength and argued that 'we should embrace as a fruitful ground of inquiry the fractured identities that modern life creates Black feminist, socialist feminist, women of colour and so on' (Harding, 1986: 28). In supporting a feminist standpoint theory, Harding argued for the 'exhilaration felt in differences in women's perceptions of who we are and of appropriate politics for navigating through our daily social relations' (1986: 163). Our questions relate to how far this is possible, or whether Harding's optimism is unfounded. Questions are also raised about the importance of some identification with woman or women, which underpins Harding's approach and whether these ideas are feasible any more.

Approaches to the private sphere have also been oppositional. Some of the most influential authors of the second wave seemed to be retracting their earlier critiques of patriarchy as located within the home and family and arguing for a celebration of the domestic sphere or at least a reflection on the positive aspects of childrearing and home-making (Friedan, 1981; Greer, 1985), which may have led to somewhat unhappy alliances between feminists and the conservative right. Debates over pornography also polarised feminist activists, with radical feminists pointing to the gender-specific exploitation of women rooted in patriarchy (Kappeler, 1986; Dworkin and MacKinnnon, 1988) and Marxist and socialist feminists arguing that a capitalist pursuit of profit was the foundation of such exploitation. Feminists have also taken very different positions on prostitution, with those who sought legal intervention to curtail prostitution being accused of failing to support those women who engage in this work and sought recognition, protection and acceptance rather than what they saw as patronisation. Different configurations of feminist political and theoretical approaches were often polarised within the same framework drawn from a nineteenth-century focus on the regulation of women and the health risks they were seen to pose, rather than their male clients as the main offenders. Second-wave feminism was neither a homogeneous set of theories and practices nor a compartmentalised and discrete discursive field. It is our aim here to review the relationship between different feminisms and explore some of the intersections between what have been called waves.

This book thus aims to bridge some of the concerns of second- and third-wave feminism (something found in Henry, 2004; Gubar, 2005; Segal, 2008), and also between academic theory and an understanding of the concerns of women on an everyday level. We wish to draw on the problematising and awareness of diversity that recent feminist theory raises, yet not allow this to lead to a fragmentation of what feminism is. This is evidenced in the way that this book is written: as two separate individuals (I-Sophie and I-Kath) who, through dialogue, also write as 'we'. Writing in this way, we argue, is one of the best ways forward for feminist thinking, as a means that allows for difference, yet also suggests the possibility of a 'we'. This is not just a question of how we write or of methodology, but is core to the theory of this book, as we are centring on reclaiming the category woman as one that is clearly meaningful in the world today. At the same time, this category can be one that incorporates and allows for difference. This approach also encompasses feminist concerns with the interconnections between the personal and the political and adopts a situated methodology resonant of some aspects of standpoint theory (Harding, 1986), which acknowledges the situatedness of the researcher in the co-production of knowledge (Letherby and Marchbank, 2007).

The debates explored in this book arise from encounters with different texts, including those found in popular culture and experiences as well as the genealogy of feminist theorising. Themes and issues that emerged in earlier feminist debates and in feminist politics still inform more recent work. The first of these which we identify is the question of silence, which has been articulated in many different ways through the history of feminist thinking, from analyses of the exclusion of women's voices and images and of women as active persons, especially sexual persons and as mothers, from western culture, and as manifested in the edifice of psychoanalytic thinking, especially based on Sigmund Freud and Jacques Lacan, which draws on Greek mythology to reinstate femininity as lack (Irigaray, 1991). Women have been absent from public life in the empirical phenomenon of being 'hidden from history' (Rowbotham, 1974), for example, as the rational individuals constituted by the Enlightenment and as active participants in public life. Friedan also identified a particular version of silence in the 'problem with no name' which has been invoked by feminist linguistic theorists (Cameron, 1992, 2006) and explored much more widely by feminisms that embrace a psychoanalytic and psychosocial dimension, for example, in the work of Luce Irigaray, Julie Kristeva and Hélène Cixous. Silence, absence and the 'problem with no name' are themes we explore and revisit.

Second, our discussion is informed by a re-examination of power in light of Foucauldian and post-Foucauldian critiques, which have been embraced by feminists (Butler, 1990, 1993; Grosz, 1994; McNay, 2000). Many of the feminist thinkers whose work is at the intersection of different feminisms have acknowledged some of the excesses of the discursive turn, notably Butler and Grosz, who have sought redress in combining psychoanalytic thought with post-Foucauldian analysis and with different materialities, including embodiment and the issue of bodies, something we also address in this book. However, some of the diffusion of power through myriad micro-practices in this discursive may have displaced some of the sources identified by earlier feminist analyses, which, despite focusing on patriarchy, a concept much more infrequently cited in the third wave, retain some complexity (Nicholson, 1984; Maguire, 1985; Phillips, 1987; Thiele, [1987] 1992; Ramazanoğlu, 1989).

Another aspect of increasing abandonment of conceptualisations of the source of power, notably at any extra-discursive site, in the move away from what was called second-wave feminism, is the destabilisation of the category woman and the implications this has had for feminist political projects and activism. The problem of the extent to which decentring and disarticulation of the subject woman and the collective women has gone and which can be seen to be threatening feminist politics underpins much of our discussion. It takes different paths, for example, through feminist phenomenology and Toril Moi's revisiting of de Beauvoir's work and through a rethinking of bodies and embodiment in light of the impact of the transformative influences of technoscience, as in Donna Haraway's work and Rosi Braidotti's reworking of Irigaray's politics of difference in relation to Deleuzian accounts of change and becoming.

These themes intersect and are interwoven through the book in our discussion of a rearticulation of a politics of difference and a twenty-first-century understanding of the combinations of the personal and the political.

Chapter 1, 'Contemporary Voices; Starting Out', opens with the voices of young female students in the UK today, in order to lay the ground for the debates with which the book engages. Students are considered here as illustrative of young people who are part of a new diasporic constituency in order to explore how they see themselves as affected by feminism and what feminism might mean to them. There is a sense in which battles are seen by these young women as having been won, but there are also concerns with routine as well as more serious inequalities. Their relationship to popular culture is a particular focus and allows us to set the context for our discussion of the status of feminism in the twenty-first century. It also raises the problematic relationship between the academy, more popular cultural forms of expression and lived experience. These everyday experiences are considered in relation to feminist activism today and what has been termed third-wave feminism (Baumgardner and Richards, 2000) and its relationship to the more problematic arena of post-feminism (McRobbie, 2008). This chapter sets the context for rethinking feminism across generations in a world in which there are opportunities for but also resistances to change, exposure of women bodies in an unprecedented way, and silences, absences and some disquiet among young women, which could constitute a new problem with no name (Friedan, [1963] 2001).

Chapter 2, 'I Said, She Said, We Said', explains the methodological approach adopted in this book in the particular context of co-authorship. We consider the particularities of writing as a mother and daughter and explain the decisions we made about how we are individually and jointly situated in the process. We outline the dialogues that constitute the book and the problems and advantages of writing as an I and as a we, and we outline our method of writing as I-Sophie, I-Kath and as a situated, cross-generational we. Feminist writers have made major contributions to methodological debates and have been concerned with the status of researchers in the production of knowledge (Ramazanoğlu, 1989; Stanley, 1997). In particular, we consider the problems of the generational divide into waves of feminism (Henry, 2004) and look at the techniques offered by different writers who have attempted to bridge this divide (Gubar, 2007; Segal, 2007). The chapter engages with some feminist dilemmas about writing as woman or as women and the relationship between feminist theorists and researchers and the field of research, and what this means for the subject and category woman.

Chapter 3, 'The Promise of Technoscience', takes up questions about the instability of the category woman in the particular context of technological and scientific interventions which might offer opportunities for liberation for women. Embodiment is used as a route into these discussions, as cyberspace is seen to allow for the absence of the body, or technoscience allows for the transgression of boundaries that seemed impermeable, for example, between human and machine as developed by Haraway (1997). We discuss the possibilities for liberation and also the continued inequalities and constraints. The chapter uses examples of web-based communications systems and medical and technoscience interventions. A key example is the field of reproductive technology, which might be claimed to subvert one of the categories most powerfully associated with women: motherhood.

Chapter 4, 'A Grown-up Politics of Difference', engages with feminist debates about equality and difference through a dialogue between different feminist theories and times and with one of the central concerns of the book, which is to develop an argument for a politics of difference. Difference has been one of the most contentious debates within feminism because it invokes tensions between essentialist and non-essentialist positions. We consider the transformations in this debate, and in particular reconsider the emphasis on difference as discussed in Irigaray and Cixous, in light of more recent transformations in liberalism and the third way (Genz, 2006; McRobbie, 2008). This chapter explores some of the routes which feminism has travelled in its relationship with the governance of difference and the implications of feminist politics having been accommodated and absorbed into a neoliberal governance that thus renders it anodyne, routine and ordinary, but less critical.

Chapter 5, 'Visibility and Invisibility, Silence, Absences', focuses on another debate that has been central to feminism and has particular implications for a politics of difference in the twenty-first century. Women may have been hidden from history and motherhood has been an absent presence, but within the language, voice and images of popular culture, women, especially those who are young, physically attractive and sexualised, seem omnipresent. This chapter uses different feminist critiques of visibility, invisibility and silence (e.g. Irigaray, Kristeva and, more recently, Levy and Paul) to explore some of the ways in which the volubility of the contemporary sexualised presence of women masks the silences which an abandonment of the speaking subject and the category woman cannot explain or redress.

Chapter 6, 'Material Bodies: Bodies as Situations', focuses on bodies and embodiment in light of the feminist corporeal turn and the major contributions which feminism has made to debates about bodies and embodiment across generations; and highlights some of the dilemmas which material corporeality poses. We look at the impact of deconstructionism and the disembodied body for a feminist politics of difference. We engage with post-poststructuralist work on the body (with a particular emphasis on Judith Butler) and also phenomenological approaches to the body from de Beauvoir to Moi and Young. We suggest a reconsideration of the intersection of lived experience and discursive regimes by seeing bodies as situations which are also historically situated and contingent.

In the Conclusion, we pick out the themes of the book and its contribution to contemporary debates about the relevance of feminism and in particular of the possibilities of a productive dialogue which has been at its core. Here, we highlight the need for feminism to take a critical stance that involves a re-politicisation of the personal. We argue for a politics of difference that can live with change and embrace its possibilities, and a recovery of some of the exhilaration of discovery and activism within feminist lives and practices that bridge popular culture and the academy and make sense in the twenty-first century.

1
Contemporary Voices: Starting Out

> The fights [of feminism] are over. We just expect things.

> I was walking down my road [at 10:30 in the morning] and these guys started shouting things at me from their car: 'Bitch'; 'Slut'. It happens all the time. Usually it doesn't bother me; you just get used to it.

> I like to wear more feminine clothes, cover up some flesh. I'm sick of the way we [young women] are shown in the media, as if we're all binge-drinking and promiscuous.

These are the voices of three young women in their early twenties and highlight the complexities of how young women position themselves in relationship to feminism. They arise out of a series of informal conversations, interviews and taught seminars with over 100 young women (see Appendix) Their responses range from those who see feminism as a battle that has already been won and is thus of no interest to young women today, to those who actively engage with feminism as something that is of relevance and importance to their daily lives. Their responses all rest on an expectation of gender equality, which in some cases develops into critical awareness and consciousness. It is worth noting that these are largely young women who have been through the pre-university education system in a political and social policy climate of anxiety in many western countries, including the UK, about the underachievement of boys and a crisis of masculinity. Girls' educational success began to surpass boys' in this period (Epstein et al., 1998; Paechter, 1998) and whilst the immediate postwar underachievement of girls, especially in maths, science and technology, warranted limited mainstream alarm, these young women will have been through school in a period of moral panic about the extent to which boys were falling behind.

The focus on students and their opinions at the outset is advantageous in two ways: first, because of the diversity of the student body; and second, because of the ways this allows a consideration of feminist pedagogy. The students discussed in this chapter are different from the middle-class white students that feminism has so often been criticised for representing exclusively. Instead, with widening participation, the opening up of universities to those from more diverse backgrounds and the increased diversity of students attending art and design colleges, this is a very different demographic. They are also doing fashion degrees and as such, fewer are from conventional academic backgrounds. The students do not represent the voices of all young women today; nonetheless they provide a route into starting to see if there are any threads in common with second-wave feminism and how these may be differently inflected in today's context, or if, rather, as some third-wave feminist writing would seem to suggest, it is defined in radical opposition.

The second concern that this allows us to address is that of pedagogy. It is a particularly timely moment to do this, given that the final BA in women's studies in the UK, at London Metropolitan University, where the last twelve students graduated in July 2008, has come to a close. The withdrawal of this degree programme was greeted with a range of responses, some of which were relatively neutral, as was the reporting by the BBC World Service (Women's Studies. 2008). Others framed the debate in the language of irrelevance, with the *Independent* newspaper describing the demise of women's studies in the teaching programme of UK universities as: 'Farewell to "predictable, tiresome and dreary" women's studies' (Lakhani, 2008). This headline raises the spectre of a worthy but boring – and hence outdated – area of study; women's studies is not sexy, and so must be boring and irrelevant. It raises the importance of considering what is happening to this form of teaching. We are not explicitly addressing those courses in women's studies or indeed courses in feminism, but trying to address the interests and concerns of those who do not necessarily explicitly define themselves as feminists. This opens a route into considering how young women may change their minds. Indeed, there is an interesting contrast to the US, where there are currently 700 courses in women's studies. Given that many other analogies between the UK and US are made in terms of the dominance of neoliberalism, the popular media and culture, it highlights the differences between these two sites and raises important questions as to why the US continues to see these courses as important while in the UK they can be seen as 'dreary' and irrelevant.

The context of change: third-wave women

As the writing on third-wave feminism notes, the gains won by feminism are taken for granted by many young women born since 1964 (the 'daughters of feminist privilege', Morgan, [1999] 2004: 59). This sense of 'entitlement' (Findlen, 1995: xii) arises from the perception that the gains made by the activists categorised as part of the 'second wave' form an expected backdrop to young women's lives today. Equal opportunities in education have been won in no small part thanks to the work of feminists who drew attention to the inequities of the postwar curriculum when education was segregated by gender, with a domestic skills focus for girls and technical education for boys and, in the UK, a selective secondary school system with twice as many places in the grammar or technical schools available for the highest achievers in the selection examinations for boys than for girls (Arnot, 1986, Arnot et al., 1999). The opportunity to do well and to aspire to a career as well as educational success is taken for granted among many of these groups of young women.

Writers in the 'third wave' (Walker, 1992; Baumgardner and Richards, 2000) shift the debate to highlight personal experiences of inequalities and the complexity of feminist experiences (Walker, 1995; Women's Studies, 2008). Whereas, for the feminist activists, the victories won by the second wave are seen as incomplete or based on problematic notions of woman, in the cases of post-feminism, the illusion of contemporary gender equality (Tasker and Negra, 2007; McRobbie, 2008) is seen to negate the need for feminism as a political movement or as a label that women can identify with. Although both third-wave and post-feminism define themselves in opposition to each other in many cases, there is still some common ground, notably in the focus on pleasure and choice and the tendency for both to distance themselves from second-wave feminism (e.g. Wolf, 1993), with exceptions such as Heywood and Drake (1997). As Henry (2004) notes, the reduction of feminism to a generational metaphor has a concomitant rejection of the mother's feminism of the second wave within an ideological framework which may acknowledge little of the achievements of this generation of feminists. These debates demonstrate the tensions that are both generational and intellectual. Understandings of feminism remain polarised in many ways and expressed as binaries, both theoretically and in terms of the mother-daughter cross-generational relationship.

The experiences of these young women are located within a new economy, albeit in a global economic recession at the time of writing, but nevertheless a world characterised by the 'knowledge economy' (Giddens, 1990; Castells, 1996; Leadbeater, 1998; Webster, 2002) in which education has been central, as demanded by the exigencies of the growth of global capital (Readings, 1996), as well as through political struggles for the expansion of social and civil rights. Although gender has not been central to most accounts of the global expansion of neoliberal governance with its incorporation of new diasporic subjects of mobile, skilled workers, including women, into global capitalism, education has been a new hub (Castells, 1996), which brings together feminist politics and social and economic change. These coalesce as a new intersection of economy, labour market, culture, education and gender with the achievements of feminist political activism. This is not to overstate the achievements of feminist politics or to underplay the persistence of patriarchal and postcolonial practices of exclusion (Spivak, 1998; Springer, 2002) or the dominance of the economic motor of capitalist economies, but it does provide some context to the voices of young women in education in the twenty-first century.

The struggles for women's rights, however conceptualised, have been long fought. What has been called first-wave feminism was not only concerned with suffrage. Feminists also fought for employment and pension rights, and educational opportunities have always been central to political and social movements that have sought to achieve greater equality. The massive expansion of higher education during the lives of the young women whose voices opened this chapter is the outcome of such struggles, as well as being demanded by the knowledge explosion of the late twentieth century. It was evident in the growth of polytechnics and new universities and a simultaneous expansion of student places. This has meant a significant shift from the elitism and dominance of a white, middle-class, male hierarchy to a much more inclusive promotion of widening participation in the university sector, with gender equality all-pervasive, especially in Scandinavia, although young women have a strong student presence in almost all faculties of HE across most of the western world, and indeed most of the developed world (Danowitz Sagaria, 2007). This is not to suggest that significant hierarchies and pockets of elitism throughout the world do not remain. There are various power geometries in play through the intersection of different dimensions of social exclusion. Racialised, ethnicised and gendered hierarchies and exclusions persist, but HE is a much more diverse place in the twenty-first century than it was in the mid-twentieth.

The advancement of feminist ways of thinking, and especially of feminist activism, made and remade within a changing economy and labour market in the period following the second world war, through the social, political and cultural changes of the 1960s and 1970s (Lewis, 1992), were influential in effecting transformation as well as reflective of these developments; feminism has been constitutive of the social changes that feminist critiques seek to explain and understand.

The role of women's studies

Another aspect of change which contextualises educational experience is the curriculum changes that have been introduced, for example, in the development of women's studies as a serious area of study and its transformation into gender studies through the development of queer theory (Richardson and Robinson, 2008) and ultimate mainstreaming or marginalisation, depending on the perspective on women's studies adopted. In the UK there has been a move from, and decline in, women's studies departments and programmes of study, and gender studies has been incorporated, to embrace the expansion of studies of masculinity and of sexuality. These have deconstructed and challenged normalising heterosexuality and can all be seen to have progressed feminist thinking, yet at the same time, to have resulted in the distancing of feminist theorising from feminist political practice and to decentre and even obliterate the category woman. Some of the criticisms of women's studies in the academy have been framed by its ethnocentricism in relation to the politics of race (Springer, 2002) and in the dominance of particular versions of the western feminist curriculum (Cerwonka, 2008). However, we argue that feminism in its myriad forms has even more relevance in the context of the contact zones of higher education in the twenty-first century, provided feminist theories remain dynamic and responsive to social transformations, by acknowledging and seeking to make sense of the lived experiences of difference. The theoretical shifts that characterise these developments have been very productive, especially in their engagement with questioning ethnocentricity and interrogating whiteness, and an acknowledgement of intersectionality (Yuval Davis, 2003; Brah and Phoenix, 2004). They have, however, also been troubling in their increasingly theoretical removal from routine experiences of inequality and discrimination and failure to engage with political activism, which has at times made feminism complicit with its own dismantling (McRobbie, 2008).

They think it's all over?

In the opening quotes, the sense of feminism being 'over' and no longer needed, and an opposing sense of dissatisfaction with areas of inequality in contemporary life, can be seen to mirror the debates in academic texts between the concerns of those who define themselves as third wave and the problematic terrain of post-feminism. It would, therefore, be very easy to 'read' the responses of these young women through the concerns of third-wave or the post-feminist. Instead, this chapter takes as its starting point the range of concerns and experiences that these young women have and uses them as a route into exploring whether what is written on third-wave and post-feminism adequately accounts for them. As Harris (2001) notes, young women have been the object of academic and public scrutiny. This interest is manifest, either in the fascination with 'girlhood' or when young women are seen as problematic and difficult. By including the discussions, experiences and opinions of a range of young women, many of whom do not explicitly frame themselves as feminist, the chapter focuses as much on the silences and absences as it does on clearly articulated feminist positioning. It raises, and later addresses, the question of whether, in the face of the proliferation of feminist discourses (third-wave, second-wave and post-feminist among them), there is a new 'problem with no name' (Friedan, [1963] 2001).

Ambivalence and messy feminism

What the opening quotes highlight is the disconnection between the statements these young women make – feminism being 'over' or not needed – and the subsequent description of an experience that makes them uncomfortable or that seems unjust. This also indicates the problematic nature of taking what these women say as somehow more 'real' – a tendency that is all too apparent in much third-wave feminism. Indeed, one of the defining features of much of the first ten years of the third wave is the confessional nature of the articles, with collections such as Rebecca Walker's (1995), entitled *To Be Real: Telling the Truth and Changing the Face of Feminism*. These articles aim to highlight the complexities of the lived relations to feminism and its 'lived messiness' (Heywood and Drake, 1997: 8); however, in doing so they have been critiqued for the absence of any theoretical advancement (Gillis, Howie and Mumford, 2007) and in assuming that the personal is political, so failing to interrogate how it is politicised and what implications this has (Gillis and Mumford, 2004).

In contrast, McRobbie's most recent book focuses in particular on young women and how they are positioned in relation to contemporary popular culture and femininity. The empirical focus of her work is popular culture, analysing films such as *Bridget Jones's Diary* and television programmes such as *Sex and the City*. However, in McRobbie's account, there is some slippage between the visibility of popular culture and the textual analysis of these representational systems, and the ways in which young women who constitute much of the audience demonstrate considerable ambivalence in their attitudes. She writes about 'young women' and makes allusions to her students, although there is little sense of what these young women actually think or the differences and complexities of their opinions and stances. Even when she discusses pedagogy, these same young women are almost absent. In doing this, McRobbie makes a strong critique of these contemporary popular cultural forms and the ways in which the post-feminist masquerade is presented, but fails to acknowledge how young women are themselves critical of the popular culture they consume and inhabit. In this book we include some of the experiences and voices of young women in order to highlight the complexities of their relationships to feminism and their experiences and attitudes to their gendered identities. However, we are not attempting to position this as a voice that helps to present a 'realness' or to romanticise the possible authenticity this offers. Instead, we are using these experiences and voices as a route into considering how this can be theorised and understood, and attempt to move past any empirical/theoretical binaries and to develop a more nuanced understanding of the complexities of change that retains political meaning and relevance to lived experience.

Women watching; women represented

One issue that the opening quotes highlight is the often troubling relationship between the label and practices of 'feminism' and the everyday experiences and ideas of these young women. Whilst young women may not define themselves as feminist in many instances, they still express a dissatisfaction and awareness of aspects of their everyday lives which is one of inequality, such as the apparent ordinariness of being called a 'slut', or the lambasting of young women as apathetic and promiscuous in over-sexualised images in the mainstream media. There is a seeming disconnect between the perception of feminism and this dissatisfaction. This points to the need to consider the voices of young women today, or indeed when they are unable to articulate or voice precisely what this discomfort is, and how they experience and position themselves in relation to feminism, media representations of them and their everyday lives. There are clear examples of accounts which bring together the voices of young women and a clear critical perspective and theory, such as Levy (2006), who manages to bridge the academic and the popular. Levy charts the activities of young women as 'female chauvinist pigs'; our book, in contrast, does not attempt to chart one particular group of women or aim to be representative of all young women in the UK today. The young women's comments that open this chapter are taken to suggest possibilities and open up ways of thinking. We are attempting to address the questions: What is feminism today? Does it relate to concerns of previous feminisms? What are young women's concerns? How do the differences in the cultural, economic and political life of these young women impact on their attitudes to feminism? We are looking at young women students as a way into raising and addressing some of the complexities, contradictions and indeed also the coherences, the silences and that which is openly articulated. This ranges from looking at those who explicitly define themselves as feminist and activists, by looking at blogs, websites and feminist networks and addressing what their campaigns are, through to young women who do not self-consciously define themselves as feminists.

I'm not a feminist, but...

One of the core issues that the quotes that opened this chapter raise is the contradiction between the attitudes that young women have and their position in relationship to feminism. When I-Sophie asked a second-year group (all female by coincidence, and the nature of the subject) whether they or any of their friends would call themselves a feminist, almost uniformly the answer was no. When I-Sophie pushed further for the reasons behind this, one response was that it has 'gone beyond that'; another agreed, stating that 'The fights have already been won. We just expect things. Even if some things aren't equal yet, I think that change just has to come over time. We are not prepared to fight for it.' This epitomises the post-feminist stance, seen in media representations such as the television show *Ally McBeal*, where the main protagonist is characterised as wanting the freedom to 'make choices... but does not want... them to impinge on her personal expression' (Gorton, 2007: 214). So, too, many of the students want the benefits of feminism (which are seen as achieved), but are not prepared to be tagged to any of its perceived negative associations. Another student stated that feminism was 'done' here, although they agreed that, in a global sense, it was needed in places like Saudi Arabia. McRobbie (2008) has suggested that neoliberalism has co-opted aspects of feminism through words such as 'choice' so that it appears that there is no need for feminism. In this climate, the possibilities of feminist activities, or the sense that women will identify themselves as feminist, are increasingly unlikely. At the same time, inequality is presented as being 'elsewhere'. This is evident in the attitudes of these young women and also in media outlets where magazines such as *Look*, a weekly for women based on fashion, celebrity and 'real stories', are resonant of the 'triumph over tragedy' narratives of women's magazines in the 1960s and 1970s (Winship, 1987). It always has a section on global stories about women, usually about issues such as female circumcision or women forced into prostitution. These run alongside sections on fashion and celebrity, which are seen to stand for the UK and the 'West' in a reconfiguration of Edward Said's *Orientalism* (1978), with feminism being interpreted in the language of the rational, progressive 'West' and set against an outdated set of earlier practices. This has resonance with George W. Bush and Tony Blair's justification of the war in Afghanistan as motivated by a desire to promote women's rights and freedoms. There is a clear opposition between the supposedly equal and liberated context as opposed to the global context and the inequalities that women are seen to experience, which are always elsewhere.

One interesting case that raises the continuities and divergences between different generations of feminism was of a young woman whose mother worked for the feminist magazine *Spare Rib*, who discussed what feminism meant to her mother's generation and how it has changed. I-Sophie asked her if she would define herself as a feminist and she answered that she wouldn't. This was after the other girls in the room had vociferously denied feminism. She looked almost embarrassed. So I-Sophie asked her why she was doing her dissertation on this topic. She replied that she hated the sexualised images of women in magazines but nevertheless said, 'My mother was a feminist but I'm not'. When pushed further she added, 'I guess it is the word. I don't want to be associated with that.' Her mother's feminist values have been instilled to the extent that there is a continuity in commitment to certain feminist ideals, as this young woman mirrors the position of many young feminists who write not of feminism being 'over', but as part of her cultural upbringing (Baumgardner and Richards, 2000). There is, however, a rejection of the label feminist, even if she expresses attitudes that could be called feminist. On other occasions, this same student was very outspoken on her views on lap dancing, or what she sees as the excessive sexualisation of women in magazines. However, when faced with a room of her contemporaries who denounce feminism she was unable to call herself by that name. The possible reasons for the dissociation with the word feminist has been discussed by Wolf (1993), Walker (1995) and Siegal (1997), and often centre on the associations of the word feminist, in terms of the assumed whiteness of the position (Morgan, 1999), or its association with victimhood (Wolf, 1993), or as Siegal (1997) notes, there is a reactionary fear of the 'radical-lesbian-man-hating-militant stigma'. Instead, the image of the post-feminist as pleasure-embracing and liberated is a more marketable notion. Indeed, as none of the students I-Sophie spoke to had heard of third- wave feminism, the majority of their ideas of what feminism is come from these media stereotypes. As Faludi (1991) notes, the image of the post-feminist (epitomised in films such as *Charlie's Angels* (Gorton, 2007)) is seen as ironic, sexy and liberated, in contrast to that of the feminist, which is characterised as *passé* and unsexy, as is manifest in the media coverage cited above on the demise of women's studies in the UK undergraduate curriculum.

Walker (1995: xxxiii) has a particular take on why the word feminist is disavowed, which is that young women 'have a very different vantage point on the world than that of our foremothers', as the word feminist signifies 'conform[ing] to an identity and way of living that doesn't allow for individuality, complexity, or less than perfect histories'. However, Walker's position only accounts for those familiar with feminist history. Given that the young women I-Sophie talked to were not aware of what third-wave feminism is, or had only a sketchy knowledge of feminism prior to this, it is unlikely that their denial of the term feminist is for the reasons Walker suggests.

There are instances of young women who do, however, call themselves feminist (these tended to be third year students and ones I Sophie talked to individually). One young woman recounted an occasion when she was in a pub with her friends, and there was a flyer for a night called 'Shag'. She was outraged, yet her friends said, 'Relax! Can't you just enjoy yourself?' as if having opinions is 'boring', tying in to the stereotype of the prudish feminist. Another young woman who identifies herself as a feminist openly discussed with friends her opinions on matters such as tabloid page 3 pictures. On one occasion at work, another woman had complained about the calendar a male colleague had pinned on the wall showing semi-naked women. 'It's just because she's a lesbian,' one man joked. The young woman expressed her outrage to me, as she is a lesbian and is known to be so by her colleague. When she challenged him he replied, 'You know I don't mean you, 'cos you're not butch, are you?' What this shows is the way that, in certain contexts, 'lesbian' is equated with 'feminist' and used in a derogatory fashion. Moreover, the stereotype is seen to be somehow operating separately from people you know and actual, everyday experience.

The examples of these two women, who are able and willing to voice their opinions in the face of sexist stereotyping, are rare among the women I-Sophie spoke to; perhaps more typical is the importance of popularity and conformity. There are, in the context of seminars, notable opinion leaders who are able to sway the direction of the debate. This can be both positive and negative, as seen in the case of another second year group. Two very vocal students defined themselves as feminist, and when they sat in seminars together, this was clearly the beginning of a kind of feminist solidarity as each gained confidence in the presence of the other. What this raises is the importance of sharing ideas in the development of critical consciousness. However, in discussing the sharing of ideas, as Louise Shapiro Sanders (2007) notes, it is important not to fall prey to the utopian ideal of the 'safe space' as Kitch suggest (cited in Shapiro Sanders, 2007: 12), where ideas remain unquestioned and unchallenged. Rather, as Shapiro Sanders notes, the sharing of ideas is not only about 'connections' but also 'difference and dissention' (2007: 12). Shapiro Sanders' position can usefully bridge the debate between the assumptions of a shared commonality that much earlier feminism is criticised for, and the opposing tendency towards individualism which is apparent in key third-wave texts (e.g. Baumgardner and Richards, 2001; Johnson, 2002). Indeed, this debate is at the core of the aims of this book: to bridge the divides between second- and third-wave feminism, and indeed consider what the possibilities are for a shared project that still allows for debate, dissent and difference.

The lack of awareness of these young women of many aspects of feminism raises questions about what happens when they are faced with feminist texts and awareness of feminist politics. Do they change their minds? Which texts prompt debate and the challenging of opinions? There are certain key texts and ideas that resonate with many of the students; these include writers such as Germaine Greer and Ariel Levy and the educational video *Dreamworlds* (Jhally, 1995, 2007). As these span the 1970s through to more recent texts, this raises an issue that is core to this book: there is no sense of a feminist past and a feminist present in terms of the ideas. There are many ideas which are still relevant to the lives of young women today, which Greer wrote about in *The Female Eunuch*. Even then the impact that this has on the students and the way they respond is particular and mobilises students in specific ways, as we show in the next two examples of students, and how these books influenced their ideas. One student, who was black British, was doing a dissertation on hip-hop and its links with youth culture. Her interest arose from the fact that this was a youth culture she participated in and a key turning point for her came when she watched *Dreamworlds*, which analyses the content of MTV videos in terms of the depiction of women's bodies (discussed in more detail in chapter 5). Previously, this student had attended lectures on femininity and negative media imagery; however, she had not seen it as connected to her own life and so did not engage with it. When she watched *Dreamworlds*, although the images and videos used are primarily of rock videos rather than hip-hop, this immediately seemed relevant to her. This then became an impetus for her to read feminist texts more widely. When asked, she never explicitly stated why she did not engage with feminist ideas previously; she clearly latches on to feminist ideas in a specific way, when it relates to something she is interested in and is part of her everyday life. This example resonates with discussions over the implicit whiteness of feminism (Lorde, 1978, 1984; hooks, 1984); and one of the key claims of those who call themselves third-wave feminists is that it is characterised by being multiracial (Morgan, [1999] 2004; Hernandez and Rehman, 2002). However, as hooks (2000) has noted, often those who are championed as the public faces of third-wave feminism (Roiphe, 1993; Wolf, 1993; Denfield, 1995) are white, as are those post-feminist icons of success and the *Cosmo* myth that you can really 'have it all'. Hurdis (2002) notes that key texts of the third wave are as guilty as the second wave in their emphasis on privileged white women. This particular student does not discuss her earlier lack of interest and later engagement in terms of whiteness, or indeed her sense of being excluded, but rather that it was through *Dreamworlds* that she first became aware of this. As Morgan ([1999] 2004: 278) notes, 'white women's racism ... may explain the justifiable bad taste the f-word leaves in the mouths of women who are over thirty-five, but for my generation they are abstractions drawn from someone else's history'.

It is important not to assume that non-white students will never prioritise issues relating to their ethnicity. Hurdis (2002), a Korean woman adopted by a white American family, writes from her own experiences that she was often asked to choose to prioritise her ethnicity, gender or class. This clearly resonates with one student I-Sophie taught, who, when selecting which fashion magazine she would do a spread for, was assumed by one of her white lecturers, through the hegemonic assumptions of whiteness, that she would want to write for an Asian magazine because of the colour of her skin. What is important is the intersection of the different parameters of identity and experience, such that they cannot be separated.

What the example of the young woman who did her dissertation on hip-hop and female objectification shows is that *Dreamworlds*, and the later feminist texts she read, changed the way she saw hip-hop videos and in turn herself. This raises something that was apparent in many other instances: that feminist texts can give young women a vocabulary in which to articulate ideas and experiences they had not been able to previously. This is clear in one of the quotes that open this chapter: 'these guys started shouting things at me from their car: "Bitch" "Slut". It happens all the time. Usually it doesn't bother me, you just get used to it.' For this young woman, reading Levy's *Female Chauvinist Pigs* (2006) was a key turning point. At first these comments did not usually bother her she states, but now that she has started reading cross-generational feminist texts such as Greer and Levy, she is aware that this is problematic and even 'wrong'. She no longer stands in silent discomfort, but now is starting to question it. The constant objectification was something that was expected, but now for her this 'invisible' backdrop has become visible. This issue is something that was raised in other examples when girls in a seminar on the gaze said that they liked being looked at, yet added that they hated it if the person was older or unattractive.

This ambivalence is apparent in I-Sophie's previous research (2007) on how women choose what to wear. Women may dress to recruit the gaze as something which makes them feel attractive, yet at the same time it can be disempowering if someone they perceive as sleazy makes an inappropriate comment. This is discussed more extensively in chapter 5 as it is a pivotal issue which emerged many times for the young women whose voices are included in this book: being seen as a sexualised object and the issues of empowerment and disempowerment. It is something that has become an ordinary part of their lives. One young woman stated that when working in a bar she had been asked to undo her top button and show her bra when she was at work. When she refused, she was sacked. The other young women in the seminar concurred that they were regularly expected to dress like this. Most of them did as it 'made life easier'; indeed, it is such an everyday, invisible backdrop to their lives they did not even think to question it. This clear sense of inequality in their everyday experiences is one that is normalised and is in contrast to the wider discourse of equality that is adopted when discussing the possible relevance of feminism in their lives. The rhetoric of equality that has been adopted politically through neoliberalism can therefore also be seen to operate at the level of everyday speech. There is a general assumption by these young women that women have achieved equality in the West, yet at the same time, when they discuss concrete experiences in their lives, it is clear that they experience inequality.

McRobbie's arguments are very instructive in understanding the empty language of equality, yet what also needs to be considered at the level of experience is the question of difference. The language of equality that is utilised and adopted leaves very little space for the articulation of difference. Whilst McRobbie herself critiques the way that the ideals of equality have been co-opted through neoliberal governance, there is little issue of difference that is raised in her work, or indeed of an understanding of patriarchy. The debate over equality and difference is one that has been central to feminist activism and writing throughout its history, over whether feminist politics is based on a desire for equality or whether differences should be acknowledged. This debate will be addressed throughout this book.

Power: now you see it, now you don't

The issue of empowerment is a core one that runs through what the young women talk about. Ordinarily this is related to dressing in a sexualised way. Many of the young women suggest that lap dancing can be seen as empowering as you are being paid to do it, and men are looking at you. There is a constant discussion of 'choice', seen, for example, in the attempt to elicit opinions on their feelings about lap dancing, or even prostitution in some instances, when the young women often stated that it is the sex workers' 'choice'. The issue of 'choice' is one that is central to both third-wave and post-feminism; Naomi Wolf's *Fire with Fire* (1993), which has become central to how the third-wave feminism has been seen, directly identifies itself with 'power feminism' in opposition to what Wolf perceives is the 'victim feminism' of the second wave. She asserts that power feminism involves being 'tolerant of other women's choices about her sexuality. She believes that what each woman does with her body and in her bed is her own business.' This notion of individual choice in many ways characterises the responses of the young women. Wood (2004, cited in Heywood, 2006) notes that choice is an 'empty word', as it has become depoliticised, and used for a wide range of reasons, seemingly uninterrogated. Choice is invoked 'not only for the right to decide whether to terminate a pregnancy, but also for the right to buy all manner of products marketed to women' (Wood, in Heywood, 2006: 423). The illusion of choice is linked to the notion that you can 'have it all', in the language of Helen Gurley Brown (editor of *Cosmopolitan* magazine in the 1980s), especially and more recently reconfigured by the 'psy-discourses' of individualism of the 'me generation' (Rose, 1996). It is as if by stating 'it's my choice' there is no need for further justification. However, the problems with this word become clear when one realises that the same young women who state that lap dancing is an individual 'choice' admit that it is something they are not comfortable with, and indeed would not watch as the environment is 'threatening'.

What emerges from the young women who do engage with feminist texts is that there is still the potential to be empowered by feminism. One young woman did her dissertation on whether women's pleasure is a priority in terms of the selling and representation of sex. She was inspired by Lynne Segal's work on pro-women porn. Therefore, what inspires and interests her is a bridge between second- and third-wave texts. Greer's and Segal's texts are not seen as part of a less knowing past, but as resources that can be used and reinterpreted through the lens of the present. She states that doing a dissertation and research has given her confidence in relationships with men to make her own pleasure a priority. There was a sense that she didn't have this same confidence before. It was apparent from watching television and music videos that women's pleasure is not a priority, and so women do not have the confidence to ask for it as they are too embarrassed.

Speaking difference; finding a voice

What the final example raises is an issue that runs throughout the discussions with these young women. In this last example feminist texts give these young women a language in which to articulate their earlier sense of discomfort. In some cases feminism highlights issues that these women had not thought about before, yet the overwhelming sense was that it gave them the words and ability to recognise and articulate feelings they had nevertheless felt. They also helped to make visible factors which had been previously invisible. In the majority of cases, where the young women had either not encountered feminist texts, or indeed these texts had not resonated with them or been of interest, there is a strong sense that there are things which made them uncomfortable, but they were unable to articulate or understand. Even if, at one level, they disavow the need for feminism, when their experiences are interrogated further, a more complex picture emerges. What this raises is that even in the context of a feminism that 'names' or has named so many of the problems or inequalities that women face, these young women still suffer from a uneasy feeling that they cannot articulate. Findlen (1995: xi) states of second-wave feminism in the 1970s when she was growing up: 'I was not a victim of the problem with no name... naming had become a principal occupation of feminists.' However, what the examples in this chapter and throughout our book show is that despite the proliferation of discourses on feminism, third-wave, post-feminism among many others, these women suffer from a new 'problem with no name' (Friedan, [1963] 2001).

Friedan's seminal text, *The Feminine Mystique*, outlined the feelings that women who were housewives in the 1950s had. These were middle-class American housewives, with husbands, children, sufficient income, yet they suffered from a lack of fulfilment, as they asked themselves, 'Is this it?' Friedan argues that this dissatisfaction is the problem with no name; it is an issue of identity, as these women have no independent self, because they exist through their husband and children ([1963] 2001: 97). They experience feelings of 'purposelessness, non-existence, non-involvement with the world that can be called *anomie*, or lack of identity, or merely felt as the problem that has no name' ([1963] 2001: 267). The context Friedan is talking about is clearly different from that of this book, a time that pre-dates second-wave feminism and centres on the American housewife and the climate of postwar, pro-natalist 'family values'. However, the sense of a dissatisfaction and discomfort that cannot be articulated clearly resonates. In Friedan's analysis of magazines of the period she notes the absence of any discussion of politics or other substantive topics but instead a focus on housewifery. That women are only interested in these topics is, in her analysis, a self-fulfilling prophesy: if this is all that the magazines cover, then this is all the women will read and be interested in. Given the current number of magazines targeted at young women, which revel in the mundane irrelevances of celebrity culture and ideal bodies, the notion that this becomes an unfulfilling cycle that women are interested in clearly has resonance. In Friedan's case the housewife is prevented from 'growing' by such magazines and the expectations of the housewife; young women today are limited from growing if the ideal occupation presented to them is to be a footballer's wife or a lap dancer. Friedan notes one of the key problems is that in her context women are seen as dependants and housewives, whereas prior to that women were seen as human beings with 'limitless potential' ([1963] 2001: 114). When women are seen in this way, there is an attempt to stop anything which is a barrier to this success. Such an argument could be applied today. The presumptions of post-feminism are that women already can 'have it all' as there are supposedly no barriers to success. As such, there are no tangible hurdles to overcome. This does not account for the paradoxical and ambivalent sense that young women may desire to be looked at in a sexualised manner, yet feel uncomfortable when this actually happens. Whilst Friedan is talking about America in the 1950s we find strong parallels, if we compare this to McRobbie's account of the UK today. McRobbie argues that in taking up some of the language of equality, it seems as if feminism is no longer necessary. However, more than this, young women are taught and learn the post-feminist masquerade (McRobbie, 2008) whereby they adopt exaggerated forms of regressive femininity, such as being silly and helpless, yet as this is combined with modern freedoms such as smoking and casual sex, it appears contemporary. It is often the women that enact this silly form of girlishness (or the alternative, the ladette) who are most vocal in their denouncement of feminism and their assertions of equality. There is also a recent striking resurgence of images of the housewife, either through popular media forms such as Nigella Lawson and the image of the domestic goddess or through the resurgence of images imbued with a nostalgia for domestic life, such as Cath Kidston's designer range of floral products and a romanticised construction of domestic living in the twenty-first century, although this is a more recent product. This return to the security of a sentimentalised domestic arena is resonant of the proliferation of domestic magazines such as *Prima* in the 1980s which provided detailed instructions on the creation of household items that the thrifty and creative housewife could make. Although these magazines were very popular, the evidence suggested that very few women actually made the items depicted in the magazines. Instead, they were read as part of a fantasy of domestic life rather than as instruction manuals or trade magazines for women (McKracken, 1989; Woodward, 1997a). There is also an interesting play on the idea of the housewife, through the appropriation of this through alternative popular cultural forms seen, for example, in the many tattoos of the image of the housewife which is, in particular, popular for burlesque stars. There is a clear sense, then, that the image of the housewife is ironic, and the wearing of the kitsch accessories pertaining to the housewife are done so in a supposedly knowing way. However, what we would argue is that this is not always as critical as it seems, as this supposed knowingness often masks a lack of criticism, as there is an emptiness to the parody. The style is adopted, and the term 'irony' is used, with little sense of the original context of the housewife and her life, or indeed that it is being worn in a subversive way. The presentation of a stance as ironic also creates problems in terms of the response or opposition that can be raised. As the ironic is 'knowing' it effectively blocks opposition as it is not being taken seriously; moreover, the presentation of knowingness is one that implies that any critique or opposition to this is naivety or being a 'boring old feminist'.

Even if, as some examples in this chapter have shown, women do experience a sense of inequality in their everyday lives, there is not necessarily any space for them to articulate this feeling in order not to appear naïve and unknowing. Furthermore, often the multiple namings of feminism are not connected to the everyday experiences of many young women as they do not identify with them, or they are obscured by the discourses of post-feminism which are more compatible with consumer culture. This issue is discussed more fully in chapter 5, as it is not just a question of 'naming' and having the words; it is also about issues of visibility and invisibility, silence and absence. The issues of silence and who is allowed to speak, and of what is made visible, raise the place of those who are not made visible, and indeed in patriarchy the constructions of stereotypical forms which women are often positioned to adopt. These can be usefully explored through Irigaray's ideas on silence, absence, visibility and invisibility as her ideas will be utilised to offer an instructive critique of the ubiquity of pornified images in popular culture, which are so visible they become invisible, something young women have to both view and embody.

Feminist activism

The next section of this chapter addresses those who identify themselves as feminist in order to address what feminist activism is today. The majority of writings on contemporary feminist activism concern the US, as many of the most prominent voices who have found an outlet in popular culture have been American writers (with some exceptions, such as Natasha Walters). In the writing on US feminist activism, there is a strong hostility often towards academic discussions, and an attempt to distance the writers from this, seen for example in *Manifesta* (Baumgardner and Richards, 2000) – such that many of their assertions are not based on a critical understanding, but reiterate issues such as 'choice', which are found in uncritical and post-feminist popular media sources. In looking at feminist activism, we want to see how it connects to the core debates in feminism more widely (including historically) and also how this relates to questions that matter to women who do not define themselves as feminist. For ordinary women there is a sense that the battles are being won, which is clearly challenged at the level of those who define themselves as a feminist. The number of feminist blogs makes it clear that feminism is far from dead as is often assumed in popular culture and indeed among the young women that I-Sophe taught. This is apparent in the number of blogs and also when we consider how frequently posts are made and the responses to them. Taking the example of Feministing.com (founded in 2004), one of the most popular US feminist websites, the editorial staff post approximately seven stories a day, which are in turn commented on by visitors to the site. For the week beginning 27 July 2008 1,247 comments were made during that week. The stories on the website focus on the dilemmas faced by younger women, who are clearly the audience and writers on the website. According to statistical data (Alexa online, 2009) Feministing.com has a traffic rank of '43,771'. Contemporary feminist voices are found most prolifically in the form of internet blogs (notably Feministing.com, Bitchphd (2009) and Angryblackbitch (2009) in the US). There is a similar proliferation in the UK, where the sites, though diverse in many ways, are often based on personal experiences and observations, which are the basis for a critique of issues such as the representation of women in the media sources, political articles in magazines and many other issues. Whilst all are clearly characterised by this critique, they need to be seen in relation to post-feminism and popular media sources. An example is on the Feministing site, which explicitly aims to give young women a voice, where the logo is an image of a silhouetted seated female with an exaggerated physique (notable very large breasts). Feministing states that this image is meant to be 'the mudflap girl' (Feministing, 2009), which they have then tried to 'subvert' by having her raise her middle finger. This subversion and use of the middle finger is actually very unclear from the image. Whilst the aims of the site are explicitly feminist there is a clear commonality between this and the ways in which post-feminism adopts sexist imagery and supposedly is ironic and critical of this. Indeed, this is a trend within much feminist activism, seen in the title of the magazine *Bitch*, and also in the use of bitch as a self-ascribed name in several notable feminist blogs (e.g. Bitchphd and Angryblackbitch). Alongside the blogs are sites which are based primarily on the discussion or issues in media sources or political issues, such as on the f word in the UK, which also has links to campaigns.

On one level there seems to be a clear contrast between this form of activism and that which characterised the second wave, often seen in terms of protests and public marches, from Miss World protests to Reclaim the Night. However, these practices still persist and, in the case of the London feminist network, this is both a website with discussion forums and a regular monthly meeting group and also a site where campaigns are mobilised – seen in the example of the recently reinstated Reclaim the Night. I-Sophie have participated in both the London feminist network and also the Sheffield fems (a Sheffield-based feminist network). Therefore, contemporary feminism is both 'global' through internet blogging, national, seen in campaigns like Reclaim the Night, and localised in terms of specific local campaigns, such as the Sheffield feminists' opposition to a Hooters bar opening in the city. Reminiscent of the clashes between second-wave feminist activism and socialist groups, the campaign against the Hooters bar involved clashes between the local socialist groups and the feminist opposition. There is a strong sense that many of the debates that raged in the second wave are still current. This can be seen in terms of the issue of who is included and who is not: whether men should be involved, and increasingly whether trans-gendered individuals should be. Interestingly, the London Feminist Network is women-only, as stated on its website:

> We are a women-only group because we believe it is vital that women have safe and supportive spaces where we can work together politically to campaign for our rights. We are the experts on our own lives and on what it is to be a woman, in all of our various identities, in a society where we do not have equal political representation, where we are disadvantaged and discriminated against simply because we are women.
> (London Feminist Network, 2009)

A different stance is taken by the Sheffield Fems, who state that they are 'primarily a women-only group. As such, we will in general limit participation in our meetings to women *identifying* as women' (Sheffield Fems, 2009). Whilst the meetings I-Sophie went to were men-only or women-only, there is still a clear sense that the group is acknowledging the ways in which the category woman is problematic to them. This problematic category is one that is taken up throughout this book, as we consider how and why it has come to be seen as problematic, and why it remains needed and relevant. The ideas of difference and equality that these debates over inclusion and exlusion raise are addressed specifically in chapter 4, as the debate is widened to consider questions of political rights and exclusions. This involves a consideration of theoretical ideas about what a woman is and the relevance of retaining the notion of collectivities of women, whether strategically as a political category as initiators of action or as constitutive of any feminist projects. These are considered throughout this book in relation to theories of difference and equality (such as Moi, Irigaray and de Beauvoir) and the everyday experiences of women, and the positions of feminist activists.

Current activism includes many of the activities related to gender inequalities and political concerns that resonate with those of earlier feminism. Modes and media of communication may have moved on, but many contemporary projects and protests echo those of the past. This is not surprising given the material inequalities that persist. This is in spite of other significant improvements in women's lives, such as women's participation in education and in the labour market. More women have joined the workforce, but women still occupy only a third of managerial and administrative posts in the developed world; in Africa, Asia and the Pacific the proportion is even lower. Of the 2 billion people living in poverty across the globe, the majority are female. Women's earnings remain significantly lower than men's in spite of equal pay legislation in large parts of the world; in the UK women earn on average 17 per cent less than men (Social Trends, 2009). Running alongside this are the insidious ways in which women are objectified and commoditised by popular culture.

Conclusion

This chapter demonstrates the convergence of concerns between young women in the twenty-first century, as expressed in third-wave texts, and those of earlier generations of feminists. They are differently articulated, for example being expressed with the language of post-feminism and of choice that arises from the dominance of neoliberal politics which are increasingly influential in most parts of the globe, and in the proliferation of introverted concerns with care of the self and individualised projects that are often incorporated into psychoanalytically constituted projects.

Feminism in popular culture may be assumed and post-feminism construed as a feminism that has been achieved so that there are no further struggles to be fought, may be superficially hegemonic, especially in representations of women in the media. However, in this climate, as a political project feminism is still seen as dangerous and even threatening, because it challenges complacency. The voices of the young women quoted in this chapter suggest that feminist battles remain live and have certainly not been won. Young women may be ambivalent about their espousal of feminism and are often negatively influenced by feminism's construction as boring or old-fashioned, but their concerns are often still with the inspirational themes of feminism of the past. Another problem is the increased distancing of contemporary academic feminism from the more routine concerns of everyday exchanges and materialities.

There is still an uneasy understanding that, however liberated western women may appear to be, inequalities are deeply embedded in social, economic and cultural practices and regimes. Feminist struggles for equal pay and reproductive rights may seem to have been won, but women are still sexualised and objectified and feel they lack control over their bodies. The intrusion of irony and parody into the language of feminism may make the identification of inequality in relation to sexuality and embodiment even more difficult to address. Power may be seen to operate diffusely at a time when there is an excess of naming, yet, we would argue, perhaps there is much less understanding. In spite of the apparent diffuseness of power, the twenty-first-century version of the 'problem with no name' might be looking for a source of the power that motivates inequalities.

The observation that women, in their daily lives, and even in the academy, have no difficulty in acknowledging their gendered situations and indeed as speaking as women with some understanding of collective concerns and shared experiences as well as diversity and the multiplicities of difference, is not a naïve, empirical statement. The problem is more about bringing together lived experience of difference with theoretical explanations through which people can make sense of their lives.

In spite of the extent of change, in terms of the citizenship rights that women have won over the last few decades and in the technological advances that have transformed communications systems in ways which women have often turned to their own advantage, there remain inequalities that suggest the continuing relevance of feminism and of a politics of difference; that is a role for feminist ideas and politics that engage with experience and provide a theoretical framework for understanding change as well as continuities. Technological advances can be overstated, but have to be accommodated in twenty-first-century feminism. Indeed, as we demonstrate in this book, feminism has not only been actively involved, but has made some of the most significant contributions to, debates about the impact and implications of technoscience.

The material discussed in this chapter highlights some of the themes which inform the book and provides some of the dialogues between different feminist theories and practices. Contemporary voices pose questions about visibility and invisibility that are both resonant of earlier feminist critiques and contradictory, but nonetheless point to the importance of providing the possibility of speaking as well as being spoken and of seeing as well as being seen, that have long been feminist concerns. The recognition of ambiguities and contradictions does not invalidate a politics that engages with difference; multiplicities demand explanation and the incorporation of difference and diversity into political activism.

This discussion raises some of the problems with which we engage in the following chapters, starting with our experience of writing together, in the context of feminist methodologies that seek to recognise gender as constitutive of a situated self and of situated researchers. By directly addressing the mechanisms through which we are writing this book as a productive dialogue, we aim to develop ideas that have been central to feminist methodologies that aim to combine respect for experience and the relationship between the researcher and the subjects and field of research with an understanding that links politics and theory. As this chapter suggests, feminist theories and approaches have themselves been involved in changing fields of knowledge and understanding and we are attentive to the ways in which feminist theories, along with all producers of knowledge, are complicit in constituting the field. Thus in chapter 2 we are going to consider the processes in which we too are implicated.

2
I Said, She Said, We Said

Speaking and writing as a woman in the academy has come to be seen as problematic in much the same way as the category woman, which has become subject to instability, questions and challenges. Even the statement 'speaking as a woman' seems oddly quaint, as it appears to be making universalising claims. This presents problems for us as co-authors of a text which is also a conversation between two different but related people, who speak from different places at different times, but who wish to speak from a situated position as women. There are questions about the strategies to deploy and the mechanics of which pronouns to use and how troubling these choices might be. If the category of woman has been destabilised and the authorial 'I' decentred, the difficulties in arriving at the decisions that have to be made are both linguistic and political.

We have both had experiences of being questioned about the use of woman and women, when problems have been suggested about either the essentialist qualities of the subject position or of the false universalism it invokes. Evidence of how troubling this is is illustrated by the example we discussed in the introduction, when I-Sophie was at a seminar discussing an empirical research project into women's wardrobes. One member of the group challenged me on the use of the term 'woman' and on the focus of the research on women's lives and wardrobes. Given that the clothing market is clearly demarcated into men's and women's clothing, and that all the women included in the ethnography identified themselves unproblematically as women, this seemed surprising. The seminar, which consisted of people who were self-identified as two men and twenty women, did not translate the self-categorisation of their gender category as men or women into the field of academic understanding. Everyone in the seminar group, except one, agreed with the challenge 'what is a woman?', which served to highlight the distance between academia and lived experience. One member assumed I was unaware of the recent subversion of the category woman in feminist theorising. Even if the actual research into wardrobes emphasised differences among women, the use of the category as a heuristic device was what my colleagues found most worrying. This raises the question of whether undermining the category woman could make it impossible to speak or write as a woman, or about women, because, apparently, use of the word woman involves the denial of diversity and difference and the assertion of a category that is universal and thus not even meaningful.

Conducting research into motherhood, as I-Kath has (Woodward, 1997b, 2003), carries particular difficulties in relation to the category woman within a framework of essentialism, because of the powerful links between motherhood and embodiment and the risk of eliding corporeal experience with biology and biological determinism. Motherhood is also problematic because of the strength of the identifications that are made, which can also be romanticised. Sometimes, concern with finding the right label is a matter of pragmatism, although the anxiety which has been expressed about using 'woman' in a meaningful way, even in relation to motherhood, might be more than inconvenient, so far are these criticisms derived from the academy from both lived experience that they deny the opportunity to express the specificities of that experience. One of I-Kath's PhD students was troubled about how to classify her interviewees in her fieldwork on maternal identities as constituted in the relationship between mothers and midwives. She opted to call the pregnant, birthing and postnatal subjects 'women' and their professional attendants 'midwives'. Several of the 'women' were also midwives, all the midwives happened to be women and many of them were also mothers. Men who work in midwifery are also called midwives and, although some mothers may express a preference for a male or female midwife, this is not the same order of debate as the identification of the mother as a woman. Discussion about the naming and classificatory process highlighted what happens when non-gender-specific terms are used – for example, 'parent' and the absurdity of 'labouring person'. To avoid 'woman' is not to be more inclusive; it is much more than using the word that the subjects would use to describe themselves. In order to address difference and explore the constitution of motherhood, you have to speak the word and accord what people call themselves some substance.

This chapter engages with the problem posed by these experiences, first in relation to the ever-widening gap between academia and experience, and second and specifically, to what it means to write as a woman, as women, about women. We are not alone in addressing this dilemma; it is one that informs feminist debates (e.g. Spivak, 1987; Riley, 1988; Di Stefano, 1990; Braidotti, 1991, 1994; Gatens, 1991; Butler, 1992; Stanley and Wise, 1993; Ramazanoğlu, 1995; Stanley, 1997; Smith 1998). Feminists have suggested the use of different pronouns to encompass different subject positions: the 'I' of personal experience, the 'we' of collectivity, the 'she' of those who are classified as women. This chapter explicitly addresses the issue of how it might be possible to write in a shared dialogic voice; how to write as a 'we' in a way that also recognises both the situatedness of that 'we' (while not eliding it with a universal woman) and also our own positioning as two individuals: I-Sophie and I-Kath.

I-Sophie and I-Kath

In attempting to write as a 'we', as this arose out of a dialogue between us, it is important to acknowledge and explore the individual situatedness of each of us, as this is the place from which the conversations arise. As acknowledged in the introduction, we have lived and experienced different periods of feminism and have lived through different times and places, although we also have a close relationship in terms of ethnicity, class and culture (as well, of course, as the embodied connection of being a mother and a daughter). These biographical specificities are mirrored in the research we have each engaged in, which has been conducted in fields that embrace both the private, intimate domestic arena and the more public spaces of policy-making representation and popular culture. For qualitative, and in particular ethnographic, research the issue of access is central and is particularly pertinent in the case of I-Sophie's research into women's wardrobes. Here, the research was taking place in the most intimate space in the home; the research was around women's wardrobes, as the focus on women was in part due to research and theoretical interests, yet also as a matter of practicality. In order for me to have access to this domain, the participants had to feel comfortable enough to be involved, and I also had to feel comfortable being present in their bedrooms. The research took place in such an intimate space and involved discussions of a very personal nature about how women feel about their bodies, and on occasion watching women getting dressed. The research was engaged in as women and was also made possible by this relationship, as a man doing the research, would have found it difficult to gain such access, or would have then found a very different subsequent research relationship. This is not to obscure the many differences between I-Sophie and the participants; for example, on one occasion, a British-Asian woman I interviewed talked at length about her saris and what it feels like to wear them. This is not an experience that I have had and therefore the position of the researcher as outsider or insider is contingent (Woodward, 2007, 2008). It is also not clear-cut, as even though I had never worn a sari, I was sitting on her bed as she told me about them, peering into her wardrobe as she tried them on in front of me and talked about her concerns over her body. This reinforces Stanley's arguments about the ways in which the position of the researcher can be used to permit research (1997; Stanley and Wise, 1993), as the conversations would not have been the same in a more formal setting, without her trying on the clothes and the physical proximity of the encounter. In this case, there were also many stories that I and my participants shared, such as the despondent trying on of an old item of clothing that no longer fitted an expanded body.

We do not want to romanticise the commonalities of 'we women', which are clearly not always shared. Moreover, the category woman is not always a cosy or easy one to occupy. It is, however, always one that matters at the level of everyday experience and is not one that can therefore be readily disbanded. Instead of attempting to dismantle the category woman and place it in quotation marks, we wish to argue that the gender trouble is not whether this category exists, but often arises from being a woman. For example, when women are sold as sex slaves, sexually assaulted as a weapon of war or otherwise, this arises out of their position as women, and as such no political action can arise from destabilising the category. In the interviews I-Sophie carried out for my research into women's wardrobes, one woman, for example, had recently recovered from breast cancer for which she had needed a partial mastectomy. Her situation arose from being a woman, yet also led her to question her gendered identity, as she had reconstructive breast surgery in order to make her, in her own words, 'feel like a woman again'. This raises the many issues that surround the category woman; for a while she was concerned she would not feel like a proper woman, yet she never questioned whether she was a woman. Moreover, the category woman for her was not a cosy or comfortable space. In spite of these problems, using the word woman still matters, and it is essential to understand what it means to be a woman through her situated experiences. No longer to talk about what it means to be a woman is neither useful nor instructive.

The notion of romanticised commonalities through exclusion is most evident in the case of motherhood, which is both an aspect of the relationship between I-Sophie and I-Kath and a focus of some of I-Kath's research. The insider status of the researcher is manifest through the essentialised embodied experience of motherhood, which might be predicated on a corporeal version of inclusion. Women often do express a preference for a female attendant during childbirth and in the care of their infants (Earle and Letherby, 2005), although such empirically based observations do not have to be underpinned by a romanticised or sentimentalised version of motherhood or a community of 'we women'. The constitution of affect need not be sentimental; the preference could be pragmatic as more women than men do this work, or affective in the expectation that those who have experienced childbirth and a close relationship with a newborn will understand the experiences and their intensity. However, if motherhood is one of the most naturalised fields of research which still invokes a community of 'we women', however discursively (Woodward, 1997b, 2003), sport, boxing in particular, creates networks of masculinity and a community of 'we men', which is nonetheless hardly ever made explicit (Woodward, 2008), except when a woman such as I-Kath researched a gym (2007, 2008) and entered this domain. Ethnographic research into men's boxing is largely carried out by men, who mostly do not explore or reflect on their situated subject positions as men (Sugden, 1996; Wacquant, 1995a, 1995b, 2001, 2004; Beattie, 1997). Participant observation with more participation than observation in sport (Wacquant, 2004), which might take Chicago School ethnography to its limits, has been noted as a tendency by men who do research into masculinity too:

> Qualitative research has its own brand of machismo with its image of the male sociologist bringing back news from the fringes of society, the lower depths, the mean streets.
> (Morgan, 1992: 87)

In sport, women are gendered. It is the gender-neutral World Cup, Open Golf tournament or Test series when men are playing, but marked as the Women's World Cup, Women's Open (or possibly Ladies') Golf tournament or Women's Test when women are participating. Athletics is more egalitarian and democratic in labelling women's and men's competitions, but the normative, ungendered assumption of masculinity in sporting practices is implicated in the sporting culture in which the researcher is immersed. In I-Kath's experience of research at a men's boxing gym, the most effective strategy for accepting a gender-specific position was initially as a white, middle-class woman who had also been involved in making a television programme at the gym, and second, as the research progressed, as an unthreatening (that is, asexual) maternal figure (Woodward, 2004). Although later in the research process this gym did start accepting women boxers, I-Kath's position as a researcher was still marked because of the particularities of this field; women have to be explicit about their gender identity in ways that men do not, in the collusive hegemony of masculinity, which constitutes the culture of sport through a complicity that is co-produced by male researchers (Woodward, 2008). Second-wave feminist studies of motherhood, which celebrated the maternal as associated with women, were subject to criticisms of essentialism and subjective approaches, whereas often male researchers in sport are seen to be immersed in their ethnographic field and thus to gain greater insights.

This is a path that has to be renegotiated between a homogeneity that marginalises differences among women and a heterogeneity that denies women a voice and eliminates sexual difference altogether. One of the major concerns of second-wave critiques of social structures and social divisions was of the relationship between public and private domains (Nicholson, 1984; Pateman and Grosz, 1987) – an intersection which is evident in our research experience, as I-Sophie was in the bedroom watching women choose their clothes in the morning, and I-Kath, was, more recently, in the gym and not in the men's changing room. Nonetheless the insider/outsider complex is much more complicated than the physical space of the research field and in each case gender has been a key determinant of the positioning of the researcher as 'inside' or 'outside'. This inside/outside binary may set up a false dichotomy linked to the similarly deceptive one of objectivity/subjectivity. As Belinda Wheaton (2004) points out, although this is an impossible distinction, the reflection on the process of how these dualisms are constructed can be useful in demonstrating the power relations in play in relation to gender. As feminist standpoint epistemologies have shown, there are power differentials in the research context and between the researcher and the subjects of research. It is about being part of the networks in which it is meaningful to speak as a man or as a woman through some of the shared experiences and vulnerabilities that are part of the gendered histories of those who speak as a man or as a woman.

Can I say something?

Debates about the subject position and especially about the use of the first-person pronoun have been central to critiques of the unified subject of the Enlightenment. Much of the argument has focused on the idea that there is an autonomous self who can speak as 'I' rather than a fragmented subject constituted by diverse social and cultural relations. The use of the first-person pronoun as the speaking subject provides an acknowledgement of experience; it does not necessarily privilege experience at the expense of interpretation or any other mechanism for the exploration of social life. Accounts of experience need not be accepted as a transparent reflection of reality, but such accounts provide a means of capturing what Bev Skeggs calls a way of 'understanding how women occupy the category "women", a category which is classed and raced and produced through power relations and through struggles across different sites in space and time' (1997: 27). Skeggs, however, uses quotation marks as scare quotes, because she is concerned not 'to argue for experience as a foundation for knowledge, a way of revealing or locating true and authentic "woman"' (1997: 27). Skeggs clearly recognises the value of holding on to women's voices as a meaningful source, but does not acknowledge that her subjects do not experience themselves in scare quotes and outside the routine practices of daily life and experience. This might be an example of a feminist theoretical position, which, in espousing the argument for the decentring of the (male) author and speaking subject, also restricts the possibility of the woman as subject, I. Skeggs is still drawing on the second-wave feminist claim that experience is the basis of feminism as a social movement and part of a process through which women, by speaking and acting collectively, were able to make sense of their subject positions and of the connections between the personal and the political.

The unified subject was the elite isolated subject, which is demonstrative of class position and status as a rational, bounded self. Postmodernist critiques have not only deconstructed this subject, but even suggested that it be knocked off its pedestal and displaced as a speaking subject that is embodied in the grammatical subject of the first-person pronoun. This clearly has some advantages for those who have been excluded from this speaking position, if those in the privileged position of the Enlightenment subject have been dethroned. This might offer political opportunities for those who had never been permitted a voice; for example, feminist positions have deconstructed the Enlightenment subject in terms of its presumed white masculinity (Lloyd, 1984; Grimshaw, 1986).

The legacy of critiques of the Enlightenment subject and its subversion by Foucauldian and Derridean deconstructionism opened up the possibilities for allowing a voice for women or other marginalised groups, just as postcolonial critiques demonstrated the ethnocentrism of anthropological accounts, where the author, supposedly academic, neutral and objective, is a man who speaks for the subjects of research (Goldberg and Quayson, 2002). Researchers too are implicated in the processes of making and remaking knowledge, but the notion of the objectivity of the person writing and speaking obscures his (*sic*) privilege and silences those about whom he speaks. Critiques of the Enlightenment subject were based on challenging and destabilising its privilege and elitism, partly through the subsuming of a particular gender, class, ethnic position in the subject I. However, postmodernist feminists, whilst acknowledging these critiques and indeed being part of them, have frequently colluded with another language of elitism and exclusion which distances the academy from experience and materiality from theory. For example, distancing has been manifest in critiques of embodiment which purport to reinstate corporeality but, through a focus on inscription, flows and mobilities, present a very disembodied body (Howson, 2005).

A destabilisation of the first-person pronoun, and especially of its assumed gender, ethnicity and race neutrality, offers opportunities for other voices and for a challenge to the power of those voices. Also, by raising the question of power and authorial power, it introduces a challenge to claims of objectivity which may not always be expressed through the first-person pronoun. This highlights the difference between the author's voice and the 'I'. One of the strategies adopted within the academy especially for dealing with the problem of subjectivity in the partial or even biased viewpoint that is seen to be inherent in the use of the first person has been to adopt the passive voice, because it seems more neutral. This can happen without an agent at all; text is written and meanings made and the *deus ex machina* is never revealed but retains divine authority.

Scholarly writing always used the third-person pronoun or the passive voice; not only were authorial voices almost always male, they were referred to as 'he' even in the limited number of cases when they were female in what purported to be the language of the academy and of objectivity. The author might have been just that; a person without a name. The use of the first-person pronoun became encoded as subjective whilst the third person assumed the epistemic objectivity of dispassionate judgement which informs the subjective/objective binary of a great deal of the academy and was articulated in philosophical thinking through much of the twentieth century (Searle, 1995). It is not surprising that the challenges came from feminist literary critics and writers. Second-wave feminism, building on the insights and challenges of creative thinkers like Carolyn Heilbrun (1989, 1991a) and what has loosely come to be called French feminism, especially in the work of Hélène Cixous (Cixous and Clement, 1986) and Luce Irigaray (1985, in Whitford, 1991), made it possible for women to speak and write as themselves. The debate continues, with accusations of over-subjectification interpreted as bias. But for many women, to be able to write as 'I' was a moment of recognition, a realisation that 'I am that name' (Riley, 1988). In postmodern times when authors have been decentred, it is hard to explain the liberatory feelings that accompanied the realisation that women could speak and write. As Heilbrun described it:

> Before the current women's movement, it was difficult to find a woman's biography of an accomplished woman that was not palpably terrified of making any unseemly claims on behalf of the woman subject. Avoiding large claims was no doubt made easier by the fact that subjects themselves were usually unable to express with full honesty the exemplary meaning of their lives...
> (1991a: 28)

Heilbrun was describing the lives of those women who were sufficiently privileged and advantaged to be literate and to have some access to the public arena of literature, a position which was criticised in feminist accounts (e.g. Jouve, 1991). However, one of the major achievements of second-wave feminism was to acknowledge the voices of women who had been marginalised in fiction (e.g. Walker, 1982; Morrison, 1989), as well as in academic writing (Minogue, 1990; Webster, 1992). Being able to speak in the first person was recognised as liberating, whether in fiction or other art forms. As Morrison said:

> We are the subjects of our own narratives, witnesses to and participants in our own experience, and, in no way coincidentally, in the experiences of those with whom we have come in contact... And you read imaginative literature by and about us is to choose to examine centers of the self and to have the opportunity to compare these centers with the 'raceless' one with whom we are all familiar.
> (1989: 9)

Morrison's first person is a collective subject; her we is not a complacent, privileged author but a first-person plural that demonstrates the power of claiming the right to speak as a woman and from the margins. She claims the right to be a participant in her experience, which reinstates both the speaking subject and the centrality of language at the heart of a feminist project. The personal is political, but this feminist slogan of the second wave retains some of its dangers, many of which are manifest in the third wave. An assertion of the personal which is framed by a bounded individual self as subject can teeter on self-indulgence and some of the more personalised and problematic aspects of identity politics. The I of the nineteenth-century black American Sojourner Truth when she said 'Ain't I a woman too?' was collective and political; a reminder of the importance of a first-person singular pronoun that is political and meaningful and the subject lays claim to being a woman, which is a category she recognises but to which she has been denied access as an enslaved black woman. In the politics of the third wave a differently inflected version of the personal is manifest in a shift from a collective to one that is more individualised. This challenges individualisms, but in the end reinstates them without a critique of power relations.

Feminist analyses of the second wave of the intersection of the personal and the political and their assertion that the personal is political put politics on the agenda and demonstrated the inextricable links between personal and political life. For example, spatially it was argued that the domestic domain was structured by the wider decision-making world, the operations of which were only possible because of the labour of women in the private arena of the home and through their reproductive labour (Davidoff and Hall, 1986). A focus on the personal which was interpreted through women's lived experience and given expression by women's voices and words was framed by an understanding of the power relations in play. More recent decentring and deconstruction within a terrain where power operates diffusely and elusively, whilst purporting to value women's experience, can also fail to identify where power is operating.

Acknowledgement of the subject position of the researcher was a key component of second-wave feminism and central to the production of accountable knowledge (Stanley 1999); knowledge defined as that, which is clearly produced from the social context, and methods used 'written accounts of feminist research should locate the feminist researcher firmly within the activities of her research as an essential feature of what is "feminist" about it' (Stanley, 1990: 12).

There are alternative accounts and knowledge can also be described as socially situated (Haraway, 1991: 188), but the inclusion of situatedness, which acknowledges the researcher as implicated in the processes through which knowledge is produced, can accommodate difference and the political dimensions of research and knowledge production. Although Stanley's reference to 'essential' might set alarm bells ringing about the fixity of the category woman, we suggest that situated research can take on board the necessity of defining the category 'woman' to focus on ontological separations as well as similarities and recognise that while oppression is common, the forms it takes are conditioned by race, age, sexuality and other structural, historical and geographical differences among women.

Feminist methodology always involves some theory of power, but with the increasing distance between feminist theories and women's experience there is a danger that a critique of the source of power will be too elusive and obscured by feminists' denial of a privileged position. Knowledge is not democratic and open to production by all. Feminists acknowledge that they are implicated in its production (Ramazanoğlu and Holland, 2002). There are, of course, options and diverse critique of power, but in order to focus on the situated speaker and the situated I, this approach points to the inseparability of knowledge and experience. We wanted to embrace the specificities of the situatedness of each of us in the personal position from which we seek to speak and the broader social and political arena in which we are working and which situates us.

Writing: I-Sophie and I-Kath

Most academics are familiar with collaborative writing; there are different strategies, separate sections, separate chapters, passing material from one to the other, eschewing the first person altogether or assuming the royal we. The latter is a strategy more likely to be adopted in teaching texts and by politicians, unfortunately one of the most famous of whom was the first and only woman to become prime minister in the UK, Margaret Thatcher, with her announcement that 'we have become a grandmother'. The first-person plural is problematic, but both necessary and useful, as is the first-person singular. 'We' is necessary for practical reasons too. We do not want to obscure a situation in which we are two 'Is', because this book is a dialogue between two times and life courses and there can only be a dialogic we as there are two situated 'Is'.

The rationale for the use of the first person is first, because of its status within feminist histories in relation to putting gender explicitly into the public arena, and second, to situate experience and demonstrate the interconnections between the personal and the political. We propose situated 'Is' rather than the notion of triangulation, which implies an equivalent relationship between author, text and reader. The notion of triangulation therefore obscures power differentials. This, therefore, is a reason to use I. The passive voice obscures who is writing or speaking because the subject is hidden. It is also elitist, as in the everyday world people speak as I, even if in academia they do not. Each of us speaks as an I who is socially and culturally constituted, but within specific and contingent situations. The third-person pronoun presents different issues. Some feminist commentators have adopted the use of she to locate women's experience (Stanley, 1997; Battersby, 1998) as an alternative, gendered strategy for situating experience as specific to women, but distancing it from an excess of subjectivity and deflecting criticism of prioritising embodied gendered positioning that could be construed as essentialist. This is an alternative version that has some purchase but is problematic in the distance it presents between the academy and lived experience. Although Christine Battersby adopts a phenomenological approach, it is largely only academics, even feminist ones, who refer to themselves in the third person as a distancing strategy which might convey greater objectivity or maybe even create a sense of importance for the author. I-Kath noted that Norman Mailer, an exponent of machismo in the literary field, wrote his account of The Ali-Frazier, heavyweight championship boxing fight, 'The Rumble in the Jungle', in Kinshasa in 1974 (Mailer, 1975), as, first Norm, then Norman, and finally Norman Mailer, which I can only imagine was to aggrandise his status (Woodward, 2007). An acknowledgement of the subject position permits its location. Thinking in terms of a speaking subject of enunciation allows the possibility of making clear the choices available to individual speakers and writers and reveals the position they take up in what Kristeva (1982) calls 'the operating consciousness' of representation.

However, having decided to adopt the strategy of identifying the situated speaker as I-Sophie or I-Kath, we found that there were two possibilities: one was to use I-Sophie as the subject but to use it as a name and prioritise the Sophie over the I and present an agreement between subject and verb in the third person, or to privilege the I and to write I-Kath with the agreement in the first person. The examples illustrate our preferences. I-Sophie launched straight into the third person and I-Kath was anxious about verb agreements and because I came first she wanted to conform to the rules of Latinate grammar and use the nominative case. I-Sophie, who is a better classical scholar, but from a different time, adopted the path that we both agreed to follow, as we decided that to use the first person and name was the first most important point and next that the third person agreement made this speaking, writing subject both specifically situated and located within a political, social terrain. (The computer spelling and grammar check preferred the strategy we adopted, presumably because the system opts for proximity and the name adjoins the verb with which it agrees; not an example of feminist cyborgification.)

The adoption of I-Sophie and I-Kath was a practical device in order to accommodate a book written by two people, yet also important theoretically and politically in terms of the aims of this book. Indeed, our device is one that links in closely to the writings of Irigaray in *Je, Tous, Nous*, where she discusses the need to create a space for mothers and daughters which valorises the relationship and does not subsume it in the patriarchal imaginary. One aspect of this she suggests as useful is when women talk to 'create sentences in which I-woman (*je-femme*) talks to you-woman (*tu-femme*)' ([1990] 2007: 43–4). The device we have suggested is an instance of this where we are given an individual identity from which to speak, which validates a distance between us and a specificity of our identities and positioning. This also involves an awareness of the fact that we both speak and write as women and thus there is both a commonality and a difference allowed within this. In writing like this we hope to create a shared voice, yet not one that overrules the possibility for the articulation of the differences between us.

This was important in terms of the actual practice of how we wrote this book, which parts were written separately and which were written together, as we decided that in order to achieve our aims it was important to incorporate both. The first stage was the conversations, as the overall plan for the book and the way we formulated ideas and came up with the chapters all arose verbally. After that, we decided that we would allocate particular chapters for one of us to lead and start writing, then the other would read the (very rough) draft and we would talk about it. This was a useful moment both to construct a shared writing voice and also to acknowledge our points of difference. Following this we would both edit it and rewrite it together. Pragmatism demands that there are sections when the first-person agreement is maintained because of the fluency of the narrative and as part of the continuity of some sections of the book. Thus our use of I is situated rather than implying an equivalence relationship between author, text and reader. We speak and write from the first-person position as an I which is socially and culturally constituted and by situating ourselves as 'I's' we acknowledge the political purpose of the book.

Why the 'we' is important

We are aware of the problems of using 'we'. The first-person plural has been at the heart of critiques of the category woman and its purported universalism in the elision in the language that classifies women as a homogeneous group. 'We' also presupposes shared experience and shared knowledge, which is not there in the academy. Researchers in the field and their subjects of research do not share the same situation in relation to knowledge. The use of 'we' can, of course, be strategic. As Caroline Ramazanoğlu (1989) argued, there is a problem in uniting so diverse a group into a collectivity but nonetheless remains vital as part of a political project. An overemphasis on divisions among women could challenge the political imperatives of feminism, even more so abandonment of a category of women who could speak as a collective 'we' at any point would subvert and destroy the politics of feminism.

The debates over the word 'we' centre on the critiques over presumptions of an identity shared by all women, in particular where this shared identity is presumed to be white, able-bodied and middle-class. With the deconstruction of the category woman that comes with poststructuralism this raises the issue as to where this leaves the possibility for feminist solidarity (Ramazanoğlu, 1989). This is also a problem that characterises third-wave feminism – that it is never seen as a coherent political movement like second-wave feminism was in spite of its divisions, most of which were classified as factions; instead, it is focused on highly localised instances of activism. This debate is often framed by discussions of essentialism, where essentialism is tagged negatively with being too reductive of difference. This is the perilous path that feminisms have had to tread. If feminists claim women have a voice and can occupy a subject position, this is seen to imply essentialism. Feminist standpoint theorists have been criticised for overstating the privileging of women's experience as rooted in essentialism, but this too is a polarisation that distorts an epistemology which foregrounds lived experience (Harding, 1987, 1993). Riley (2005) locates this problem in language and suggests that shared experience can be productive; indeed, what has been vilified as essentialism could be productive. The possibilities for collective action can then be framed in terms of Spivak's 'strategic essentialism' (also discussed in Stone, 2007). Chakraborty makes a case for this in considering the relationships between race and feminism, as she argues that woman is an 'essentially racialised category' (2007: 102). This question of feminist solidarity is considered in this book in particular by discussing the category woman. This question is epistemological and also raises the question of language – that is, the use of the words 'we' and 'I'. The use of we is political because it suggests a collective identity and some sense of agreement or at least points of connection. It does not preclude the possibilities of dissent, yet it does pave the way for a critique.

'We' could express solidarity (as in political campaigns) or it might subsume differences into a collective hegemony that further marginalises those who have been denied a voice of their own. 'We' might suggest a social world of 'we women' in which particular intimacies are inherent, for example, in the domestic sphere or the private, as opposed to the public world of many women's lives or as if the two spheres were separate and distinct. As Janice Winship (1987) wrote in the context of women's magazines, they invoke a security of 'we women' that insulates against the pressures of the public arena. 'We' can also be strategic, of course, as in the case of this book at points where we (*sic*) have agreed about the organisation and structure of the book and its division of labour. 'We' also identifies the co-authors who are speaking to the readers. There are clear critiques of texts which presume a 'we', especially those that focus on women's particular embodied experiences such as childbirth and mothering as many radical or material feminists of the second wave did, whether framed by corporeal, historical or metaphorical constructions of women. Irigaray has been accused of essentialism for foregrounding women's embodied experience and its possibilities for the reworking of language and symbolic systems (Whitford, 1991). In this book, when we are writing as a 'we' this is a 'we' of two people. Although this 'we' is clearly still partial, given that the particular 'we' is based on two individuals who are white, middle-class, British, well-educated, it raises the possibility for inter-generational dialogue and the bringing together of ideas. The possibilities of collective action and this dialogue are what this book is about.

We are arguing that writing as a we is not a peripheral or a coincidental matter, but is in fact pivotal to redressing certain issues that have hindered the advancement of feminist thinking. In particular, we are aiming to think past the opposition of the third and second waves of feminism. We have used the wave classification strategically and as a shorthand for temporalities, but are concerned to question their ultimate usefulness, especially in providing boundaries between different feminist theories and activism. As Astrid Henry notes, referring to the 'third wave' signifies that there is 'not only a resurgence but also includes the notion of progress on from the second wave' (2004: 24). Indeed, this is often seen in the supposed 'knowingness' of feminism now in opposition to an assumed naivety of a feminism that used the term woman. This is seen markedly in the example of poststructural feminism, where, as Henry suggests, this is particularly marked in strands of lesbian feminism, where the alliance with queer theory allows more discussions of fluidity and the inherent assumptions of sophistication. However, as Henry adds, this alliance with men through queer theory moves away from the consideration of women as something that needs to be critiqued. Henry argues that the same charge can be levelled at the seemingly opposing form of post-feminism as it both celebrates heterosexuality and is anti-academic (seen in magazines such as *Bust*).

Post-feminism, third-wave feminism and poststructural feminism are predominantly characterised by the positioning of the second wave as naïve and uncomplicated. As is evidenced in *Catching a Wave* (2003), Dicker and Piepmeier argue that 'we' live in a different world from the second wave and third wave which are 'concerned not simply with "women's issues" but with a broad range of interlocking' issues (2003: 10). Here there is an interesting commonality between the women of the third wave in opposition to the 'they' of the second wave. Indeed, the third wave often defines itself as pro-sex and multi-ethnic, as a critique of the perceived whiteness of the second wave. However, as Henry notes (2004: 32), what this obscures are non-white second-wave feminists. Indeed I-Sophie, well versed in the critiques of the second wave, was surprised when I first saw I-Kath's collection of *Spare Rib* magazines, from the 1970s and early 1980s, which she keeps in her wardrobe, and noted how prominent the discussion of race and accusations of racism were in these magazines.

In the most extreme formulations some writers (e.g. Roiphe, 1993; Denfeld, 1995) are openly hostile to the second wave. Whilst there have been strong academic critiques of these texts, these are all writers who achieved high media profiles and therefore became part of the popular consciousness of young women as they become aware of what feminism is. As Henry has argued, this hostility to the previous wave is often written about it in the language of the mother–daughter relationship. For instance, if one considers Naomi Wolf, in the *Beauty Myth*, she is pro-'peer-driven feminism' (1991: 281), because 'no matter how wise a mother's advice is, we listen to that of our peers'. In the case of both Rebecca Walker and Naomi Wolf, this is in a literal sense, as both of their mothers were involved in second-wave feminism. Henry uses Rich's notion of 'matrophobia' and women's desire to 'become purged once and for all of our mothers' bondage, to become individuated and free' (Rich, cited in Henry, 2004: 41). In this case the use of 'our' suggests the institution of motherhood, which Rich explored in *Of Woman Born* (1977). Our book is an attempt to move beyond this to a more productive consideration of the mother-daughter relationship. Without romanticising or demonising it, we aim to see how it can provide a new way of thinking inter-generationally, one that focuses on situations and takes advantage of the points of contact between two women and that are part of a relationship that spans generations. Such examples of mother and daughter co-authorship are hard to find. A particular instance is the article by Alice and Rebecca Walker in *Essence* magazine (1995). This is based more on exploring the specifics of their relationship (as, for example, Rebecca Walker discusses how she grew up trying to be the good daughter and therefore the good feminist). Whilst this is an interesting and instructive exploration, our book is somewhat different and we are using our different positioning, in terms of generations and also experiences, to start a shared dialogue. The aim is not to privilege the dialogue between us as two individuals but to use it as a route into considering the wider position of feminism. In our project feminist texts are presented in dialogue and we seek to recognise and reinstate the dynamic of feminist work across the generations to which each of us belongs.

Bridging the divide

There are instances of writers who attempt to bridge this divide, two of whom will be considered here in terms of imagining how to write inter-generationally. We have a different way of doing it, but this is also something that builds on others. In some cases this involves standing outside and analysing why there has been a divide, such as Henry and her discussion of the mother-daughter trope as this comes to cement different periods of feminism in opposition to each other. Two other attempts to engage with this, – Segal (2007) and Gubar (2007) – will be discussed here as they offer ways of thinking about this bridging of generations. Segal uses her own experiences over the decades to chart the shifts and continuities in concerns. This is related through her personal narratives. She aims, in doing this, to 'reclaim' 1970s feminism by challenging how it has been characterised, through her own memories and experiences; indeed, as she notes, 'decades are never simply chronological, serving instead as powerful metaphors for their most salient moments, usually constructed retrospectively' (2007: 125). She does, however, still write chronologically, as a device to challenge and problematise how things have been constructed since.

What is interesting when her material is viewed through the lens of our project is that many of these problematisations can be directly linked to the feminism of today. For example, she discusses the passion and vigour of much of the early feminism, as a 'surge of strength and purpose that animated women when, for the very first time, they linked their own discontents to those of other women' (2007: 67). This is seen in the impact that it had on specific women, some of whom are quoted as saying: 'I was bowled over. I was no longer alone'; 'Changed my whole life... I learned who I was [through the women's liberation movement]' (cited in Segal, 2007: 68). There are clear refractions between these phrases and what young women who become feminists today state (as told to I-Sophie by her students or in conversation with other young feminists). What is perhaps different is that there is no longer the same sense of being part of a wider movement, even if, on reading key feminist texts, some young women do state that it makes them realise that their experience is shared, and indeed gives it a name. What this highlights is that the project outlined by the two of us is one that can build on what writers such as Segal have started. By using two individuals from different generations it is possible to consider even more closely the relevance and potentialities of a reconsideration of the ideas of the second wave, which certainly accords with I-Kath's experience of many women in the movement and as students of women's studies. There was also camaraderie, or even a sisterhood, within the academy. For example, some of I-Kath's strongest and best memories of working in women's studies in the 1980s were of friendship and, especially, laughter.

In terms of how it is written, Segal suggests that, like all of her writing, it 'has a political inflection, attempting to address both an academic and a popular audience' (2007: 128). Indeed, in this light she is critical of writers such as Slavoj Žižek and his 'metaphysical excess' as not being the 'soil for renewing either cultural or political agendas, serving more as a form of high entertainment and rhetorical posturing confined to academia' (2007: 130). Segal's position is, therefore, one that mirrors our own in its aim to be political, to reinstate the ideas of the second wave of feminism, and indeed to reconnect the academic with lived experience and even the popular.

One other possible route into exploring the links between then and now is taken by Gubar in a fictitious account that shows how women with money and 'rooms of their own face bewildering but unprecedented prospects today' (2007: 6). She writes in a manner that manages to avoid abstract or theoretical language which could exclude many. A virtue of Gubar's approach is that she is avoids oversimplification and explores the ambivalences and contradictions of many feminist positions, which were not resolved in the 1970s; nor are they resolved today. For example, she discusses the 1960s and birth control as it was linked to women's greater employment, and the concomitant assumption that women's lives would not be determined by the sexual division of labour. She raises the possibility that these assumptions no longer hold true.

Her decision to write clearly and lucidly is one that resonates with our own aim, as she critiques postmodernists in terms of how they write, using certain language such as 'subjects... constituted by discursive practices' (2007: 39) and how 'other words were put "under erasure" through quotations (like "women") they somehow seemed inadequate, robbed of reality' (2007: 40). This is problematic in the politics of social exclusion where language is hotly debated; 'race' in scare quotes might disappear, but racism certainly has not. Indeed, this is very relevant to our own writing, and the ways in which women can be reintroduced, unbracketed, fully real yet not as assumed only through an essentialised biological sameness, which mirrors discussions of race, ethnicity and subjectivity. In Gubar's book, the fictitious character finds herself questioning 'what politics could possibly arise from post-structuralism, with its obeisance to all those Frenchman (like Lacan, Derrida and Foucault), its arid abstractions (derived from Lacan, Derrida and Foucault), its smug sense of glamorous sophistication...' (2007: 40). Indeed, this points to the need, politically, not to succumb to the opacity of language – a comment that mirrors Segal's. This is not to deny the enormous contribution that French poststructuralists have made and that feminists have taken up with enthusiasm (as illustrated in Greene and Kahn, 1985, for example), but rather to indicate the problems of excess and the dangers and the extent to which obscure language and opacity have come to masquerade as explanation. Gubar and Segal are pointing to some of the over-elaborations and oversimplifications that might have distracted or even deceived some feminist theorising.

Gubar's character works in a university, and she cites one example of a younger colleague who is trying to get tenure as a route into exploring how feminism relates to academia, as she discusses how early feminism was predicated on the notion of solidarity, which starts to fall apart in the face of the hierarchy and individualism of academia. She discusses how women came into academia to transform it, but in the end are part of it, 'pandering to the insularity, parochialism and elitism' (2007: 151). Instead, she asks: 'Ought not the education we advance emphasize the activism that bought us into being, our efforts to make intellectual work personal and political through our strong sense of community'

(2007: 151). Appropriate for our book is how she discusses the ways in which feminists can live with difference 'by forging alliances and coalitions based upon the political goals they share' (2007: 216). Gubar offers important insights into the problematic relationship between feminism and academia and possible fragmentation. However, the only problem with how it is written is that, by writing as a fictional character, she seems to step outside the debate as if she is bracketing her own 'I'. This is an approach that has been explored within what could be temporally positioned as second-wave feminism where a fictional account has been combined with a feminist critique in order to permit the speaking 'I' (e.g. Oakley, 1984). In our book, we are aiming to be different. In our writing, there is an I, a we and a she, although, as stated above, our preference is for the integration of the first and the third person in our proposed device.

What these examples raise are both the sources of thinking and knowing for this book, the particular situatedness of the author, and also the ways in which the book is written. In writing as a mother and daughter we are attempting to continue the attempts at bridging that previous writers have made, yet extend them in novel ways. What an exploration of writers such as Segal and Gubar raises is that a crucial aspect of bridging any kind of theoretical and generational divide is how the book is written. Indeed, one of the characteristic features of the divide and hostility between different strands of feminism is in terms of how the work is written. Much of what is characterised as third-wave feminism is written in a popular style when it is written in book form (e.g. Wolf, 1991; Denfeld, 1995) and these are the books that get widespread media attention, or in feminist magazines such as *Ms* or *Bust*. What is characterised across these texts is that, quite often, the source material is the young women's personal lives. In particular, a core emphasis of many third-wave feminist writers is their own sexual fantasies and lives (inspired by the earlier work of Gurley Brown, 2003), as they discuss in great detail particular desires or thoughts in order to raise the contradictions of experience. This has clear resonances with the discussions of the personal being political of the second wave. What is problematic in the third wave is that this is often separated from the political dimensions – an intimate discussion of the desire to give blow jobs or explore the liberatory potential of bikini waxing is hardly the basis for new feminist politics. Whilst an engagement with social and cultural transformation and the contextual changes and mobilities of popular culture is what appears to make feminism contemporary, there is a tension between populism and relevance, a danger that, in the headlong rush to be popular, the outcome may be superficial and too ephemeral to be relevant.

However, in other instances the discussion of how to write from personal experience is a stronger political stance. As Joan Morgan writes in *My Life as a Hip Hop Feminist*, for feminism to be relevant to black women it needs to 'move past theory and become functional, it has to rescue itself from the ivory towers of academia' (1999: 76). Her stance is like that of many other writers who critique academic feminism; however, what Morgan does assume is that academia is always whitening, and also that it is somehow in opposition to the 'real'. There are important dualities to overcome. The notion of the 'real' also relates to questions of authenticity and for whom you are allowed to write. Henry cites one group who state that 'no one will speak for us but ourselves' (2007: 162). It is clearly important to ensure that representation is not merely in the hands of the powerful and privileged; yet at the same time, it is important not to descend into the limitations of identity politics and the subsequent fragmentation of feminism.

This divide is also between the empirical and the theoretical. One of the challenges this book attempts to take up is the inclusion of the voices of young women, as well as theoretical positioning. It is crucial that the advancement of feminist thinking is grounded in experience. McRobbie's (2008) notable book about the state of contemporary feminism today focuses on young women and how they are 'positioned' by offering a very instructive critique of *Sex and the City*. Yet what is problematic about her account is that she does not include the voices or experiences of young women themselves. When I-Sophie have talked to young women, it is evident that they are able to critique such TV programmes for themselves, and it is important not to disregard their voices in the name of 'theory'. Theoretical developments do not fall in opposition to everyday experience, as the latter is the ground from which theory can develop, which engages with the world these young women inhabit. The construction of subjectivity through discourse, even one that has young women as its key protagonists, can still be removed from lived experience.'McRobbie presents an instructive example of a contemporary feminist polemic which retains a political situatedness, yet the sources that this polemic is based on seem to be not influential feminist writings, but the current fashion for Deleuzian philosophy within the academic mainstream.

What we are aiming to do in our book is to chart a passage between these various oppositions and polarities: between the empirical and the theoretical, the academic and the experiential, and the different generations. As we have illustrated, the ways in which the ideas for this book have been formulated are through discussions between us. They arise out of experiences, which in turn impact on how we consider theory.

Conclusion: feminist dilemmas

This chapter has posed some dilemmas. These are ideological, political and methodological and illustrate the tensions between different ontological and epistemological positionings. Feminist epistemologies are marked by diversity, with different criteria for the constitution of legitimacy, but, in outlining our approach, we have suggested that there are some necessary connections between knowledge and experience; research methodologies cannot be independent of the social situation of the researcher or from the political, social and ethical context in which knowledge is produced. Similarly, epistemologies are implicated with ontological positions, the most important of which in this book relates to claims that are made about the category woman. It is possible, and necessary, to assert the lived experiences of women as speaking subjects without resorting to an essentialist, fixed or naturalised category of person, who is either nonexistent or only constructed in relation to a speaking male subject. This chapter, whilst focusing on the experience of writing and the situation of the subject who speaks and who writes, has also raised particular contemporary intellectual dilemmas. Feminism has always been predicated on an elision of a theoretical critique and taking up an ideological position and a commitment to political action. Ways of speaking and who can speak are deeply embedded in the feminist dilemmas that are presented in the tension that is increasingly emerging between the theoretical and political praxis. Writers and researchers are implicated in the process of constructing and circulating knowledge, yet to do so without acknowledging the situation could be construed as dishonest. It might also be a betrayal of feminist political struggles to be allowed to speak. Thus we have adopted the strategy of I-Kath and I-Sophie in order to make our positions explicit and to acknowledge our situations and situatedness.

Active feminist critiques have material effects and engage with materialities. By taking a stated position we seek to challenge the postmodernist bracketing of who we are in order to regain sufficient confidence to take a stance. Concealing the first-person position, whether singular or plural, is something that will confine feminism to academia and not allow it to engage with or be of interest to the real world.

Destabilising the first person has been effected only to replace it with an even more elitist way of talking and the performance of academia; using the 'constituted subjects' or other such phrases is reiterating the norms of poststructuralist academia, which doesn't destabilise power – in fact, it is constitutive of its own discursive field and even its own regime of truth.

3
The Promise of Technoscience

Cyberspace has become routine; you can shop there, organise your social life, your financial life, even your working life. Globally, the web is the workplace for many people, offering seemingly multiple possibilities for changes in employment and entrepreneurship, yet these same possibilities are also perniciously exploited through cyberspace in the interests of international capital. The advent of the internet and web-based technologies is one of the most marked transformations in our lives. I-Sophie grew to adulthood in this world, whereas I-Kath didn't have a mobile phone or an e-mail address until she was in her forties (although she has been making up for the earlier lack ever since). Such developments have accelerated in recent years and currently the average age for getting a first mobile phone is eight. Taken-for-granted communications technologies have had an impact on lived experience and on embodied experience and appear to present a trajectory of change that is understood as progress. One of the aims of this book is to challenge such straightforward narratives of progress, or indeed the assumption that current technological advances can be seen to mark a rupture with a less knowing past. There is a clear analogy between the narratives of technological progress and the presentation of feminist histories as a similar trajectory of development from a naïve past to a more knowing present. Cyberspace is pivotal to the articulation of much contemporary feminism, as feminist voices are heard through blogs, websites and discussion groups. When we consider the differences in I-Sophie's and I-Kath's experiences of the expectations of technoscience and cyberspace, it would be easy to map this onto the model of a generational rupture. However, this would mask the continuities, given that our knowledges and experiences are not fixed in the world in which we grew up, with cyberspace now being routine for both of us. The mother-daughter relationship is therefore a useful route into thinking about how we can create a dialogue between us and so start to challenge ideas of rupture in feminist moments, or pre- and post-internet worlds.

Advances in science and technology have delivered significant improvements to women's lives, for example, through medical technologies that permit greater reproductive safety and possibilities for the control of fertility. These advances have also opened up all sorts of possibilities for rethinking the category woman. There has been a shift in feminist debates. Earlier, second-wave feminists discussed of the tensions between the advantages and liberatory potential on the one hand, and the constraints and disadvantages, on the other, of new technologies in polarised positions of those who embraced the liberation of technoscience versus those who saw them as new versions of patriarchal control of women. More recently, postmodernist feminism has questioned the boundaries not only of sex and gender, but also between human and animal and human and machine, which subvert the category human as well as the category woman. We argue that there is a strong case for retaining a political focus, which could draw on elements of feminist standpoint epistemologies, which might have seemed naïve, but which offer a way of being attentive to the specificities and contingencies of women's experience by retaining the category woman and the inequalities in play in these experiences.

In this chapter, we explore how debates over the internet involve revisiting many debates that have always been central to feminists, such as the relationship between the body and gender. The fact that it is not necessary to be physically present when interacting with others has led to both optimism about the liberating potential of the web and the idea that this could be an escape from the body and liberation from corporeal constraints. This has particular resonance for women who have for a long time been reduced to their bodies in a reinstatement of Cartesian mind body dualism, which also translates into that of nature–culture and woman–man (Cixous, [1975] 1980). Nature and the body, as part of what is classified as the natural world, have been devalued in their association with women in a binary logic that has elevated the mind and the soul as superior, male attributes. In the area of clothing, fashion and appearance, women are associated with artifice and superficiality, rather than with nature. The clothed body occupies a somewhat paradoxical position: the body associates women with nature, yet care and attention to the body surface associate them with artifice. In both instances, neither the clothing nor the body is associated with the mind, the soul or rationality. In this vein, science and technology are associated with patriarchy, and as such, have been treated with suspicion by many feminists, who are only too aware of the control that has been exercised over women. Developments in science and technology and what Haraway (1997) has called technoscience have been central to feminist debates, whether framed by the explosion of reproductive technologies from the later part of the twentieth century or the language and communication networks of cyberfeminism and the deployment of the web to transmit feminist ideas and practices. Debates about technoscience have been framed by the 'promise of monsters' (Lykke, 1996) as well as translated into the hope of technoscience. Technoscience challenges the certainty and the fragility of the body and its boundaries and presents some very positive (as well as negative) aspects of culture with which to shape and re-form nature. Woman's position in relationship to questions of what is natural is a long-standing feminist debate, yet new dimensions are now being raised.

In this chapter we draw on different aspects of technoscience and change which have been of particular concern to feminists, at least in part because they engage with the problem of bodies and embodiment. Communication technologies offer an apparently disembodied cyberspace in which participants are liberated to be who they want to be unconstrained by gendered, racialised or disabled corporeality. Increasingly, voices that have been silenced are able to speak on the web to engage in debates that acknowledge who they are and are not shrouded in anonymity (Janmohamed, 2009a). Similarly, reproductive technologies have been of particular interest to feminists for the liberatory possibilities they offer from what has been called the 'tyranny of reproduction' (Firestone, 1970). If much of the constraint, limitation and exploitation that women have experienced historically has been attributed to their physical ability to bear children and lactate, it is not surprising that those who seek to loosen the chains have turned to the promise of technoscience. This, however, also raises the question of how technoscience relates to the power geometries of social and political change.

In this chapter we focus on technoscience, first, because it has been the focus of feminist debate and also the medium of feminist activism. Second, science and technology are strongly linked to ideas about change and concomitant ideas of continuities in inequalities and also the core issues that matter to feminism, such as the relation between embodiment, gender and selfhood. Third and finally, due to the specific concerns with embodied selves to feminism and to technoscience, we highlight that the debates over embodiment and its relation to cyberspace and technoscience offer a productive field in which to explore the tensions between challenges and resistance and the reinstatement of corporeality and its differences. Technological and scientific advances might be liberatory, but also and even at the same time involve the re-establishment of inequalities based on embodied differences and anatomical bodies. This chapter focuses on the impact of technoscience, both as part of lived experience and as integral to feminist dialogues through which transformations take place. We explore the status of debates about technoscience in feminist analyses and the relationship between this thinking about science and technology and rethinking the category woman. The material on which we draw on also challenges the notion of chronological, sequential waves of feminist thinking by demonstrating the relevance of critiques from different moments and various perspectives within feminism, which can accommodate change. Our concern is to explore how different feminist approaches, at different times, speak to each other. Even in the field of technoscience, change is not represented by a single, linear march of progress.

Techno-change

The very use of the words technology, science and cyberspace immediately invokes notions of change and, especially, very rapid change, where insecurities as well as possibilities are created through the speed at which changes are taking place in the field of technoscience. Change can be so fast that legal and moral frameworks, policies and practices cannot keep up with the rate at which science is creating new possibilities and new ways of being human. This is evident in contemporary debates about cloning, IVF and the status of the parent–child relationship in a complex field in which there are diverse genetic, physical, legal and social implications in the making of human beings: one woman's egg, another woman's womb, one man's sperm and one, two or maybe more social parents. The governance of cyberspace and of medical ethics often lags behind what technologies have made possible, whether through the speed and unregulated spaces of the web or through medico-scientific inventions and techniques that create new ways of reproducing and sustaining life. As we shall demonstrate, it is, of course, possible to exaggerate the extent and scope of change and ignore important continuities. Change also operates dialogically and technoscience does not operate in free-floating cyberspace, unconstrained by materialities which include corporeality and social, economic and political forces. New technologies offer opportunities and benefits for those who experience impairments that restrict their mobility or access to other fields, although the extent of the advantages is contested. Cyberspace is often represented as following a generational progression. New technologies are associated with youth and the speed at which those early on the life-course adapt to change and embrace new technologies. 'Grey surfers' may be the butt of humour and are always represented as a specific category of internet users as if their utilisation of new technologies and occupation of cyberspace were remarkable and somehow different from those of the young. Technology seems to follow a linear generational path too. However, lived experience does not follow a linear path into the technological future, but reproduces some of the disruptions and irregularities of everyday life. The period covered by our conversations in this book covers some significant transformations in new technologies and in women's lived experience but, as is argued in this chapter, there are productive exchanges that can be made between different feminist positions that have been developed across this time-span and, rather than an epochal shift, we propose a creative dialogue among as well as between feminist theories.

The problem of bodies

Feminist theories of the body and embodiment have been central to the development of conceptualising and understanding bodies and embodied selves. 'The body' and, more especially, bodies have always played a key role in feminist thinking and activism. The body and ways of thinking about it have an unsettled history in feminist thought, however. At times it might have appeared that, by focusing on the gendered body, feminists were falling into the trap of associating women with 'nature' and, by implication, linking men to 'culture', with all its connotations of superiority and rationality and the cultural devaluation of the body that has arisen historically from its associations with biology, within a dualistic polarisation of the biological as opposite to the social. How feminists have responded to the clothing, fashion and beauty industries has been characterised by the problems of working within the nature/culture binary. An example can be seen in Daly's (1979) argument that women need to reject the 'false' masks imposed by patriarchal values through make-up and fashion and get back to 'real women's values' (1979: 27). However, as I-Sophie has argued elsewhere (Woodward, 2007), this implies that women have a real, authentic self that exists outside of culture. Whilst the critique of the beauty industries is an important one, by celebrating nature as somehow 'authentic' merely serves to reinforce the association of women with nature. Feminist critiques have been haunted by the ghost of biological reductionism and the unhappy and unrealistic binary of nature and culture. One of the major projects of second-wave feminism was to disentangle the binary, even if by doing so the outcome was sometimes to reinstate it.

Bodies matter to feminists, but they are troubling. At the level of common sense, bodies appear to set the limits of the self; 'one body one self' (Fraser and Greco, 2005: 12). If the body and the self are one, as Bourdieu argues, following Merleau-Ponty (1962) and 'we are our bodies' (Bourdieu, 1993), this suggests the possibility of exercising some agency over the embodied self. If our bodies are almost always clothed, then there is a sense that, to paraphrase Bourdieu, we are our clothed bodies. Clothing could therefore be seen to offer possibility for the exercise of agency. However, the first attempts to reclaim the body and see it as a positive source of identity and value centred on the body itself. The assumption that the body and the self are one underpins much feminist activism, as illustrated in the feminist-inspired handbook of the second wave *Our Bodies, Ourselves* (Boston Women's Health Collective, 1969) and suggests that gaining control of your body means gaining control of yourself, and that the body is an intrinsic part of the self. From the 1970s, this book not only had an enormous impact on feminism in the US, but has been taken up, translated and adapted by women across the globe (Davis, 2007). Drawing on Said's concept of 'travelling theory', Davis has argued that the worldwide travels of *Our Bodies, Ourselves* shows how the book was transformed in the process of its many border crossings. *Our Bodies, Ourselves* has not only been US feminism's most successful and popular export, it also provides insights for feminist scholarship, in particular, for how we think about history, the politics of knowledge and transnational feminism (Wells, 2008).

This handbook was important in connecting sexual politics to knowledge and part of the process which set in motion the proliferation of self-help guides and the growth of such material, for example in women's magazines (Winship, 1987; Woodward, 1997b). What started as a practical, political programme has also been appropriated into the explosion of introspective, self-help advice, which demands attention to the original critiques and political projects of earlier feminism. This emphasis on knowing the body is very different from more recent aspects of cyberfeminism when it seems the aim of the project has been to escape the body. Feminist activism in the 1970s and 1980s, as in earlier times, focused on the idea that providing information about how women's bodies worked and were experienced was a route out of ignorance and lack of control; knowledge and thus control meant liberation. However, feminist critiques (Martin 1989; Battersby, 1998) have shown how the body in western thought has often been denied or dismissed, with the mind or the soul occupying a 'higher' status position than women's embodied experiences, such as those of menstruation, birth, lactation and the menopause.

More recent analyses have developed in what has been called the 'corporeal turn' in feminism (Howson, 2005) as part of feminist engagements with the 'problem of bodies' and with rethinking materiality through an attempt to counter some of the apparent disembodiment of some poststructuralist approaches (Butler, 1990, 1993; Grosz, 1994, 1995, 1999). For Butler, everything is discursively created, including sex, gender, desire and body, which could well lend itself to an exploration of disembodied cyberspace, but fails to address the materiality of embodiment. Social constructionism, however articulated, generates the problem of the absence of the anatomical body as a relevant factor (Lloyd, 2007). Butler argues that people are sexed at birth and thus 'being sexed and being human are coextensive and simultaneous' (1993: 142), in a view which has the advantage of synchronising existence and essence by prioritising the social processes of sexing the body. However, as we shall argue, this still runs the risk of a body that is entirely inscribed and thus immaterial and itself uninterrogated. This rethinking of bodies and the intellectual concerns with 'the body' has often been framed by social constructionism, which retains a strong, explicit presence in many contemporary feminist critiques that engage with ethnographic research into gendered experience (Hargreaves, Vertinsky and McDonald, 2007), as well, of course, as underpinning most of the post-Foucauldian feminist debates, albeit in diverse and complex ways (Butler, 1990, 1993; Gatens, 1991; Grosz, 1994).

By deconstructing the 'natural' body, it has been possible to identify the sources and mechanisms of oppression. Feminism, in many ways, has necessarily privileged social constructionist accounts because the exploration of gender as social and cultural provides a social explanation of difference, and, importantly, inequalities that can be changed by political action. Social constructionism seems to challenge the fixity of embodied difference, which was often understood as biological and reductionist (Witz, 2000). The idea of biological reductionism was a powerful concept to be challenged in the 1970s, especially. Social constructionism was largely adopted because such approaches assert the necessity of stressing the ways in which gender is social and that therefore the field of study is social life. This is not to say that there are no problems with an overemphasis on the social construction of the gender. As the feminist biologist Linda Birke argues (1999), biology was seen by many feminists as oversimplifying the complexity of human beings and many, like her, have addressed bodily experience and put material bodies and biological bodies back on the agenda. As has also been shown, social life is a male-dominated field and overwhelmingly masculine in character and is constituted by the suppression of difference, in which male embodiment is normalised and female embodiment ignored or pathologised, so that female bodies are perceived as matter that is out of place (Douglas, 1963) in the anthropological sense (Witz, 2000)

Whatever the strengths and advantages of social constructionist approaches to gender and the sex/gender distinction of the 1970s and 1980s, it also ran the risk of reinstating the very fixity it sought to challenge. Although poststructuralism aimed to unsettle binary fixities, there is also a danger of the establishment of a new orthodoxy expressed in the unequal dualism of privileging fluidity and flexibility over belonging, social constructionism over corporeality and materiality and a postmodernist dogma expressed in its own metalanguage. As Linda Nicholson (1994) argued, the distinction between sex and gender fixed the body as a biological construction and failed to note the myriad and complex ways in which bodies are implicated in the construction and experience of gender. Feminists have been critical of the problems of over-enthusiasm for social constructionism and the more recent corporeal turn (Howson, 2005) and have incorporated much fuller analyses of materiality and the complex networks which constitute embodied selves. Howson describes the diversity of approaches which permeate feminist accounts and arguments. Materiality includes biology and specific gendered bodies across generations (Rich, 1977), economic materialities (Barrett, 1992), bodily resistance and stubborn immutability (Bordo, 1989, 1993, 1998), everyday practices of phenomenological accounts (Young, 1990, 2005), residual facticity (Witz, 2000), as well as postmodernist attempts to reinstate materiality (Gatens, 1992, 1996; Butler, 1993, 2004; Diprose, 1994).

There has been an expansion of a feminist focus on science and technology which demonstrates the inextricable and co-constitutive interrelationships between bodies and culture, including technoscience, which challenges all the theoretical boundaries (Haraway, 1985, 1989; Franklin, 1997), as well as creating detailed analyses of bodies, inside and outside social productions; sexuality is part of embodiment, and culture and gender are even in our bones (Fausto-Sterling, 1992, 2000). Particular issues emerge within the corporeal turn, including problems of agency and control, and the boundaries of the body and concomitantly of the self. Too much stress on the body may mean limited scope for change or for intentionality. The problem remains one of how to incorporate action into an analysis that also embraces the physical experience of the material body and how bodies are marked by difference. A possible route into this is through understanding the body as a clothed body. Given that the body is almost always dressed (as evidenced historically and cross-culturally), it raises the importance of considering the body and clothing together. Clothing, understood prior to the bodies it adorns, can be understood within a social constructionist paradigm as being something that constructs gender and creates meanings around the body. It could also be seen as a possible domain for agency, as the clothing that is selected and worn offers a route out of the apparent fixity of the body. A classic example of this could be seen in the gender parodies of cross-dressing. However, clothing does not just help to construct the body, as the body itself gives meaning and form to clothing. The relationship between clothing and the body offers a fruitful route into breaking down boundaries between essentialism and social constructionism by considering both the body and clothing as forms of material culture. Another particularly productive approach which has been deployed in feminist critiques of cyberspace and of technoscience as it impacts on women's experience of embodiment is Irigaray's conceptualisation of difference, which includes the possibility of speaking the body and of a female imaginary that reinstates women's voices and bodies, including motherhood into culture.

Speaking the body

Although Irigaray's own work, especially that which has been most frequently cited in the context of cyber-futures (Plant, 2000) and technoscience, does not deal with technology at all, her work on the female imaginary and speaking the body has been used to develop ideas about how cyberspace might be a place where women can speak. Irigaray ([1980] 1992) argues that we cannot know what a feminist technology would look like until culture and the symbolic order have been transformed to permit the expression of a feminine symbolic. She suggests that one route into reappropriating negative patriarchal accounts of women is to valorise them. Irigaray's work argues for the recognition of the absolute absence of women's bodily experience, which is knowledge from the inside, in the metaphors that generate the language of knowledge production. For example, in *Speculum of the Other Woman*, she argues that Lacanian psychoanalysis presents woman as 'other' because men see women from the outside. Women, conversely, could see themselves from the inside, using the metaphor of the speculum (the instrument for looking at the internal cavities of the body). Thus women could be other to men and men could be other to women, rather than women occupying the eternal position of 'other'. Her work is predicated on the need for new symbolic structures, incorporating body metaphors as a means of invoking a female symbolic. She emphasises the need to explore how women relate to themselves and to each other, and how social, global conditions enable some exchanges but not others. There are, of course, questions about how this can be conceived and put into practice; the scope for speaking women's bodies may be more limited.

Eve Ensler's play *The Vagina Monologues* can be seen as an example of an attempt to speak women's bodies, which also demonstrates some of the problems. Such attempts are situated in the context of the repetitions of popular culture, where resistance and rebellion can be reappropriated and re-presented as part of the mainstream. The play was first performed in New York in 1996, but has since been performed across the globe and so could be seen to have entered the mainstream and language. Indeed, the language of the mainstream can be seen as one of Ensler's political concerns in promoting the possibility of women reclaiming their own bodies; three women speak in the play delivering monologues which are based on the words of a wide range of ordinary women. The women regain control over their bodies and themselves, our bodies and ourselves, in some monologues speaking the words that are used to objectify women (such as 'reclaiming cunt', Ensler, 2001). In other cases the monologues attempt to give voice to that which is culturally absent, either in terms of experiences or through words. Greer (2003) was very critical *of The Vagina Monologues* after she appeared in it. In part, her criticism centred on the use of the word vagina, which she argued was used incorrectly (sometimes women were actually referring to their vulva or labia). Whilst many of the criticisms Greer makes of Ensler herself may hold weight, ordinary women using the word incorrectly is surely a sign of how little they know their own bodies. Greer criticises the use of the word vagina as it has negative connotations – the etymology of the word being the Latin for sword sheath (Greer, 2003) – and also argues that this attempt to speak women's bodies is hardly new. Given that the word that is now commonly used for women's genitalia ('pussy') is an incredibly misogynist one derived from pornography, this highlights how much further we need to go in terms of the creation of a female symbolic order, which allows for language that is not derived from patriarchal representations such as pornography. Moreover, whatever word is used, there is a serious issue about the most offensive swear words, which are often those which relate to female genitalia – an underlying patriarchy that needs to be addressed. Greer (2003) notes that the overall range of monologues represented was somewhat disappointing in its failure to address many important issues, such as the herpes virus acquired by people having unprotected sex. Importantly, she also notes that in the book there is a consideration of female genital mutilation in Africa, but no mention of episiotomy in childbirth, a common procedure in the US and the UK in the routine management of hospital deliveries. Even if Greer's criticism is balanced against the more positive impetus behind *The Vagina Monologues* to speak women's bodies, we would argue that although the monologues give voice to some cultural silences, they also perpetuate other absences and silences.

As theatre it is entertainment, but in the agitprop, political theatre tradition of aiming to make a difference and effect change. The play has generated a movement called 'V day', which aims to publicise and support the work of organisations that have mobilised against violence against women. I-Sophie saw *The Vagina Monologues* at the Arts Theatre in London when it was first performed in the UK and we went together to see the play in Sheffield in 2009. I-Sophie's assessment when she first saw the play was that it was a positive piece, which for both the audience and her raised serious issues yet also was a point of identification for the predominantly female audience. By 2009, the play was being promoted as a fun night out for the girls, although the programme made much of the V Day movement and, as with other performances across the globe, the monologues included distressing violence as well as amusing and bitter-sweet accounts. When we went together, the monologues included a harrowing account of multiple rape experienced by one woman in war and a case of sexual abuse. There were also two monologues by lesbian women with very positive narratives, which were clearly appreciated by the audience. It was, however, an unsettling and sometimes disappointing experience. It may be that the language has become mainstream and this particular form of women's expression of their sexuality is now routine. Women simulating orgasm has lost the power to shock or surprise. The emphasis in the publicity on a 'girls' night out' may have created some of the tensions. In spite of the diversity of the monologues, the audience's reaction suggested some contradictions. Responses appeared embedded in a hegemonic heterosexuality that seemed programmed to elicit laughter and collusion with a heterosexual women's intimacy, framed by familiar stories of most straight men's inadequacies (apart from 'Bob'). Sexualities, like gender, seemed polarised by the attempt to speak women's bodies; there is thus the danger that attempts to subvert the patriarchal devaluation of women's experiences can always be accommodated and reconstituted to reinforce aspects of control. The Sheffield audience seemed to have responded in the most vocal ways as part of what has been termed the ladette culture, almost as a form of what Levy (2005) terms female chauvinist pigs, where women internalise the bawdy behaviour that often serves to objectify women. These experiences were absent when I-Sophie saw the play in London. The experience is contradictory though, with eruptions of anarchic enthusiasm and participation from a largely female audience that would be unlikely in an audience in which men were not in such a small minority. The final monologue, by Eve Ensler herself describing her daughter giving birth, is a good example of the ambivalence of the relationship between audience, text and actors. What appeared to be an uplifting and positive reclamation of women's bodies was greeted with laughter, as if the only possible responses were laughter at the amusing aspects of sex or silence at the account of brutal violence. Reclaiming speaking embodied selfhood is difficult and the experience is, of course, temporally and spatially bound. Cultural and social specificities influence what is possible; what was radical in the 1990s may seem less so in 2009 and the dynamic of language use and cultural change has different effects and affects.

The Vagina Monologues is an example of a contemporary attempt to make a political statement which encompasses and frees women's body experiences of being in the world. Such attempts are also seized on by mainstream popular culture and absorbed into its practices through processes that may also serve to depoliticise them. Just as feminist activism has been translated into the ordinariness of neoliberal governance, women's attempts to subvert the normalisation of sexual orthodoxies that exclude or marginalise them have often been appropriated by popular cultural forms and made anodyne, or at least lost some of their dynamism. The monologues use the resource of women's accounts of their lives as women through their bodies, and our experience as part of the audience was productive in the discussion it generated in reflecting on what was expressed and what was not. The contradictions of the experience and effects of the play in no way undermine the project, but do point to some of the difficulties of speaking the body. However, what is most important about Irigaray's work in this context is first, that she points to the cultural and symbolic absence of a female symbolic and the masking of gendered difference that permeates cultural exchange. Second, she suggests an alternative approach to re-creating culture through the expression of a culture that makes motherhood and the mother–daughter relationship explicit rather than subsumed and silenced under a Lacanian Law of the Father. *The Vagina Monologues* make it explicit; but it was a disappointing that the particular attempt to engage with an aspect of the mother–daughter relationship in the final monologue failed to work as effectively as I-Kath in particular might have hoped. Irigaray's argument about the cultural absence of motherhood has particular resonance for a discussion of the techno–scientific interventions that are implicated in assisted reproductive technologies, but is equally powerful in addressing the possibilities of cyberspace, because the silencing of motherhood and the mother–daughter relationship impinges on the silencing of women. Motherhood, however, presents a particularly powerful site from which to challenge psychoanalytic phallocentrism, because it combines embodiment, silence and outrage.

Criticisms of Irigaray as representing an essentialist position suggest that she purports that there are categories of women and men that pre-exist the cultural and social processes through which gendered identities are constituted, because of her emphasis on the primacy of embodied differences. However, as we would argue, she is focusing on metaphors and the cultural construction of women as 'other' through the silencing of women's embodied experience and women's voices and challenging the absence of women and of embodied difference from culture; women's inclusion and presence could be productive. Irigaray is not claiming that women's bodies would speak them, as Lacan avers, through the prime signifier of the phallus, but is arguing for a female imaginary through recognition of embodied difference.

Mothers, monsters and reproductive technologies

We start in a place that has particular resonance for us as authors and remains a relationship that accords with most people's lived experience across the globe, where it is still the case, as Adrienne Rich argued, in the title of her book on motherhood as experience and institution, that we are 'of woman born' (Rich, 1977). This is in spite of the periodic media hyperbole about men having babies, as in the case of the American Thomas Beatie, who was born female and kept her reproductive organs, but, following hormone treatment, grew a beard and achieved legal male status, gave birth to a baby in 2008 and, at the time of writing, is pregnant again, having temporarily suspended the hormone treatment. Such examples, although exceptional, inevitably occupy media space, although they do little to challenge gender binaries or transgress sexual boundaries, because they are always represented within the male/female binary; 'man has baby', or more recently, as if to go one better in the tradition of hegemonic masculinity's competitive edge, 'man has twins'. Each case involves someone who was born with female reproductive organs, wanted to become a man, but delayed removal of the uterus and ovaries (but not breasts) until they could give birth with a male identity. Breasts clearly occupy a particular space in the cultural and embodied construction of womanhood. Women who want to be men have their breasts removed as the outward manifestation and visible evidence of female gender identity, just as some women who want to be more attractive women may have their breasts enlarged. Giving birth as a legal man naturally requires a uterus and ovaries, but breasts are presumably incidental to the natural experience. This illustrates something of the contradictions and ambivalences that are in play in the technologised reconstruction of gender in the twenty-first century, but contributes little to challenge either gender binaries or the power relations which marginalise women or reconfigure nature. Beatie's own self-categorisation is male, which carries the shock value of a man who can give birth 'naturally'. Also, of course, he must have felt he could not identify with the sex he was born and could only be himself as a legal man. How 'natural' a man with a uterus and ovaries is however is problematic and this case may do more to challenge the strategic use of the language of nature and the natural to reinstate a polarisation of woman and man, than to subvert embodied gender differences or identities, or even to suggest that there may be more than two sexes, as Fausto-Sterling (2000) argues.

The case is not only typical of the sensationalism of the contemporary media and the practice of performing private, personal acts in the public arena for gain, but is also an illustration of some of the ways in which essentialist ideas are reinforced as well as transgressed. The experience and constitution of motherhood present a significant site for the exploration of essentialism since motherhood is an aspect of experience, especially embodied experience, that has been central to feminist debates across generations and within a wide range of social and political contexts. Motherhood involves traditional ideas about gendered, essentialised embodiment which new technologies question and may subvert. Motherhood, more than many other areas of life, has been troubling for feminists because of the tensions it presents between the naturalisation of embodiment and the promise of reconstitution through the possibilities offered by technoscience. Motherhood and maternal embodiment present a particular focus on the interconnections between the body and technoscience which is an important dimension of the debates in this book about the meaning and resilience of the category woman and the destabilising possibilities of, for example, reproductive technologies. Reproductive technologies present a particular illustration of the interrelationship between embodied gendered identifications and cultural interventions and between certainties and insecurities: 'Nowhere is the relationship between gender and technology more vigorously contested than in the sphere of human reproduction' (Wajcman, 1991: 54). Motherhood might seem to be both embodied and natural, a biological fact in which technologies intervene, but still reducible to what is called natural, as well as a cultural practice in which women are not only the bearers of children globally, but also, in the majority of societies, are their primary carers and nurturers (Wajcman, 1991). What constitutes technologies too are inseparable from the value-laden practices through which they are implemented and enacted, none more so than in the field of reproductive technologies. Control of the body, in childbearing and birth control, has been central to feminist movements for women's rights and equality (Steinberg, 1997). Feminist campaigns and theoretical critiques have put motherhood on the political agenda and retrieved it from the silent space of naturalised, cultural assumptions. For example, older women, lesbians, black and ethnic minority women, migrant women and the poor have all been denied access to assisted reproduction technologies. The case of the octuplets born to an unemployed single mother of six in the US in 2009 (Octuplets, 2009) might suggest a more inclusive egalitarian approach, but seems more likely to raise issues about the power relations between medical practitioners, pharmaceutical and medical technology companies, and the media and women's bodies, where women's bodies could be construed as vessels for reproduction.

Mothers are women, but this is not to say that all women are mothers, which raises important social points about the merging of femininity with the maternal. There has been an elision between empirical, lived experience and cultural assumptions which have passed unstated and unexpressed. Motherhood remains in many ways unquestioned and an 'absent presence' (Kaplan, 1992; Woodward, 1997b). Irigaray has stressed the 'unacknowledged mother' of western thought and culture in which it has been repressed as 'the dark continent *par excellence* [which] remains in the shadow of our culture' (Irigaray, in Whitford, 1991: 35). Irigaray has argued that the silencing of motherhood and the elision of woman with motherhood have been challenged by the campaigns through which women have sought control over their own bodies. For example, 'Contraception and abortion raise the question of the meaning of motherhood, and women (notably because of their entry into and their encounters within the circuits of production) are looking at their sexual identity and beginning to emerge from silence and anonymity' (Irigaray, in Whitford, 1991: 36).

Irigaray's argument is also useful to our project because she demonstrates not only the absence of motherhood and the mother-daughter relationship in western culture, but also the ambivalence and contradictory representations of the maternal where it is present. As the 'dark continent', motherhood is also subject to primitive fantasies in ancient and contemporary mythologies, not least within psychoanalytic theory. Archaic projections of the devouring mother who threatens madness and death are symptomatic of the unanalysed hatred and disgust from which women suffer as a group culturally. Within the binary logic of the Madonna and the whore, mothers are constructed relationally as either 'good', that is, self-effacing and silent or 'bad', that is, selfish, sexualised, even monstrous. The woman in her sixties who defies nature and demands unnatural motherhood, women who freeze their eggs for later use and women in same-sex relationships who seek assisted reproduction have all been represented as dangerous. Of course, this is a much more complex system of beliefs and practices than such dualisms can accommodate, but the silence about motherhood and the maternal feminine is an important area of investigation and debate because it is constitutive of some of the denial of positive representations and experience of all women, not just those categorised as mothers. As Irigaray argues, this is also a silence that creates monstrosity.

Sci-fi monsters

Feminism shares some features with science fiction in its diverse relationships with science and technology. Just as science fiction as a genre that is strongly present in a period of rapid technological change has posited a destabilisation of sexual identity where newly re-formed bodies and selves emerge from scientific interventions, so too have feminist theorists been attentive to the disruptions and constraints of science as well as to its liberating potential (Doane, 1990). Motherhood and monstrosity also meet in both of these areas, in which science fiction 'is more hyperbolically concerned than ever with the question of *difference*, typically posed as the difference between human and non-human' (Penley et al., 1991: vii). However, motherhood has a particular place in the genre. Although it has traditionally been concerned with monstrosity, Penley argues that 'new pressures from feminism, the politics of race and sexual orientation and the dramatic changes in the structure of the family and the workforce seems to have intensified the symptomatic wish to post and re-pose the question of difference in a fictional form' (Penley et al., 1991: vii); she also cites advances in genetic engineering, bioengineering and cybernetics that have had an enormous impact on science fiction and on representations of gender difference – a confluence of pressure. There is a clear tension between the potent liberatory potential of Haraway's cyborg metaphor translated into science fiction and the tendency in the genre for it to be appropriated and reproduced in ways that actually reinforce gendered, racialised stereotypes.

In the narratives and language of science fiction fears have been projected onto the monstrous feminine, especially the monstrous mother; so too the language used to describe and reconstitute maternity through the lens of technoscience invokes monstrosity as an outcome of unregulated intervention, such as multiple births, irresponsible motherhood, often at one or other extreme of the lifespan, or women who seek 'designer babies'. Motherhood in science fiction and in lived experience negotiates a troubled path between monstrosity and sentimentality in an ambivalence expressed in the case of the octuplets born in the US, mentioned above. The media coverage ranged from demonisation of the irresponsible mother who requested assisted reproductive technology and the even more irresponsible authorities which granted it to a woman who already had six children, to the images of delightful tiny babies who would raise the spirits of a world deep in the gloom of an economic recession. The debate was also framed by the discourses of technoscience, which celebrated the technology through which it was possible to deliver eight live babies (Octuplets, Times online, 2009).

The maternal space, as Kristeva has argued, is 'a place both double and foreign (Kristeva, 1977: 409). Motherhood represents a heterogeneity that creates confusion. It is the very double identity of motherhood that makes it troubling. Haraway puts it differently by suggesting that the idea of the 'individual' is more closely associated with men, whereas 'women have so much trouble counting as individuals in modern western discourses'; 'their personal, bounded individuality is compromised by their bodies' troubling talent for making other bodies, whose individuality can take precedence over their own' (1988: 39).

Anxieties about technology have been projected onto those about the female body and reproduction in the genre of science fiction in ways that are instructive to an analysis of the intersections of femininity, motherhood and technoscience. The genre brings together (for example, in the *Alien/s* series) the representation of the conflict, not with a symbolic father, but with an extension of the maternal feminine, which is shown to have assumed monstrous proportions. Motherhood can be monstrous because mothers may also give birth to what are classified monsters. It is this categorisation of impairment in the newborn and stillbirths historically that informed the persecution of midwives as witches (Donnison, 1987) and also plays a big part in science fiction and in the elision of horror films with those of science fiction (Doane, 1990) (e.g. *It's Alive*, the *Alien/s* series, *The Brood*, *The Fly*).

The politics of reproduction

Reproductive technologies embrace a huge array of practices ranging from the control of fertility, through contraception, the management of childbirth and screening technologies, to the promotion of conception through egg and embryo donation, *in vitro* fertilisation (Stanworth, 1987) and, most recently, cloning (Franklin, 2007). Motherhood might appear to be a biological fact, but its regulation, control and the massive range of interventions designed to prevent or promote it ensure that reproductive technologies are embedded in moral, social and political fields. It is hardly surprising that feminists have seized on its possibilities and threats and, especially, engage with the elision between femininity and motherhood that underpins the policies and practices. In the 1960s and 1970s this was largely framed by a polarisation of views, for example between those of Shulamith Firestone, who celebrated the possibilities of release from the brutality of childbearing afforded by technological developments, to the those of FINRAGE (Feminist International Network of Resistance to Reproductive and Genetic Engineering).

More positive approaches to reproductive technologies argue that they subvert traditional hierarchies and offer opportunities for the reconstruction of gender identities in an approach which frames the debate in terms of gender identities. Progress does not necessarily have to involve the subversion and undermining of the category woman. Although earlier approaches to reproductive technologies were underpinned by an oppositional approach to the positive versus negative aspects of such interventions for women, they all assumed that woman was a meaningful categorisation of the key players, or at least the major recipients, of the interventions of such technologies. There has been some slippage in the debates that have followed in which the gendered subjectivity of women has been questioned. Revisiting the critiques of reproductive technologies which pointed to their reflection and reconstitution of gendered inequalities in the wider arena is productive for the contemporary political debate.

As Deborah Lynn Steinberg (1997, drawing on Harding's critique of feminist standpoint and feminist empiricist theories) pointed out, it is possible to acknowledge the oversimplification of the polarised positive versus negative positions, but to hold on to a politics of difference. Steinberg challenges the inevitability of claiming a homogeneous category of women by shifting the emphasis from gender as the overarching focus to permit a reclassification of women that can accommodate power and differences among women. She deconstructs some of the categories produced by the use and application of reproductive technologies and explores the specificities of women's experience. She does this by developing an anti-essentialist critique of postmodernism and through an anti-oppressive approach developed from feminist standpoint theory which encompasses difference and a political agenda of change. Steinberg is concerned to retain a feminist politics within the tradition of political action and premised on the acceptance and assertion of a meaningful category woman and the will for change, for example, in challenging racism and social exclusion and what is constructed as 'normal' (white, straight, middle-class) and what could be seen as the eugenic underpinnings of some IVF practices. Steinberg's approach belongs to a tradition which reworks feminist standpoint theory and opens up the possibility of crossing boundaries through differences among women rather than challenging the very category. Cyborgs offer a more radical transcendence of boundaries; between as well as among women.

Cyborgs

Haraway's development of cyborg thinking was pivotal to rethinking the boundaries of what is human and the relationship between the human and the machine, which has had significant impact on feminist reconceptualisations. Her *Manifesto for Cyborgs* (1985) set in motion new ways of thinking about crossing the boundaries of the embodied self which have been very important in engaging with the problems for feminist politics that have been created by technoscience, whether in cyberspace, through communication technologies or in biotechnologies (for example, those used in the field of reproductive medicine). Although her work has since moved into different fields, she still deals with interconnections and the possibilities of science and technology for feminist politics. Her earlier work on cyborg thinking is cited here because of its influence, her arguments that inextricably link the gendered body to diverse materialities, including technoscience, and because Haraway's work on cyborgs challenges the idea of sequential waves of feminist thinking that follow on, rather than being in dialogue with, each other. Cyborg identity is predicated on transgressive boundaries and resists models of unity. As Anne Balsamo (1997: 82) argues, for Haraway, technoscience offers tools for re-crafting our bodies. Haraway's cyborg thinking also offers the means of transcending some of the more restrictive boundaries of being human and of explaining the intersections of the human and non-human which no longer privileges the rational, bounded subject. The fluidity of boundaries is not, however, unproblematic and in particular raises questions about the extent of the liberatory potential of technoscience.

A key area in which it is important to raise questions about the liberatory possibilities of technoscience can be seen in cosmetic surgery, where the capabilities of scientific developments are now utilised as a means to alter the body. The initial premise of cosmetic surgery was that those who suffered some form of disfigurement would be able to return their bodies or faces as closely as possible to their original appearance. Even in such cases where the positive aspects of these procedures are evident, there is an underlying normalising discourse, which assumes that bodies and appearances which are outside the norm need to be corrected. This is far more marked when we consider what has happened to cosmetic surgery in the UK and US. This is extended in many countries to being an orientalising discourse in places where women who do not have white skin are having their skin bleached and their features altered to look more western (as in Japan, where surgery on the eyelids is one means through which this is effected). Perhaps what is most alarming is how normalised invasive cosmetic surgery has become in terms of how many people are having procedures and the openness that often accompanies this. In the US, in 2008, the most popular procedure for women was breast augmentation, with 355,671 women undergoing it (American Society for Aesthetic Plastic Surgery (ASAPS), 2008). The significance of this, as it becomes more mainstream, is made apparent when this is compared to the figures for 1997, when 101,176 received breast augmentation (ASAPS, 2008). Whilst cosmetic surgery is not the sole domain of women, the statistics make apparent how much more prevalent it is for them. The most popular procedure for men in 2008 was lipoplasty (liposuction), with 31,453 men having the procedure; in the same year 309,692 women had the procedure (ASAPS, 2008). Cosmetic surgery needs to be situated in the wider media context, where images present unrealistic models of women's bodies, yet simultaneously present these bodies as something to be altered. As Bordo (2003) has argued, this leaves no part of a woman's body untouched, as even the majority of women who do not have cosmetic surgery engage in some beautification rituals.

Cosmetic surgery and beautification rituals are body projects (Turner, 1984, 1992; Shilling, 1993), which have been located within a discourse of choice as well as of self-regulation. As Shilling (2003) has more recently argued, such interventions seem to demonstrate the body's plasticity and to highlight the contradictory nature of such practices. Cosmetic surgery seems more akin to practices which train the body in docility in that, like diet and exercise regimes 'they are experienced as empowering practices that enable women to feel they are in control over their own bodies and lives' (Howson, 2005: 76), but nonetheless, in the case of cosmetic surgery, involve subjection of the flesh to particularly invasive practices. Cosmetic surgery and body modification practices, in suggesting the operation of some agency on the part of the women who subject themselves to such regimes, may mask power over women's bodies, which effaces difference and normalises idealised, racialised bodies (hooks, 1992; Kaw, 1994). Even less intrusive interventions suggest fragility in the boundary between self-empowerment and containment (Bordo, 1993).

Now that procedures like Botox or do-it-yourself chemical peels can be carried out at home, the boundaries between ordinary practices that most women engage in and the more extreme practices are increasingly blurred. These forms of body modification exist on a spectrum from those who pluck their eyebrows and have their hair cut and styled, through to those who have their bodies cut upon and remodelled. This highlights the impossibility of seeing any body as existing as natural or outside of culture. What was once either a medical procedure for people who had suffered a disfigurement or the domain of the very rich has now started to seep into the mainstream. Not only are women valorised through their appearance, there is also a clear sense that they are expected to valorise themselves through it, although this is not a new phenomenon, as historically women have been given value through their appearance, with men being positioned as the primary viewers. However, this has become even more marked in the contemporary world. A case in point is the example of Kelly Rowland, a former member of the group Destiny's Child, and an example of a high-profile woman having breast enlargement. Her reason for undergoing it was that 'I was sick of not fitting into my tops'. The ideal body thus needs to be understood as a dressed body; Rowland was not only trying to actualise the perfect body presented through media sources, but experiencing her body doubts and inadequacies through her clothing. After the procedure, she is able to fit into her favourite top and states, 'I'm so happy. I feel complete' (*USA Today*, March 2008). This is a far cry from the example discussed earlier in the chapter 'Our Bodies Our Selves', which suggested that knowing the body is the route to self-awareness as women. In this example the self and body are only complete when the body has been cut open and silicone bags inserted into the breasts. The parts of the body, the breasts, associated with lactation and motherhood, are reduced to their sexualised function. When this is considered in light of the previous discussion of motherhood, it demonstrates cultural contempt for motherhood. There is a deeply embedded misogyny apparent, where the ideal woman's body involves being mutilated in order to be removed from any actual connection with womanliness.

Cybergrrrls; riot grrrls

The liberatory potential of technoscience has been most enthusiastically embraced through new communication technologies. It is this aspect of feminism which has been used particularly strongly to support a generational model (Gillis et al., 2007). One of most voluble aspects of the third wave is the cyberfeminism that arose out of feminist responses to the theoretical developments of Haraway's cyborg thinking, although cyberfeminism is not embraced by Haraway, and Sadie Plant is sometimes excessive in her support for the weaving of women and the web in an outburst of disembodied liberty. Plant's expression does not always lapse into hyperbole and she has made the important point that

> Network culture still appears to be dominated by both men and masculine intentions and designs. But there is more to cyberspace than meets the male gaze. Appearances have always been deceptive... Women are accessing the circuits on which they were once exchanged, hacking into security controls, and discovering their own post-humanity.
>
> ([1995] 2000: 265)

80 *Why Feminism Matters*

However, it is in her attempts to mobilise Irigaray's work on speaking the female body that Plant has more difficulty in retaining her challenge to malestream language and thought on the web. She uses the metaphor of weaving to entwine different aspects of women's experience and history, endeavouring to deploy Irigaray's entreaties to reconstitute or make anew the symbolic order.

Like Haraway, who has pursued a different path out of the cyborg and moved most productively into the intersections of the human and the animal, Plant sees the transgressive potential of the web and has presented one of the most positive takes on the internet in her ecstatic vision of the liberating possibilities of web-based technologies which combine 'the actual and the virtual. An interface which is taking off on its own: no longer the voice, the gap, or the absence, the veils are already cybernetic' (1995: 63).

Plant's over-enthusiasm and essentialist reading of Irigaray lead her into difficulties which do not necessarily suggest that it is not possible to present liberatory arguments about the power of new technologies. Plant was typical of earlier arguments that

> The greatest freedom cyberspace promises is that of recasting the self: from static beings, bound by the body and betrayed by appearances, net surfers may reconstruct themselves in a multiplicity of dazzling roles, changing from moment to moment according to whim.
> (Stallabrass, 1995: 15)

The web is not, however, a disembodied or gender-free space, as Adam (1998) and Wakeford (1998) have both argued, in their research on artificial language and web use, in Wakeford's case in cyber-cafés. Wakeford is attentive to the many landscapes we inhabit that are mutually constitutive. The promise of freedom in cyberspace may indeed be seductive, especially for women when other spaces present dangers, including physical risks. Across the globe many women may be much safer in cyberspace than anywhere else, but this is not a simple message embedded in a binary logic of risk and security; both are material and both are in play.

The blog 'Girl with a One Track Mind', first started in 2004 (Lee, 2004), is a clear example of the limitations that accompany the supposed freedoms and liberations that are presented by the internet. The blog details the sexual exploits of a young single woman living and working in London, including her fantasies, as well as a series of one-night stands and a variety of sexual acts, which are described relatively explicitly.

When the blog started it was written under the pen name Abby Lee, and the young woman clearly enjoyed the anonymity of the internet as a means through which she could express sexual fantasies and ideas in a way in which she felt she could not in everyday life. In 2006 a book with the same title was published; soon after, her real identity, Zoe Margolis, was revealed (Mikhailova, 2006). The young woman initially refused to comment and went into hiding as she left the safe and anonymised space of the internet and she was subject to social censure. Margolis herself, in an interview later in the year, stated that the internet appealed to her as she could write 'freely' and 'honestly' about her experiences (Margolis, 2006). There is an interesting dual process of liberation and sexual freedom, which runs in tandem with a fear of judgement and a sense that such liberation is only possible in the anonymity of cyberspace. It also highlights that there are clear connections between the internet and life offline. This example raises serious questions about how possible it is to be liberated through sexual activity, when in fact this example demonstrates that it can be highly constraining. Interestingly, the Girl with a One Track Mind site continues, and Margolis professes that she herself is a feminist (with a link at the side of her page to the f-word). Her self-definition as a feminist comes from what she feels is an absence of female-centred perspectives on sexuality in the mainstream media. Her articulation of feminism is therefore strongly linked to sexual liberation, and as such can be seen in light of the arguments of feminists who question whether sexual liberation is not just reinstating the associations of women with their sexuality. Indeed, as Levy (2006) argues, rather than being liberating it merely serves to objectify women, by adopting the stances and terms of patriarchy. This is true whether it is present on the internet or offline. The very decision to write anonymously highlights the sense of shame that accompanies this expression of sexuality and indeed how strong the social constraints on women may be offline.

The web is a site for the proliferation of blogs and also for those with an explicitly feminist edge. Cyberspace has also become the metaphoric home of new brands of feminism, as exemplified in fashion and music, one of the most spectacular of which was the riot grrrl phenomenon in popular music in the early 1990s. The riot grrrl feminist underground punk movement, which began in the US, challenged the hegemony of fawning femininity of the girl backing group and the cheer leader who conforms to a stereotypical femininity and substituted piercings and tattoos for pink dresses. Riot grrrl lyrics focused on social mistreatment of women, including domestic abuse, rape and political demands for abortion and reproductive rights, equal pay and safer streets (Barton, 2009).

The phenomenon was presented as political and seen as radically new in its musical innovations and, more especially, explicitly political message (Marcus, 2010). Sharon Cheslow, guitarist with Chalk Circle, was reported as attributing her politics in music to her study of feminist theory at university (Barton, 2009: 16).

Although riot grrrl has stamped its message on the language of contemporary resistance, as appropriated by the cyber-grrrl movement (Gillis et al., 2007), the extent of its ability to develop a coherent feminist challenge has been undermined by its associations with fashion and a more male tradition of sensation, but what is important is the public expression of the need to articulate feminist resistance and the spontaneity of its use of the contemporary cultural practices to reclaim and reverse the sexualisation of women as well as their cultural marginalisation, by linking popular culture and feminist politics.

As Gillis et al. argue, a new (cyber-)feminism would have 'to interrogate more carefully its politics and histories', which, she argues, 'is best achieved by disentangling cyborg feminism, gender and technology studies, cybertheory and e-activism' (2007: 179). She also notes, in the context of Haraway's much quoted preference for cyborgs over goddesses as a desirable identity for women, that the idealisation of the cyborg that is part of the utopian views of cyberspace embraced by feminists also needs to be challenged. One way of doing this would be to pursue Irigaray's politics of difference, which acknowledges gendered, embodied difference, rather than pretend that cyberspace is disembodied and revisit some of the critical analysis which does foreground gender and is attentive to where women are in these spaces. Disembodiment could be close to the disappearing body in the operating theatre, which surrenders itself (often herself) to interventions whilst unconscious (Akrich and Pasveer, 2004).

Conclusion

This book is presented as a dialogue between two women who grew up in very different historical moments; if we consider the differences between the periods when Kath became a woman (1950–78) and when Sophie did (1980–2009), they are periods which are strikingly contrasting. Not only are there significant changes within each period, there are also changes between them – no less so than in how feminism is articulated and also in developments in science and technology. This chapter has addressed the area of technoscience, first, because it is so important to women's lives and also to feminism, and second, as it is an area which raises particular challenges to the idea of a cross-cultural dialogue. The particular areas of focus have been those of the development of the internet, and the scientific intervention in bodies through reproduction and maternity. These developments are crucial to how feminism is articulated through blogs and websites, and the challenges that it faces, such as through the spread of internet pornography (see chapter 5). The internet is also one of the media for many people's lives today, and technoscience is now central to how women's lives are lived, as in the ability for some to have IVF or cosmetic surgery amongst other things. Given that technology is often a pivotal medium of change, it raises interesting questions that are at the core of this book about whether feminist ideas from the 1970s or before can be relevant to a world or riot grrrls and feminist blogging. Technoscience has particular relevance for our discussion, because of its associations with the generational model of feminism and the relationship between change and continuity. However, as this book is based on a dialogue, we aim to challenge the idea of straightforward progress by proposing a dialogue. Neither seeing feminist history nor technological progress are teleologies and we suggest the ways in which certain issues of inequalities persist and others are merely reconfigured in different ways. We have suggested the need for a more nuanced exploration of both the uneven paths of transformation and the exchanges between different feminist moments.

One of the main focuses in this chapter has been the body and materiality: this is the subject of intervention in a medical arena, yet is also something which many seek to transcend in cyberspace. Technoscience offers dramatic and powerful ways of transforming the sexed body and the category woman which are sometimes translated into an attempt to escape the body or to reconfigure the embodied self. There are increasingly strong arguments for holding on to the body and to the political project of feminism in however many diverse forms it may take to accommodate differences among women and a sexual politics which uses technoscience to enhance embodied experience rather than escape it. In discussing the body in this chapter, we have aimed to challenge essentialism within the context of the impact of technoscience, yet at the same time we wish to hold on to the importance of the materiality of the lived body. We have argued that bodies and difference matter and can be accommodated without resort to essentialist or reductionist theories and this argument has been developed through different engagements with biology and a rethinking of the relationship between techno-scientific cultures and practices and embodied experience.

A theme that has run through this chapter is that between liberation and constraint: whether developments in technoscience can be seen to liberate women, to give them more opportunities or to restrict them. Indeed, it also raises the question of the relationship between cyberspace and life offline, and we wish to suggest that we do not see the two spaces in opposition. Technoscience is developing at a rapid pace, but problems are rearticulated in similar ways, which in this chapter we have used to highlight that bodies are still problematic, and we still need a politics of difference that engages with life offline. Web technologies reinstate offline distinctions, for example of generation, gender, disability and racialisation, as well as challenging them. The offline world still manifests the same inequalities and, as is demonstrated by the feminist websites, the same concerns that shaped those of feminist groups in the 1970s and 1980s are present in current debates amongst feminist activists. There are problems related to seeing technoscience as value-free or ungendered; some of the tensions related to the claims of being freed from corporeal constraints. This is taken up in chapter 5, where we look at the persistence of pornography and at what has been called the pornification debate. Cyberspace creates opportunities for anonymity for more exploitative activities as well as liberatory ones of self-expression for those who have hitherto been silenced. The regulation of cyberspace is also problematic. Cyberspace, like all aspects of technoscience and new technologies, offers moments of opportunity and others of constraint and exclusion; technoscience is at the intersection of other axes of power and not a separate space. Even cyberspace is not free-floating, but firmly embedded in power relations that operate across all areas of life. The manifestation of existing inequalities in the practices of technoscience also raises questions about the extent to which change is either linear or part of a metanarrative of epochal transformation. Change can be uneven and incremental, even in the field where one might expect it to follow a particularly rapid march of progress.

Reproductive technologies are also part of the wider social context and reproduce and represent inequalities and materialities, but motherhood has histories and resonances that are culturally specific and contradictory, as is apparent in the configuration of motherhood as an absent presence. We have to move beyond the cyborg/goddess binary, or that of the earth mother/techno-mother; they are not the only alternatives. Change and social transformations, as illustrated by the discussion of new technologies, do not exist in a vacuum but have to be located within a politics of difference. This is the subject of the next chapter.

4
A Grown-up Politics of Difference

> Although the Fems appreciate the role of men in feminism, we are primarily a women-only group. As such, we will in general limit participation in our meetings to women identifying as women.
>
> (Sheffield Fems, 2009)

> We are a women-only group because we believe it is vital that women have safe and supportive spaces where we can work together politically to campaign for our rights.
>
> (London Feminist Network, 2009)

These two statements are taken from currently active feminist groups in the UK, and show the positions taken in relation to the participation in the groups and who can attend meetings. A slightly different policy is adopted in each case, with the London Feminist Network opting for 'women only' and the Sheffield Fems adopting the stance of 'women identifying as women'. The former has come under scrutiny in the organisation of the Reclaim the Night march in London, because the event is exclusively for women (not only does it not include men, it also excludes transsexuals who were born male). The Sheffield Fems are clearly aware of potential questions of inclusiveness and as such have adopted the slightly more ambiguous stance of those who 'identify' as women, thereby protecting themselves against this accusation. This follows a debate over whether men should be included or not (for the last two years men have been allowed to attend). What these two examples highlight is that questions of difference matter, yet these same questions are also difficult and problematic to negotiate. Difference, as expressed in terms of differences between women and men, remain politically relevant in the twenty-first century, in a manner which does not deny the blurred spaces between gendered identities identified in earlier feminist accounts of difference (Maguire, 1985) or of the scope of differences which intersect in contemporary cultural, political and social spaces.

The politics of difference has travelled a troubled route through structuralist emphasis on binaries, the problems of equality and the poststructuralist virtual abandonment of any version of gender difference that could inform a political position. Difference has been celebrated, set against equality or combined with it to produce diversity, reconstituted as *différance* following Jacques Derrida. It has been coupled with a different preposition as in 'different to', instead of the more grammatically correct 'from', all in the name of escaping the devaluing of one side of the relational equation which is seen to produce difference. Difference is always implicated with sameness and homogeneity, however limited. If people see themselves as different from one group, there are questions about what makes the group with which they identify the same. The identity politics of the 1980s was largely based on a sense of community of those involved in a particular category of self, marked out as 'different from' and the 'same as' (Woodward, 1997a). Identity politics is in dialogue with post-feminism, just as second-wave ideas about difference and structuralism, and its concomitant community of women, however defined, is in dialogue with postmodernist fluidity, destabilisation and poststructuralist diversity. As the opening quotes to this chapter highlight, these questions are far from resolved. Women in the twenty-first century still engage with the problems of difference and, implicitly if not always explicitly, with what was called the equality difference debate. Women's groups and feminist websites still address the problems of categorisation and the exclusion of men and inclusion of pro-feminist men or those who self-categorise as women. Postmodernism and the hybridity of classificatory systems have not eliminated the problems of speaking or acting as women. Contemporary debates by activists about the inclusion or exclusion of men reflect and reconstruct many of those of second-wave feminism, for example, in women's peace groups, such as those organised at the cruise missile base at Greenham Common in the UK in the 1980s. I-Kath recalls debates among activists and in higher education about the status of women-only groups and how providing safe spaces for women to reflect on their experiences outside the delivery of the curriculum (e.g. in optional sessions) could be reconciled with the equal opportunities to which educational institutions are committed. The debate within the academy was framed by ideas of fair play and equity, but it often raised important questions about providing women-only spaces, which was theorised in a variety of ways, including the strategic necessity of recognising the need to address difference in its particularities within a feminist political framework (Ramazanoğlu, 1989).

Contemporary questions are raised about whether the group should be women-only, or if meetings should alternate between mixed and women only gatherings. In the case of the Sheffield Fems, a group that I-Sophie has attended on several occasions, whether or not to include men has been a topic of debate. The resolution is that men wishing to be involved can be part of specific campaigns but not attend the weekly meetings, as a way to allow for all possible perspectives: men are not excluded, nor are transsexuals. The only position not taken is that of a women-only space, as the category woman is perhaps seen as too exclusionary, or there is too much uncertainty over what this entails. This kind of questioning of categories and uncertainty about who counts as a woman is resonant of earlier debates about feminist activism, but is now inflected with the instability of postmodernist subversion and undermining of the category woman. Contemporary debates are not so much concerned with whether events and feminist politics even should privilege women as a distinct group of people with gendered histories and recognisable boundaries of gendered selfhood, but whether new boundaries can be established by expressions of interest, so that being a woman is a process of self-classification or even arbitrary and disembodied.

Debates about difference were central to feminism in the 1980s and recognised as such. When third-wave feminists celebrate the advantages of difference and of contradictions within feminism (Shapiro Saunders, 2007) or suggest that getting to grips with difference is a more recent venture (Dent, 1995) they may be underestimating the extent of second-wave engagement with these issues. However, what is particular to third-wave discussions of difference is the suggestion that the second-wave contribution to the debates about difference is framed by utopian discourses, a conflict-free zone unsullied by difference to which feminists have aspired (Kitch, 2000). The desirability of a utopian agreement has been located within a generational relationship within such critiques, with the suggestion that second-wave feminism speaks in the parental, maternal mode. This is predicated on the model of generational conflict, with the daughters of the third wave rebelling against their perception of the previous generation and expressing a desire to assert their own autonomy. What is most important for our project is the need to engage with the diversity of feminist critical thinking and to explore rather than reject a whole host of feminist interventions which so productively address the problems and the possibilities of difference. Difference, although temporally and spatially specific and contingent, has enormous relevance and resonance for feminist politics.

This chapter takes up the debate and looks at how current engagements with marking gender and the experience of difference encounter earlier debates at points of interconnection. Difference and some process and acknowledgement of gendered differentiation are central to the concerns of feminism, which do not have to be based on a fixed or oversimplified biological notion of sexed difference. It is possible, as Irigaray argues, to suggest that

> Without doubt the most appropriate content for the universal is sexual difference... Sexual difference is an immediate natural given and it is a real and irreducible component of the universal. The whole of human kind is composed of women and men...
> Sexual difference probably represents the most universal question we can address. Our era is faced with the task of dealing with this issue, because across the whole world, there are only men and women.
> (1996: 47)

It may appear that Irigaray is overstating the case and minimising the ambiguities of sexed differences, including intersex and transgendered identifications, as well as marginalising other significant aspect of differences, especially race. However, as Grosz argues, Irigaray's claims do not place sexual difference

> outside historical or biological transformations, nor does it render it any more significant than any form of oppression in explaining the complexities of social and cultural evolution; it simply insists that whatever other factors are at work, sexual difference must be a consideration, a relevant factor.
> (2008: 50)

Assertion of the universality of questions of sexual difference is based on the empirical manifestation of sexual difference across time and space. However, the embedded powers of differentiation based on sexual difference, including the centrality that is given to embodied difference, does not mean that it is immutable and fixed. As the discussion of technoscience in chapter 3 showed, bodies are increasingly plastic. The opportunities afforded for blurring the boundaries between body and machine and corporeal plasticity does not eliminate gender differences though, and technoscience presents another field in which inequalities based on gender are perpetuated and reinstated as well as new opportunities and transgressive possibilities. The purpose of constructing an argument built on the ubiquity of sexual difference is to recognise its temporal and spatial impact on social relations and to deconstruct the processes through which difference is made, remade and lived as part of being in the world. Failing to engage with the primacy of sexual difference may serve only to reinforce and reinstate its greatest and most entrenched inequalities.

This chapter looks at the status of the politics of difference through feminist encounters in the political terrain of activism and practice as well as through attempts to reclaim the lost category 'woman', for example, in the diverse approaches of what was called French feminism in the work of Irigaray, Cixous and, differently, by Kristeva, in Butler's work (1993, 1997, 2000, 2004) and the development of queer theory, and in critiques of the more disembodied aspects of the cultural turn. Postmodernism and postcolonialism have strong ties with feminism and this chapter looks at how these conversations play out in the development of feminist theorising and in particular in relation to the articulation of differences and inequalities that include sexual difference. Butler, in critiquing the heterosexual matrix and the normalising of the heterosexual woman and man, opened up the space for theorising queer identities and other previously marginalised identities and redirecting the feminist spotlight from the centre to the margins; in doing so, the marginal and the transgressive become the new feminist centre. Whilst the transgressive raises questions about the naturalisation of the body and associated gender and sexed identities, in this book we are keen to focus on the category woman. This is not merely an academic interest, but it is something which is essential to the way that sexed difference is lived in everyday experience, as well as being a political strategy and the conceptual basis of feminist theories.

The chapter focuses in particular on the question and the language of difference in the political terrain and through the practices and policies of differentiation, starting with feminist debates about the tensions between equality and difference which powerfully inform contemporary discussion of post-feminism. Second-wave feminists agonised over the difficulties for women of claiming political and social rights to particular treatment as women and the complexities of wanting to be both equal and different. Women have fought for the right to control their own bodies and sexuality and to equal civil, legal and political rights, including equal pay with men. Many of these struggles may have been won *de jure* but certainly have not been achieved *de facto*, as is evident in the disjunction between legislation on equal pay and against discrimination in the West and actual pay rates and incidences of harassment and discrimination in all aspects of human rights that still persist. The particularities of the equality and difference debate are worth exploring because of the liberal assumptions that, legal battles having been won, sexual difference is no longer a relevant field for political engagement in neoliberal countries and only has any purchase in a few recalcitrant repressive regimes globally. Women in neoliberal states are presented with the dilemma of a post-feminist climate in which the battle is seen to be over and, women's rights having been won, there are no collective resolutions to be gained. All that remains for contemporary young women is lifestyle choices and individual solutions. The chapter examines the implications of the gendered identifications that are made and remade through the construction of difference and through social, cultural and legal institutions, in order to reinstate the materiality of difference and the ordinariness of sex as a category into feminist political thinking that can embrace difference and contingency.

Problems of difference; problems with difference

A politics of difference is and has been problematic for feminist theorists. As was demonstrated in chapter 3, difference is dangerous, partly because it is associated with corporeality and what Butler (1993) calls anatomical difference and also because difference seems to invoke binaries and the polarisation of opposites. Binary logic may also invoke negativity and lack that are contrasted with more positive, active attributes, as expressed in psychoanalytical theories, especially Lacanian, in which the desiring subject is male and woman is represented as lack. Cixous took up Derrida's point about the unequal distribution of power in the logic and language of dualisms which underpin and underline gendered social divisions.

Thought has always worked by:

Opposition.
Speech/Writing
High/Low...
Does this mean something?

(Cixous, [1975] 1980: 90)

She goes on to present a poetic table of differences which still has resonance in the gendered experience and practice of difference.

Where is she?
Activity/passivity
Sun/Moon
Culture/Nature
Day/Night
Father/Mother
Head/heart
Intelligible/sensitive
Man

Woman

([1975] 1980: 90)

Cixous's project is to demonstrate the inequitable constitution of binary logic and many feminist critiques arising from feminist theories in the 1970s and 1980s focused on the constraints of dualisms, both conceptually and in lived experience in the practices of women's lives. These become problematic when the binaries of sex are mapped onto other, hierarchical, binaries. Binaries foreclose the muddied waters of ambiguity and, especially the contradictions and ambivalences of sexual difference, by insisting on only two categories of gendered person. However, in emphasising the limitations of the idea of opposites and of dualisms and positing more fluid classifications that even deny the possibility of any categorisation, there is a danger that the political edge and the relevance of feminist analyses have lost their focus on power and the power geometry of sexual difference. It does not allow for the possibility of interrogating inequality which is experienced by woman as women. Feminists are complicit in the processes through which new sets of knowledge are produced and become established. The task in this book is to present some evaluation of the impact of feminist knowledges at different historical moments and in different places, by concentrating on how the category woman is reproduced, reconstructed, denied or deconstructed. In the disarticulations of contemporary feminism that McRobbie notes, feminism can be seen as dismantling itself in the breakdown of alliances through what she calls the 'disarticulation [which] devalues or negates and makes unthinkable the very basis of coming-together (even if to take part in disputatious encounters), on the assumption that there is no longer any need for such actions' (2008: 26). We argue in this chapter that this process of dismantling is inextricably imbricated in the abandonment of a politics of difference that requires the reinstatement of the category woman. The kind of difference that was invoked in earlier feminist critiques, however, reproduced a polarisation which also ran the risk of reinstating the very unequal oppositions they sought to challenge, especially those which deployed corporeality to celebrate the female side of the equation. Motherhood represents one such problem. The celebration of motherhood, in particular when constituted in a pro-family rhetoric, has been strongly linked in some critiques (e.g. McRobbie, 2008) to a political conservatism. This raises a core debate for this chapter, which is how to acknowledge difference in a critical manner which does not simply reinstate existing stereotypes or inequalities. It is important that in advocating a politics of difference, we are also strongly challenging the naturalisation of women's or men's capacities, which is what frequently happens within conservatism. We aim to take up the question of difference in a theoretically informed and critical way.

The mother of all differences?

Motherhood is an aspect of embodiment which has created particular difficulties within feminist thinking. Motherhood is still largely a set of activities, embodied experiences and a relationship associated with women, not least because it is women's bodies that carry and deliver the child. Chapter 3 addressed one of the most troubling aspects of difference, namely motherhood, and drew attention to the absence of motherhood and the mother–daughter relationship in western culture. We cited Irigaray's complex arguments for their reinstatement, or maybe instatement, within a political framework that has been subject to claims of essentialism, but could not be defined as conservative in any way. Since Irigaray is not appealing to an historical pre-symbolic in a temporal chronological narrative, as some feminists of the second wave in particular have done (Stone, 1991), for example, in the much criticised celebration of the goddess and the matriarchal societies that pre-dated patriarchy. Irigaray's critique is theoretical and concerned with the narratives and symbolic systems through which meanings are reproduced and with the embodied practices which constitute social life and social inequalities. The feminist relationship with motherhood as a site at which difference is marked has not always featured sophisticated complex arguments, which may be why some feminist forays into the maternal have been so speedily dismissed. Attempts to engage with the more positive dimensions of maternity as a female identity that could be celebrated have been associated not only with the dilemmas of biological or corporeal reductionism, but also with an unhappy alliance with conservative, pro-family politics.

Some feminist approaches have attempted to point to the particularities of women's experience. Even those who had previously argued strongly against the constraints of the nuclear family, and especially of motherhood within it, have recanted and noted the specificities of the experience of motherhood which are not necessarily repressive and could be reconfigured even within existing social relations. The most notable of those who appear to have retracted earlier criticisms are Betty Friedan and Germaine Greer, with her celebration of the extended family. McRobbie (2008) is very critical of the pro-maternal/maternity thinking of some earlier feminism which, she argues necessarily promotes a conservative political approach which denies the fluidity of personal and sexual relationships and the possibilities of a re-articulation of women's social and sexual identifications. However, in this book we are arguing that recognising sexed difference in an arena such as motherhood does not have to promote conservatism. Indeed, acknowledging the ways in which motherhood is gendered is important in, for example, challenging existing maternity laws and in how we conceive of the workplace. It does not just mean that this will involve the repositioning of women in the home.

Neoliberalism: contexts and dilemmas

One of the problems for feminist politics which has already been identified is the incorporation of feminist policies and objectives into the mainstream, which has been a feature of neoliberal governance and has been read positively by some feminists who have welcomed gender mainstreaming (Walby, 2002). Some feminists have argued that feminist and gender equality aspirations have been met and the many conditions which made feminism relevant as a social and political critique of the structures and institutions that created the problems have now been superseded. In government this has been challenged, in spite of public hyperbole about the apparent explosion of women in government, as in the UK Blair administration in 1997, when the increased number of elected women Members of Parliament were celebrated as 'Blair's Babes', the nomenclature being a pretty dire warning of how frivolously this was seen. The so-named Blair's Babes form an interesting contrast to the terminology surrounding Britain's first and only female prime minister, who was known as the Iron Lady. Both represent different ways in which gender difference have been dealt with or positioned within the mainstream of political life: in the case of Thatcher, she was seen as a strong political force, yet she notoriously did very little that would be advantageous to women. By contrast, Blair's Babes are trivialised and feminised by being reduced to their appearance: both in their own bodily appearance as women and as a group of women, who gave Blair's government a semblance of gender equality. The superficiality of this is revealed when we look at what has happened since then: the number of women MPs has fallen and, under Blair's leadership, even women who had espoused feminist politics earlier in their careers were unable to put feminist politics onto the agenda in a regime characterised by macho tactics, practices and policies (Campbell, 2007).

In some instances third-wave feminism has been complicit with some of the assumptions that the battle has been won and gender mainstreaming means that the problem for young women in the West today is earlier 'feminism rather than patriarchy' (Baumgardner and Richards, 2000: 65). This is an argument framed within debates about consumerism and individuality, but still suggests that political struggles and feminist critiques are redundant in a climate in which women have more choice and more control over their lives. This is usefully illustrated by the contrast in I-Sophie and I-Kath's lives. I-Sophie was born in 1979 (three months after Margaret Thatcher became PM), and despite having a feminist mother, I did not see feminism as something that had anything to do with my life. I grew up with the illusion that gender equality had largely been achieved, and whilst there were instances in my own life that countered this, they were brief punctuations in a context otherwise characterised by gender equality. It was only when I was in my early twenties and had graduated that feminism moved from being an interest of mine to being something which framed how I saw the world. Although I had grown up implicitly influenced by the attitudes and ideas of feminism, I had previously not seen them as being relevant to my world. This is in many ways typical of those around me. After I had changed my attitudes and started to recognise the huge gender inequalities in terms of pay, employment and the sexualisation of women, what struck me was how my attitudes were seen to be somewhat extreme when compared to those around me. The expectation and assumption of gender equality had become so pervasive, despite the evidence to the contrary, we had become in many ways gender-blind.

Third way, third-wave, post-feminist problems

Some third-wave feminists have argued that the recent articulation of neoliberalism, which has been called the third way, provides a framework for exploring and analysing what has been termed post-feminism and what Gillis (2004) calls feminist micropolitics. The third way, which was associated with the sociologist Anthony Giddens' (1998) input to the reconceptualisation of social democratic politics, was influential in reshaping the British Labour Party and in the strategies of New Labour which came to power in 1997. As outlined above, Blair's first administration was celebrated for the increased number of women MPs, unfortunately labelled Blair's Babes by the press, suggesting a somewhat insubstantial change in the hegemonic masculinity that had characterised Labour politics at many moments in its history. This movement in politics was linked to the shift from the class-based politics of labourite, socialist and social democratic politics in Europe and based on the rearticulation of the relationship between the state and the market and the severing of links with the trades union movement, especially in the UK, and the opening up of a politics based on consumption rather than production (Sassatelli, 2007) in the context of globalisation (Giddens, 1999; Held et al., 1999), technological development and the expansion of the knowledge society (Woodward, 2004). UK developments echoed with those of other neoliberal states across the world and the shift towards an emphasis on consumer choice and markets rather than state control which had been dominant in the US and UK from the 1980s has grown across Europe and the former Soviet states. The opening up of identifications for women as part of a new framework that incorporated consumption and popular culture within third way neoliberalism might be seen to resonate with feminist micropolitics. Gillis argues that micropolitics offers a depoliticised model of political action or even inaction – certainly, non-traditional, limited action. Gillis distinguishes between post-feminism and third-wave feminism in her critique of micro-feminist politics.

Third way politics also emphasised choice and the possibilities of participation for women in the public arena; choice and consumption were clearly linked to paid work, because the policies of neoliberal governance within the trajectory of the third way stressed the importance of involvement in the labour market as a route into independence and autonomy for women. Stephanie Genz (2006) focuses on the centrality of paid work in the policies of the third way regimes in the US and parts of Europe (notably the UK and Germany) as an individualist route into social belonging and citizenship which appeals to the consumer-led, individualistic version of feminism of many young women. According to Genz, post-feminism, with its reaction against earlier socialist versions of feminism, fits in well with these pluralist, fluid identifications, which are also consonant with much poststructuralist, postmodernist feminism, including some of Butler's theoretical arguments that lend themselves to a decentred, fluid conceptualisation of activists included within feminist projects. Genz's arguments suggest that the destabilising of the category woman could not only undermine feminist politics, but also lead to more individualistic neoconservative politics, which accords with Gillis's distinction between post-feminism and third-wave feminism, although the dividing line is not always easy to see and it may be a nice point to argue for clear-cut boundaries.

The US context is different and neoliberalism belongs to a particular genealogy in which socialism and social democracy are differently inflected from the European context. However, as Lisa Duggan (2003) has pointed out in the context of the US, neoliberalism has encompassed everything and has appropriated identity politics into its own remit. However, as she argues, liberalism in its more recent expanded form is not always so liberal and has increasingly been under attack, for example in the dismantling of welfare and the cutbacks in spending, which were strongly evident in the conservative politics of the George W. Bush administrations, often masked by the guise of economic policy, but nonetheless heavily value-laden. Previous administrations had mainstreamed elements of identity politics, such as gay rights and equality feminism, so that they appear to have been normalised and integrated into the neoliberal project, but as Duggan demonstrates, this is not a linear progression of the enhancement of a rights agenda. Economic recession notwithstanding, the future of welfare and social policies in the US looks more positive in 2009. However, it remains to be seen how far Barack Obama will be able to counter some of the reduction of rights, notably women's rights, although he has already acted on women's reproductive rights and moved to allow the use of stem cells in medical research and treatment. These actions suggest a politics that is much more consonant with neoliberalism and led to its incorporation of a more feminist agenda. In the contemporary climate the relationship between the state and the market, although recently strongly weighted in favour of markets, has begun to move back again in light of recent market failures and global economic recession. This may place severe restrictions on the ways in which the state is able to support different

Liberalism and feminism: dialogues past and present

The apparent benefits of the spread of neoliberalism have been subject to feminist critiques for a long time, well before the resurgence of feminism in the West in the 1960s and 1970s. Mary Wollstonecraft, whose *Vindication of the Rights of Woman* was first published in 1792, pre-dated the suffragette movement in pointing to the social and cultural discrimination which women suffered, and the suffrage movement of the early twentieth century also included demands for social inclusion, in terms of rights to higher education. Neoliberalism is, however, a force to be reckoned with and its global spread cannot be assumed or pass unquestioned. The almost global mainstreaming of neoliberalism has become one of the 'universal pretensions' of political thought (Philips, 1992). This is not a simple story, but the language of neoliberalism increasingly seems ubiquitous. Liberalism as a political ideology is founded on ideals of critical, rational thought, self-reflection and the value of self-determination and individual liberty, and has been critiqued by many of those who have not been included in the Enlightenment project of the unified rational subject (Hall, 1982; Pateman, 1988; Barrett and Philips, 1992).

Liberalism is universalist, if not universal, but it too has a troubled history through its failure to embrace everyone, all women, working-class men and those in particular ethnic or racialised groups, for example, being only lately included with rights of citizenship and still not in all places and under all circumstances. Liberalism evokes a unitary political subject who has a right to freedom and shares this right with other subjects who are alike in this respect. The role of the state is to ensure access to liberty and self-determination and to provide a framework in which people can make free choices. However, there are a number of interrelated tensions within liberalism, notably those between equality and freedom, equality and hierarchy, and sameness and difference. For example, if people are free to do as they wish, some may exercise their freedom at the expense of others. Feminists in the second wave pointed out the liberal failure to interrogate underlying inequalities in power relations, especially those implicated in the relationship between women and men. Equality of opportunity is almost inevitably in tension with equality of outcome. Neoliberal thinking suggests that liberalism is premised on equality of opportunity, but persistent inequality of outcome inevitably suggests that opportunities are not actually equal. There may be equal pay legislation in most democratic states and increasingly across the globe, but women's pay is almost always well below that of their male colleagues and women still do not occupy positions of power or receive such high average remuneration as men. The media celebrate success stories of women such as Nicola Horlick, hailed as a city 'superwoman' who was spectacularly successful in her career and also had five children, fulfilling the dream that you can have it all. The few women who manage to succeed are used as a model to suggest that meritocracy works, and manages to obscure the massive inequalities that underpin this. The media pounced on Horlick's divorce with similar relish, as part of a more recent conservative backlash that repositions women's primary role as homemakers.

Liberalism, like feminism, is also fraught with dissent as well as inequalities. One aspect of the apparent freedom of liberalism is freedom of speech; speech, debate and deliberation are central to democracy and to neoliberalism. John Stuart Mill notably defended free speech in *On Liberty* and this has remained a key if contested tenet. However, as the debates within liberalism and feminism about censorship demonstrate, this debate raises important issues about the protection of vulnerable people and about the extent to which words can be violent acts. Within feminist exchanges the debate has extended beyond ideas of protection by the state into both the nature of injurious speech and the relationship between actions and behaviour and symbolic systems. Debates have been particularly powerful in the context of speech acts and representations of race hate and violence expressed against women, as Catherine Mackinnon has argued in the case of pornography, which, she claims, is more than symbolic; it constitutes an act of violence against women, just as the racist symbol 'whites only' or 'no blacks' is more than speech (MacKinnon, 1994). Whereas MacKinnon argues that social inequality is substantially created and enforced and is not merely inscrcribed. Butler (1997) has explored the problems linked to claims that we may have been injured by speech acts and argues against the claim in favour of censorship and protection through the legislative system, that symbolic systems can be the equivalent of actions. This debate illustrates some of the contradictions within the neoliberal project that have particular resonance within feminism and signpost some of the specific problems, in this instance, about the relationship between words and things in the context of the liberal tenet of free speech.

One of the assertions that has been made to explain the inequalities of outcome that appear invariably to ensue is to appeal to the unequal starting point of those involved as rooted in some kind of natural base. Friedrich Engels' observation in *The Origins of the Family, Private Property and the State* (1884) that women were the first proletariat and exploited because of their role in reproduction has informed a variety of feminist approaches as it combines the materialities of social organisation and collective experience with a critique of power imbalances that connect the individual to the wider social structure. There is a limit, however, to what can be explained by claiming that inequalities arise from unequal natural abilities, although it has often been 'nature' that has been invoked to explain unequal outcomes. In fact, pursuing the opportunities open to individuals can lead to a structural hierarchy of unequal outcomes which itself constrains equality of opportunity at a collective level, which has always been the aim of feminist activism to challenge.

Lastly, the ideal of equal rights and obligations as a citizen, in relation to the state and other citizens, implies sharing the same values about what rights and obligations are, that is sharing a moral worldview. Different worldviews can generate different conceptions of what is rightful and obligatory for citizens, which are related to the existing inequalities between subjects. This is another instance of the underlying tension between sameness and uniqueness. If liberalism means that each individual has the right to autonomy and self-determination, then everyone is the same in this respect and sameness rather than difference is central to its trajectory. Sameness might also have been underplayed in the identity politics of the 1970s and 1980s when groups sought to mark their difference and particularity (Woodward, 1997a).

However, at the same time, ideas of personal autonomy lead quickly to ideas of personal identity and the desire that one's selfhood be recognised by others, which implies differentiation and distinction (Taylor 1992: 43). Such an approach could be seen as a Romantic gloss on Enlightenment liberalism, which suggests a concern with the particular character or spirit of persons, nations, places, which have a more powerful purchase for understanding ethnicity and diversity than gender differences. The autonomy of the self can only be realised when others recognise you as distinct and thus different. The autonomy that all individuals desire, and that liberalism vindicates as the key value which we share equally, is paradoxically a condition that depends on differentiation. Differentiation carries differential weightings and values; that, however, makes it a more politically subversive concept.

Another linked tension that underpins liberalism is whether liberty is a natural phenomenon in which governance should be minimal and non-interventionist, a view suited to classic liberalism; or whether it is an elusive construction that needs to be carefully and diligently nurtured, protected against other people's wilful exercise of their 'rights' by an interventionist state, which in social democratic regimes can not only regulate markets but also guarantee rights, and thus difference, for those who have been marginalised or excluded, such as ethnic minorities and women, which implies an approach more consonant with a civic republicanism and might invoke charitable discourses that emphasise the individual's place in a collective (Heater 1999).

The third way has developed a range of legislative interventions within states to embrace different aspects of discrimination on grounds of race, ethnicity, gender, disability, age and sexuality, albeit quite late in the day in most cases. So successful have these strategies been seen to be in the lexicon of neoliberal governance that states too have assumed the battle has been won. It is not only the practice of legal, quasi-legal and voluntary bodies to group all aspects of social exclusion together, as if there were no particularities on the margins (Woodward, 2007). This has also been formalised in the bodies that deal with difference and equality. In the UK, the Commission for Racial Equality and Equal Opportunities Commission have merged to become the Equality and Human Rights Commission. Whilst the decision to return to the language of rights is commendable, the existence of a single body, although having practical advantages, might obscure differences and construct a category of homogeneous disadvantaged people, and may counter the more political project of promoting human rights.

As Duggan (2003) argues, there has been some exaggeration of the ubiquity of neoliberalism. On the one hand, repressive regimes remain, whatever the opening up of markets, and on the other, neoliberalism takes multiple forms, some of which would have been described as socialist or social democratic: states still intervene in welfare programmes as well as, if not more so, in markets, especially as demonstrated in the credit crunch of 2008–9. Violence against women still operates on a massive scale across the globe (Gangoli, 2006, 2007), a phenomenon that is not restricted to what could be called repressive regimes. In the UK, for example, it is estimated that a quarter of all women have experienced domestic violence. There are different strands of liberalism with different emphases and neoliberal economics is not the only aspect that has to be considered. Before the election of President Obama, Coles (2005) argues that political liberalism was no longer the dominant ideology in the US, and an increasingly anti-democratic politics had been replacing the ideals of equality that underpin liberalism through the right-wing backlash of the early twenty-first century, although a critical deconstruction of neoliberalism and an exploration of its component parts, including engaged activism, might offer a more optimistic reading of its democratic possibilities.

Since the establishment of liberal thought, usually traced back to the Enlightenment, regimes based on liberalism, which have evolved into what is still an increasingly ubiquitous form of neoliberalism, have dealt with these tensions in a variety of ways. The most common has been to confine political rights and the rights and freedoms enshrined in liberal ideals to particular groups of citizens – predominantly white, upper- (and later middle-) class men. Various others have been excluded or limited, usually by virtue of a supposed incapacity to exercise such rights or discharge the accompanying obligations. Thus, women, children, people who lack literacy and diverse ethnic and racialised minorities have all, in different places and at different times, been formally or informally excluded from the basic rights of citizenship, including the right to vote. These histories inform the transformations of neoliberalism, an ideological form of governance that can be seen as increasingly dominant across the globe, which is not to deny the perseverance of repressive regimes and masquerades of liberalism. Neoliberalism has embraced the concept of equal opportunities in its defence of the benefits of meritocracies that could emerge, by rationalising the advantages, not only to the economy, but also to the wider political, cultural and social terrain of social relations and social order.

Economic rationality is fundamental to the neoliberal project, although the economic is extended to encompass all aspects of social, cultural and political life. Wendy Brown argues that neoliberalism

> entails submitting every action and policy to considerations of profitability... human action [to] entrepreneurial action, conducted according to a calculus of utility, benefit, or satisfaction against a micro-economic grid of scarcity, supply and demand and moral value-neutrality... Neo-liberalism normatively constructs and interpellates individuals as entrepreneurial actors in every sphere of life. Moral autonomy is measured by their capacity for self-care. A fully realised neo-liberal citizenry would be the opposite of public-minded, indeed, it would barely exist as a public. The body politic ceases to be a body but is,rather, a group of individual entrepreneurs and consumers.
>
> (2003: 3–5)

Brown's argument draws on utilitarian views of the liberal state and a conceptualisation of the state as a collection of individuals and points towards the possibilities of Foucauldian regulatory practices which provide one route through understanding the operation of policies of diversity and cohesion which have increasingly become part of neoliberal governance. She also points to the centrality of the entrepreneurial actor who used to be called the sovereign consumer, which is one of the problems identified by Genz in her critique of third way post-feminism. Polysemic, multiple identifications reiterated through the practices of consumption are everything in this new paradigm. One way of exploring feminist dilemmas in this terrain of neoliberalism is to revisit the equality and difference debate that pre-dates contemporary feminist discussion.

Equality and difference

The debates about equality in contemporary neoliberal political theory and governance have a considerable impact on social relations and the experience of gendered lives. Liberal egalitarian theory is characterised not only by a debate between equality of opportunities and outcomes, but by different sorts of equal opportunities. The notion of equal opportunities is problematic in different ways. What sort of opportunities? How can people be given such opportunities and what happens to those who are unable to do anything with the chances they are given? Meritocracy has attractions in the labour market, education and the wider consumer society. But the meritocratic implications of equal opportunities might lead to an extremely unequal society with large disparities between a highly paid successful elite and a group of disadvantaged people who come to be classified as victims of their own lack of ability. As John Rawls has argued, this sort of equality might be the 'equal chance to leave the less fortunate behind in a personal quest for influence and social position' (1972: 108). Another dimension of this discourse emphasises effort and the desire to succeed rather than talent, although effort is clearly important to success. Although Rawls was writing well before the explosion of reality TV, the emphasis on the desire to succeed over talent has a particular resonance in an age when reality TV is the really real. Shows like *The Apprentice* have followed *Big Brother* down the path of rewarding overconfidence without substance. The entrepreneur Sir Alan Sugar presides over a panel and one by one whittles down a group of eager young people who all seek the ultimate accolade of being his 'apprentice'. Those most likely to succeed are increasingly those who may lie in their curriculum vitae (as was the case in 2008) and definitely who express the most ruthless ambition. *Big Brother*, the 24/7 televising of routine domestic life, was itself based on the attraction of ordinariness – or possibly, and increasingly, as the show progressed, on the attraction of repulsion (Stallybrass and White, 1986) and of the freakshow. Popular culture increasingly reinstates the practices that inform neoliberalism.

The debate has shifted within the wider political terrain but in those places social inclusion is part of the citizenship agenda; participation emphasises the role that individuals play in taking responsibility for themselves. The free market is seen as the best route to social egalitarianism and justice, but it is tempered by the recognition that people need additional resources on the grounds of need, as, for example, in the case of disability. Equal opportunities for women may work through market forces or operate in tandem with social inclusion programmes which are both an intrinsic part of neoliberalism and part of its masquerade. Each of these areas is concerned with one of the debates which have informed discussion of equality and equality of opportunity in the past, namely the tension between equality and difference, although discussion has been most vociferous in the field of gender studies, especially within the framework of feminist theories.

Gender equality and difference

The distinction between equality and difference (Scott, 1988, 1998) poses questions that have informed the debates about equality that precede those about diversity but are still very much part of its discourse. This discussion has been framed by what, in feminist literature, has been called 'Hegel's dilemma' (Pateman, 1988), which suggests that equality and difference represent conflicting and incompatible aims; if you recognise difference, you cannot have equality. Hegel was the first political theorist to set out the moral dilemma that arises when citizenship is undermined by the working of the capitalist market. Hegel did not address the problem in relation to women, but Pateman applies the dilemma to women and welfare, because of the assumption that the public and private spheres are separate and that patriarchy assumes this to be a sexual division of labour. The market leaves some citizens without the resources for political participation. The women's movement has engaged with the tensions between at one point claiming equality and at another requiring the recognition of difference. Questions have been raised about who women might want to be equal to, especially given the hegemony of the white, middle-class male who is assumed to be the norm of the rational individual at the heart of liberalism. What is also particular about this debate is that it includes a focus on embodied difference (e.g. between women and men in employment law), in terms of women's capacity to bear and breastfeed children. Feminism has been nervous about recognising the possibility that difference matters at some moments and not at others and that it might be possible to construct an agenda in which women's distinctive voices are heard without having to resort to a rationale of cultural differences where women might be universally defined as nurturing and hence subordinate to the male norm of rationality. Feminist nervousness persists in the twenty-first century, as illustrated by the case in January 2009 of the French Justice Minister Rachida Dati's decision to return to work only five days after giving birth by caesarean section. Her decision received a great deal of media coverage, with several references to the five-inch heels she wore on her first day back at work. Ms Dati has since resigned her post, but it did appear that as an ambitious, successful woman of 43, she was anxious about showing any signs of weakness. Feminists within popular culture entered the debate, expressing concern about the disregard with which hard-fought rights for women had been disregarded; the rights that women have fought for to protect their physical wellbeing as mothers, but also the relationship between the mother and her child which represents emotional intimacy, much less important than career success (Bunting, 2009). Bunting's feminist political argument is countered by French claims that things are different on the other side of the Channel; French women view themselves as women first, mothers second and don't see maternity as their sole *raison d'être*: 'You could call it feminism' (Poirier, 2009). This case raises issues about equality and difference and invokes many of the tension of contemporary feminism; between the recognition of embodied difference and being equal and receiving equal treatment. This is also a demonstration of what is culturally constituted as an assertive equality position in western culture, which suggests some disjunction between feminist theoretical explanations and lived experience, especially in the public arena.

Feminists have made considerable progress in deconstructing the equality/difference binary in most productive ways. As Joan Scott has argued, 'When equality and difference are paired dichotomously, they structure an impossible choice. If one opts for equality, one is forced to accept the notion that difference is antithetical to it. If one opts for difference, one admits that equality is unattainable' (1998: 765). An alternative position deconstructs the division, so that neither aspect is privileged. Grosz has suggested an alternative to this dilemma which avoids the negative effects of reversing the equation and privileging one side or the other, by arguing that a better strategy is 'not to privilege one term at the expense of the other, but to explore the cost of their maintenance' (1994: 32). If difference means putting women at the centre, Grosz's approach aims to deconstruct the centre and thus subvert the dominant, unequal norm, without assuming an additive model. Thus women are not 'added on' to the existing social structures and norms, which would lead to integration into the malestream (Daly, 1979), but are part of a transformative process.

This debate, seeking to go beyond the politics of equality versus difference, has been very important in feminist theory. In policy-making and the processes of governance, these debates can be seen as linked to stages in feminist thinking, from first-wave feminism which focused on rights of suffrage and liberal principles of equal treatment before the law, through second-wave feminist demands for positive action and sometimes separatism, to a third-wave concern with diversity (Rees, 2002), although as the theoretical debates indicate, this is not a linear path and second-wave concerns with equality and the language of rights are integral to any feminist politics.

Equal opportunities for lap dancing

An example of the interplay between equality and difference can be seen in the debates surrounding the licensing of lap dancing clubs in the UK. They currently fall within the remit of the Licensing Act 2003, which means in terms of obtaining a licence to operate, they are placed under the same conditions as bars or cafés. They are not seen as sex-encounter establishments. Lap dancing clubs employ female dancers, and the majority of clients are men – perhaps with the exception of Levy's (2006) 'female chauvinist pigs' or the uncomfortable female city worker forced to go with clients. They are based on selling women's bodies and performances, yet this gendered aspect of the trade is not present in the application for a licence. Object and the Fawcett Society have launched a campaign to change this licensing, as, with the law as it stands, it is extremely difficult to oganise opposition to the opening of a new lap dancing club. There are currently only four grounds on which this can be opposed: public disorder, public nuisance, crime and disorder, and the protection of children. There are no grounds for opposition on the basis of gender inequality, despite being locations that clearly objectify women's bodies and present them as a commodity to be bought. Interestingly, there is a clear legal contradiction, as Cooke (2009) notes, between this legislation and the Gender Equality Duty 2007, which requires that local councils consider gender in all decision-making. There is an issue of inequality as women are being objectified and not men; however, this is also an argument about difference, as it is part of a wider culture where women's bodies are systematically objectified and exploited. The question of equality here is also one that points to the differential experience of men and women in this example of the sexualisation of women's bodies as a service to be purchased.

Whilst the question of difference is not necessarily one of innate and essentialised difference, it is, however, a question of the experience of embodied gendered difference in the context of the contemporary UK. Lap dancing clubs do not operate in isolation but are part of a wider climate of the expectation of the sexualisation of women's bodies and behaviour. In this instance the critique of the legislation is that of inequality, which is also a question of gender difference. The campaign by Object and the Fawcett Society has had some success and the government has announced that changes in legislation will be instigated as part of the Policing and Crime Bill. The licence will be stricter, having to take account of local feeling, and be renewable annually. However, there are still problems with the legislation which will not make this mandatory, and will therefore be at the discretion of the local authority. Not included are venues that hold a lap dancing event less than once a month. When we move beyond the law and consider these issues in practice the issues become even more muddied. This is shown in the case of the proposed opening of a Hooters bar in Sheffield in 2008. Hooters, an American chain which is not expressly a lap dancing or sex trade establishment, is criticised by many for its strongly sexist attitudes and practices. All of the waitresses are female, dress in the Hooters uniform and, in the US, have to sign a contract that states:

> I hereby acknowledge and affirm that the Hooters concept is based on female sex appeal and that the work environment is one in which joking and innuendo based on female sex appeal is commonplace... I also expressly acknowledge and affirm I do not find my job duties, uniform requirements or work environment to be intimidating, hostile or unwelcome.
>
> (Bindel, 2008)

There are clearly issues here of the sexualisation of women as an explicit expectation of their job which raises questions about where the boundary between flirtation and the expectations of the job and harassment lie. Indeed, this is the basis on which the Workers Liberty group in Sheffield stated their opposition. However, there were clear issues surrounding how the local feminst group, Sheffield Fems, could articulate their opposition. Despite the fact that in reality and practice they opposed the opening on the grounds of it being sexually exploitative of women and reinforcing sexist stereotypes, at the level of practice they mounted their opposition on the grounds that it was sexist, yet primarily that it was a 'tacky' and inappropriate (Sheffield Fems, 2009) for the location that had been proposed. The use of 'tacky' is a tactical strategy appropriate to the discourse of appeals against planning decisions, whereas 'sexist' would carry less weight in this context. There is here a sense that the bar was being opposed on the grounds of inequality and also the need to recognise sexed difference in terms of experience, yet at the level of getting local support this was not deemed to be a popular enough tactic. The relationship between equality and difference becomes even more complex when moving beyond how this is enshrined in law and we consider wider attitudes. Indeed, we could argue that the ways in which the language of neoliberalism has taken up ideas of gender equality and supposedly made these mainstream has meant that we have become gender-blind. The apparent freedom to lap dance masks structural inequalities that neoliberal governance seems unable to address, despite its commitment to social inclusion, cohesion and diversity.

Bodies of difference: different bodies

Much of the debate about equality and difference was underpinned by embodied difference, and some of the troubling concerns that feminists have had about arguing and fighting for equal treatment and equality of outcome and opportunities whilst also wanting to argue for recognition of difference that is located in embodied experience. This is seen in the example – perhaps the only example – of women's capacity to bear and give birth to children. However, as Rita Felski (1997) has pointed out, equality versus difference may indeed be a fallacious dualism; they are not opposites. The antithesis of equality is inequality and the opposite of difference is sameness or identity. The error arises from a slippage between equality as identity and difference as an absolute social value rather than a relational concept, which does not require a fixed notion of embodiment that determines gender difference. It is also very unlikely that a politics of equality would insist on equivalence and identical treatment of all subjects. Need is also contingent and related to corporeal differences which do not have to involve identical treatment. However, association between embodiment and difference remains problematic because of the hierarchical and unequal value systems that are in play. The body is still the ghost in the machine in this debate, which may account for the attention which has been given to the nature of embodied difference and how it might impact on the equality and difference in the context of governance and politics.

One of the big questions here, which has particular resonance for our concerns in this book, is the status of women in this debate. Genz suggests that the more instability there is about women as a category of person, the greater risk there is of a diluted politics, framed by individualism rather than human rights. The dismantling of the sex/gender dualism and even sex as a distinct aspect of life that is itself a social constriction and inscription has some very positive possibilities in terms of challenging inequalities and constraints (Butler, 1990). Bodies are inscribed with social meanings and culturally and politically constituted, even in *Bodies That Matter* (1993); sex, which might have appeared to be a biological manifestation of gender difference that informs some of the equality and difference debate, is thus misplaced and belongs with all other iterative social practices. This has two relevant implications. First, corporeality and the lived body, especially as differentiated by sex, are no longer relevant or important. Second, women as agents and collaborators in feminist activism and politics are undermined. Politics becomes more than reconfigured; politics is both disembodied, which may be productive, and disoriented, which could be disastrous. If, as Butler argues, sex is performative and produced through the iteration of particular acts and practices there can be no stable, unitary conception of women as the basis for gender politics. Thus, writing of the category woman, the project for feminist politics, is not to struggle for recognition of difference, nor to fight for equal treatment, but to 'challenge the place of the category as part of a feminist normative discourse' (1990: 325). Butler's intention is to open up the possibilities of feminist politics, but as she has more recently acknowledged, the movement of deconstructionism and of dismantling the category woman and of distancing feminist intellectual debate from what was constructed as naïve oppositional thinking may have had unwanted political implications as well as challenging some of the more restrictive practices and policies of governance and of social and sexual relations.

Conclusion

This chapter has explored some aspects of the interrelationship between the spaces in which political action takes place and some of the concepts which inform contemporary debates. As the young women quoted in chapter 1 suggested, initially it might appear as if some of the political battles have been won. Not only have issues over which feminists have long fought been addressed and incorporated into the language and practice of neoliberal governance, but contemporary politics seems to be framed by a discourse of choice. Politics has moved on to embrace the rational, free woman as well as the autonomous man of the Enlightenment. However, much of the articulation of feminist principles and policies by liberal governance masks the inequalities that persist and the choices available to women in this landscape seem to focus on practices of consumption and what masquerades as sexual freedom and especially individual choice that is taken out of context and not located within the power relations that are in play. This expresses the other aspect of what was said by most of the young women in chapter 1; battles *seem* to have been won and this is the problem.

As third-wave feminists have argued, postmodernist and even postfeminist engagements with the politics of difference are complicit in the dismantling of feminist explanatory frameworks and feminist activism. It is as a result of the rhetoric of equality being adopted that it makes it very difficult to mount an effective opposition or criticism. As the material in chapter 1 illustrated, almost all of the young women adopt this language of choice and empowerment, yet it is evident that there is something missing. Lurking behind the claim that the battles *seem* to have been won, profound inequalities persist. At the level of women's lived experience, feminist academic writing and feminist being in the world, there are some commonalities. There are, however, important disjunctures between them, which are exacerbated by the failure to address difference. This chapter has focused on politics and the question of difference; the next chapter focuses on how popular culture and representational systems have adopted a similar illusion of equality.

We have suggested, however, that a politics of difference can be reconstituted through an exchange between different versions of feminism and different feminist voices. It is possible to revisit some earlier debates and note that equality and difference are not alternatives and that an exploration of how they interconnect can be productive in revealing some of the ways in which feminism too might be implicated in the dismantling, not only of feminism, but also of women as acting subjects. Retaining a category woman is not only useful and empirically relevant, it is intellectually and conceptually necessary for the maintenance of a feminist politics.

5
Visibility and Invisibility, Silence, Absences

> If we keep on speaking sameness, if we speak to each other as men have been doing for centuries, as we have been taught to speak, we'll miss each other, fail ourselves. Again... Words will pass through our bodies, above our heads. They'll vanish, and we'll be lost. Far off, up high. Absent from ourselves: we'll be spoken machines, speaking machines. Enveloped in proper skins, but not our own. Withdrawn into proper names, violated by them.
>
> (Irigaray, [1977] 1985: 205)

Irigaray argues in *This Sex Which Is Not One* that, as language is patriarchal, in order to speak, women must speak in a language which alienates them and distances them from themselves. As language speaks the body, and as speakers are embodied, this silence is simultaneously an absence, and women are unable to express their embodiment in language. There is no space for the articulation of women's bodies within patriarchal language, where women are constituted as a 'lack' within a Lacanian psychoanalytic framework, which Irigaray has strongly contested. Not only does Lacan claim that language speaks us and we are spoken rather than speak, but also that the key signifier of meaning is the phallus (Lacan, 1977). This absence from the imaginary is applicable to language and its relation to the body, and also to imagery and the question of visibility, and what is therefore rendered invisible and absent. This is the focus of this chapter. Here, we consider the relationship between silence, absence and invisibility in terms of how women's bodies are represented and how this links to how women see themselves and their ability to express this through words. A focus on invisibility may seem somewhat surprising given that, in the contemporary climate, there is a proliferation of representations of women's bodies seen in any brief perusal of a magazine rack of popular magazines and newspapers, on the web and in film and television. However, this same explosion of sexualised images of women, we argue, can be seen as part of the reiteration of 'sameness' that Irigaray identifies in the quote that we have selected to open this chapter. The proliferation of imagery does not necessarily equate with diversity, but can be seen in terms of the same patriarchal dominant form of representation. In this chapter we have chosen to explore some of the ordinariness of such largely heterosexualised representations within popular culture.

Debates over representation have been central since Mulvey's (1975) seminal account of the male gaze as it operates in Hollywood cinema. Mulvey's exposure of the extent to which narrative cinema was dependent on patriarchal ideology has been enormously influential and has generated a whole genre of criticism in the critical school of thought associated with the journal *Screen*, which could be seen to constitute 'cine-psychoanalysis' (Gledhill, 1984). Whilst there have been challenges to Mulvey's stance, including her own (Mulvey, 1989), with much criticism focusing on her earlier neglect of the possibilities of a positive female gaze and the presumed heterosexuality of the gaze, the questions she raises are far from redundant. Indeed, concerns over the ways women are represented and issues of exploitation can be traced from the debate Mulvey opens, through to contemporary feminist and post-feminist writings. When the more recent literature is considered, what is perhaps most concerning is that there has been a marked shift away from the critique of these forms of representation and towards an emphasis on pleasure. Writings within what has been termed the third wave equate, and justify, the emphasis on pleasure in terms of empowerment; in doing so they seem to suggest that earlier feminist work does not consider pleasure, which is certainly not the case, given that the major focus of critical feminist film theory has been on reclaiming women's pleasure. Despite the prevalence of terms such as empowerment and the idea that it is a question of choice what women engage in sexually, there has not been enough interrogation of what these words actually mean. In embracing empowerment there has been an abandonment of any understanding of power, or indeed of patriarchy. Postmodern, post-Foucauldian critiques point to the diffusion of power with no extra-discursive location, as power exists in a constantly reiterated circulation. In this chapter, we aim to interrogate how words such as empowerment are used and consider what this obscures. We draw on recent feminist literature critical of the dominant and homogenised representations of women (e.g. Levy 2005; Paul 2005) and consider these in terms of the ideas of visibility, silence, absences, in terms of language, the body and imagery as these all intersect. We consider the implications this has for women and whether it leads to woman being, in Irigaray's terms, 'absent' from herself.

Empowerment?

Within popular media discourses, the term empowerment is commonly invoked in relationship to appearance. As the opening chapter highlights, along with I-Sophie's earlier research (2007), at the level of everyday experience and discourse, the link between appearance and women's self-valorisation is evident. As I Sophie's research shows, when women choose what to wear from their wardrobe and try it on in front of a mirror, this is often an act of questioning 'is this me?' Therefore, when women consider items of clothing this is never simply a question of appearance, as this ties in to how the item of clothing feels on the body, and the notion that the selection of colours and styles also constitutes a personal aesthetic, as an externalisation of selfhood. A crucial part of the process of considering an outfit is also imagining how the outfit will look to others. The act of dressing, apart from when this involves wearing habitual clothing which is worn in an unthought-out and routine manner (also discussed in Woodward, 2007), is almost always considered in relationship to the imagined or remembered gaze of others. This becomes more explicit and deliberate for some women as they dress in order to actively recruit the gaze of others. In some cases this is for a generic male gaze: women I worked with felt valorised by the admiring looks of others. This is often talked about in the language of empowerment. The application of this term ranges from women dressing up for a night out, through to more extreme permutations, such as lap dancing or 'pole-exercise', where empowerment is invariably invoked as a justification, and also as linked explicitly not only to appearance but also to feeling sexy (Holland and Attwood, 2009). In the examples, ranging from a woman trying to look sexy on a night out with friends or on a first date, through to a woman pole dancing almost naked, this same sense of empowerment can easily give way to feelings of vulnerability. The same sexy outfit that attracts admiring glances from potential sexual partners can also elicit unwanted gropes from leery men or inappropriate comments. On such occasions the control that comes with feeling sexy is lost, as the terrain of empowerment is also that of disempowerment.

The current use of the term empowerment is problematic because it is reductive of women's identity to their capacity to appear 'sexy', and also more perniciously as it conceals material inequalities between women and men. It is also a widely used term as it is frequently invoked in popular feminist discourses and has seeped into the media promotion of post-feminism. It is invoked as a defence, and often celebration, of a woman's right to lap dance, where it signifies sexual power (and also control) that women dancers have over men. We would argue that this is a very particular kind of power, which is not permanent, but rather relies on the maintenance of the appearance and manner of being 'sexy' and so transitory and context-specific. These sexualised feelings of control and power over men can easily be undermined, as a woman is left feeling vulnerable in the reversal of power relationships. What emerged from the discussions with young women outlined in chapter 1 is that even if the word empowerment is often used, when women discuss their experiences in more depth, these same women clearly feel an ambivalence about the word. We are therefore not arguing that young women are dupes and do not understand what they are doing. Many of them do understand, yet this may run in tandem with a feeling of uncertainty and ambivalence. They adopt the rhetoric and sometimes behaviour that celebrates empowerment as it is linked to sexuality, yet they also express a discomfort with this. This was discussed in chapter 1 as the new 'problem with no name'; when, for instance, a male employer looks at a woman employee's breasts when he is talking to her, this gives rise to an embodied discomfort that is experienced and is constitutive of sensation and affect. This idea is elaborated in this chapter in terms of the thinking of Irigaray and her ideas of what is absent and what is made visible or not allowed through masculinist discourse. Although her philosophical writing on difference and the empiricist basis for Friedan's work are divergent and rarely discussed together, they both address the issue of that which cannot be articulated in language.

Power dressing?

Sexualised power is both limited and reductive of women's capacities. This will be discussed in the context of paid work – that is, largely activity for remuneration in the labour market that is perceived as legal and legitimate, rather than the more blurred categories of legitimacy that apply to work carried outside or on the margins of legality, such as sex work. Even as the boundaries of work dress become more fluid and inclusive, the wearing of overtly sexualised clothing is considered inappropriate for most kinds of work. 'Power' dressing (a style of dressing that is typically characterised with the 1980s and is now seen as somewhat outmoded) derives its 'power' from the large shoulder pads and structured shape. The presumption is that to be taken seriously in the workplace masculine clothing is needed. In *Je Tous Nous* ([1990], 2007), Irigaray argues having a voice as a woman is only possible when you are reduced to a feminine stereotype or speaking through the dominant masculine structures as a man. Thus, Irigaray subverts Lacan's Law of the Father as part of the make-up of these structures, rather than, as other feminists have done in the past (Mitchell, 1974; revisited in Mitchell and Mishra, 2000), using Lacanian psychoanalysis as an explanation of how patriarchy works.

Irigaray's arguments at the level of language can be extended to a consideration of clothing, where equality is conceived in patriarchal terms; women can become 'equal' to men by adopting masculine aspects of dress and demeanour. There has been, in more recent years, a notable relaxation of the normative dress codes in most workplaces, where more feminine or fashionable details are permissible. However, this does not signify an absence of restrictions, as the wearing of sexualised clothing at work is either disapproved of or undermines the seriousness of how the woman is seen at work. The expectation of what is worn in the world of work falls in contrast to the dominant representations of women's dress in media outlets, where the emphasis is on sexualised modes of dress for women. This highlights a contradiction in attitudes to women's appearances: the valorisation of women through the appearance of being sexy, and the moral and aesthetic codes of the workplace. The mainstream associations for women's appearance may be linked to those of sexiness (especially and primarily for the young), yet in the area of work this does not hold true. The crossover of sexy clothing in the workplace has significant consequences for how women are seen. The sexualised power that comes from clothing is seen to be so strong that women are reduced to this particular capacity. When the same clothing is worn in another context, such as on a date or a night out with friends, this can, in the words of popular culture, 'empower' a woman. In the context of work, however, it does not allow women to be seen as serious members of the workforce. It obliterates all other ways of being seen, other than as sexy. This is not empowering but limiting and restrictive, as all the other possibilities that a woman could be are obscured.

The problematic relationship between what is present and what is concealed, invisible or absent, is usefully expounded in *The Forgetting of Air* (Irigaray, [1983] 1999). In many ways, this accords with Kristeva

(1984, in Cavallero, 2003), as she argues that language, which is spoken, always conceals and contains the traces of all other possibilities. Irigaray uses 'air', as an element and as a concept, to critique Heidegger and strands within western philosophy as air seems to elude classification through its fluidity.

> Metaphysics always supposes...a solid crust from which to raise a construction. This is a physics that gives privilege to...the solid [place]...And its abysses...doubtless find their explanation in the forgetting of those elements that do not have the same density as solid earth.
> (Irigaray, [1983] 1999: 2)

Air is perhaps the most interesting of the elements, Irigaray suggests, which is missing as it is impalpable, and raises the relationship between 'presence and absence' (Irigaray, [1983], 1999: 9) as well as the interplay between 'visibility and invisibility' (Cavallero, 2003: 92). The visible involves isolating one element from all of the other possibilities; it is often difficult to see what gives rise to that which is present (Eagleton, 1990: 289). Cavallero, extending Irigaray's argument, suggests that Being is imposed rigidly in terms of metaphysics and language, which 'efface' (Cavallero, 2003: 92) this absence and invisibility. These arguments can be powerfully extended to understand how the sexualised can serve to erase all other possibilities, as if they are invisible and not present. The sexual body that conforms to the representational stereotypes of female sexiness comes to such prominence, and apparent fixity in meaning, because it is firmly sedimented within western and patriarchal ontology and representational systems. Women are aware that there are numerous other possibilities for who they can be and their attributes, but these are not present in the sexualised moment. Furthermore, the sartorial and bodily expression is one that is almost universally understood in this cultural context, as it is a dominant form of visual and embodied language. Irrespective of what a woman's particular desire is, if she is trying to be taken seriously, this is effectively erased and made absent as it is not part of the 'language' or dominant visual codes. In her critique of western culture, Irigaray suggests that this is the only language that is available to many women, as it is present in multiple forms, including those that permeate popular culture. However, her challenge to Lacanian phallocentrism and criticism of Lacan's stress on the Oedipal stage as the key point of the entry into language and the symbolic system of representation, has also posited an alternative female imaginary, based on the pre-Oedipal stage (Irigaray, 1985).

Or just power?

This dominant representational form will be explored more fully later in the chapter. However, before this, we suggest that it is necessary to interrogate further what is meant by the word 'power'. It is a term that is employed within a range of feminist discourses, and, equally, within the terrain of post-feminism. There is a slippage in what is meant by the term which resonates with postmodernist conceptualisations of the dispersal of power to myriad sites, with sources that cannot be located, which raises questions about the relationship between feminist theories and practices and some of the ways in which feminism might be dismantling itself.

Feminists have drawn on a wide range of conceptualisations of power, including structuralist accounts which identify a material source of power, for example as inspired by Marxist theories of the economic determinants of social relations and cultural forms. Radical feminists replaced the economic base with patriarchy as the major determinant of social relations. Following the explosion of Foucauldian critiques, such approaches began to appear naïve in their failure to accommodate the multiple points at which power operates or the dual aspects of power as both productive and constraining. Such approaches drew attention to the problems of recognising power and opened up a whole field of investigation in order to make visible the ways in which power can be exercised. This highlighted the complexity of the operations of power and notably the difficulty of recognising not only how power works, but also when it is being exercised (Nicholson, 1984). It is, however, worth rethinking the location of power and earlier critiques, which may not have been as simplistic, as has been suggested in the rush for complexity and new language of explanation. Beverly Thiele drew on Lukes' idea that power has three faces, one involving coercion and even violence, one that is more subtle and prevents debate, for example, so that women's concerns are invisible and not even on the agenda and the third, most insidiously, because it is hardest to locate by controlling our perceptions of ourselves (Thiele, [1987] 1992). The last face of power is resonant of Michel Foucault's notion of self-regulating techniques of the self, but even the subtle injunctions of this face of power are located in a social and cultural system through 'a patriarchal understanding of women, of sexuality, of the family and of a consumer oriented economy [which] conspire to create a feeling of inadequacy...a very effective method of controlling them' ([1987] 1992). Self-regulation may not be an entirely circular process.

More recent experience of the enabling as well as constraining effects of power and of power as effects has been framed by a concern with sexuality as reproduced within popular culture. Within feminism power has been used in both positive and negative ways, as Wolf writes about and identifies herself with 'power' feminism, in *Fire with Fire* (1993), which is defined as being 'unapologetically sexual'; understands that good pleasure make 'good politics' and is also pro 'choice' in sexuality (cited in Heywood, 2006: 15). It is this version of power in popular feminist and post-feminist discourses that has become more prevalent, seen in 'do me' feminism, and, for example, in popular feminist magazines such as *Bust* and also activists such as riot grrrls. The emphasis is not on critiquing power structures, but more about supposedly reclaiming terms such as bitch or girl. Indeed, there is a critique of feminist writings which are centred on critiques of implicit patriarchy (in Wolf's case this is more explicit). Wolf refers to these writings as 'victim' feminism, which she defines as anti-sex and something that does not allow for women's agency. Examples she cites are writers such as Dworkin and Rich, who, amongst others, stress the constraining aspects of power as manifest in its coercive face and tend to discuss the ways in which patriarchal power subjugates women. Although they both offer alternative strategies for women to assert and affirm their subjectivity, Wolf's critique is certainly simplifying of strong positions within feminism, which make important challenges to understanding how power, in particular patriarchal power, operates through analyses of rape, domestic violence and media representations which echo some earlier feminist concerns with coercion and the problem of violence against women (Dworkin and MacKinnon, 1988). Indeed, Wolf's emphasis on the desire to look at 'power' as a positive thing that women have has been the more popular usage of the term, as the word 'empowerment' is one that has a strong current currency generated by, first, the apparent success of feminism and the feeling that battles have been won and second, located within a popular culture of choice and psy-discourses (Rose, 1996) and of 'getting what you want'. The word has become so widely employed and overused that it is now devoid of meaning, analogous to the word 'choice'. It is employed positively, by ascribing agency to women, yet equally each term gets bandied around in a range of situations and fails adequately to challenge the power structures that operate. Even if one woman may be paid a fortune as a high-class prostitute, there are far more women who are trafficked into prostitution or who do it through an abusive and controlling pimp, women for whom this is certainly not at all 'empowering'. McRobbie (2008), writing about post-feminism in the UK, discusses the focus on girlhood and the ways in which young women are made visible. She uses Deleuze's concept of luminosity in order to explain how and when this visibility occurs. Her ideas have clear resonances in our book, as McRobbie makes a powerful case for the ways in which the languages of feminism have been co-opted within political and social discourses such that feminism itself no longer seems necessary. As ideas such as 'choice' are taken up by consumer culture, this involves the 'undoing' of feminism as it is no longer needed.

'Empowerment' and 'choice' are utilised in an individualistic manner. This same individualism can be seen to have colonised the feminist slogan the 'personal is political', turning it into an empty phrase, which merely encourages an explosion in the detailing of personal lives in public, which is completely divorced from wider contexts or indeed politics. In considering questions of power there is still a need to understand and interrogate patriarchy and retain it as a critical concept. Veronica Beechey (1979) defined patriarchy as the dominance of older men over younger men and particularly of men over all women, within a broadly structuralist framework that draws on anthropological conceptualisations. Other definitions, such as Heidi Hartman's, elaborated the idea as 'a set of social relations between men, which have a material base, and which though hierarchical, establish or create interdependence and solidarity among men that enable them to dominate women' (Hartman, 1981: 14–15). This reading of materiality draws on a Marxist base–superstructure paradigm which is located within what was broadly called Marxist feminism. Sylvia Walby (1990) emphasised the economic basis of male power as control over women's labour and developed a complex system of explanation based on six structures, which constitute patriarchy as a system of oppression and exploitation. These structures are: the patriarchal mode of production, patriarchal relations in paid work and in the state and violence in sexual relations and in cultural institutions (others accorded more weight to sexual control). These definitions are rarely cited or acknowledged now, partly because of poststructuralist critiques which challenged them for failing to accommodate the plurality of modes of power, the differences among women and the instability of structures. These critiques, however, whilst instructive in pointing to the problems with structuralist universalisms, have come to assume something of a meta-theoretical and universal status, which was seen as so problematic in such structuralist theories. As some of these structures seem remarkably resilient, it is worth revisiting some of these ideas and reconsidering how they might inform third-wave thinking and the political possibilities of feminism in the twenty-first century.

In the new turn towards materialities, which take diverse forms and trajectories, we suggest holding on to the material as embedded in and arising from social relations and having effects and affects. Materialities challenge the ever-shifting mobilities of virtual spaces, which are understood discursively as sites for the production of meanings. They are not synonymous with structures in that they are not bounded and include the intersection of different materialities; embodied selves are material too. We are also not distinguishing between symbolic materialities and those that are part of the social and economic fabric of structures and institutions. Instead, they include the social relations and the symbolic meanings and permit a location of power, one of which is patriarchy.

Patriarchal power?

The concept of patriarchy is far less frequently invoked by twenty-first-century feminist critiques, although the interrogation of the concept was seen to have considerable significance in the 1980s. An understanding of patriarchy was seen as vital to a feminist critique of social relations; in one of the biggest women's studies courses in the UK, which I-Kath taught in the early 1990s, one of the initial exercises was to offer a definition of patriarchy. Even at this time, the concept was seen as part of the genealogy of feminism and women's studies, and was already being questioned for its universalising classification of women and for its failure to acknowledge the significant differences among women, notably of race, ethnicity and disability, which any theoretical conceptualisation based on a female/male binary was seen not to accommodate. Patriarchy, however, occupies a particularly important place in the feminist lexicon of explanatory concepts, and its absence from postmodernist theories is part of the destabilisation of the category woman as a politically motivating dimension of feminist politics.

Gayle Greene and Coppélia Khan (1985) use a story by Isak Dinesen to illustrate how patriarchy works and became part of the assumed norms of social exchange. *The Blank Page* is narrated by an old woman to demonstrate how 'silence will speak' (Dinesen, 1975: 100). The story is about medieval nuns who were charged to supply fine linen bridal sheets for the princesses of the royal house; blood-stained sheets were then displayed the morning after the wedding as proof of the virginity of the bride. Subsequently, the blood-stained portion of sheet was framed in gilt and displayed, each 'adorned with a coroneted plate of pure gold, on which is engraved the name of the princess (1975: 103). The narrator describes the gallery in which the gold-framed sheets are displayed:

> In the midst of the long row there hangs a canvas which differs from the others. The frame of it is as fine and as heavy as any, and as proudly as any carries the golden plate with the royal crown. But on this one plate no name s inscribed, and the linen within the frame is snow white from corner to corner, a blank page.
>
> (1975: 104)

As Greene and Kahn argue:

> This tale, like the linen of Convento Velho, is woven from the social fabric of western European patriarchy. It can be unraveled only by a reader who understands that patriarchy in its social practices, psychological dynamics and symbol- making and in its powers to mould women and men as social beings.
>
> (1985: 6)

With the image of the sheets, Dinesen evokes patriarchy as an ideology, built on male control, through social institutions, notably marriage, within which women are exchanged and regulated, as their sexuality is controlled. This analysis emphasises the sexual dimensions of patriarchy, although these aspects are clearly imbricated in the economy of kinship ties and socioeconomic relations. This has a clear application to some of the sexualisation that permeates social relations and the social worlds young women, all women, inhabit in the twenty-first century.

If we consider patriarchy in the context of sexualised power which is being discussed here, then it is possible to start to explain the ambivalences that young women feel: the admiration from others that makes them feel 'empowered' and the leery glance, or inappropriate comment, that makes them feel uncomfortable. They are fitting themselves into a pre-existing power structure, which defines what is 'powerful' or not with its own material effects, not only on how they see themselves, but also what they are able to do. Therefore, there is no agency in defining the terms, which is clearly seen in the narrowness of the definition of what is attractive or sexy, something which becomes even narrower in the current context. Despite the proliferation of images of the body beautiful, they all reinforce the same normative ideas of beauty. This raises the question: why is 'power' valued in positive terms? This critique of power fails to acknowledge its constraining or relational force. In the claims to accommodate agency and challenge the notion of false consciousness, whereby, as argued by the Frankfurt School, popular culture is seen as distorting and manipulating the minds of a mass audience, another deception is effected: the myth of 'having it all'. There are critiques of the way that power operates independently, but power surely implies the subjugation or exploitation of someone else. When applied to the relations between men and women, or women and women, it is incredibly negative and damaging. Taken through the example in which it is often employed, lap dancing or pole dancing, women can be seen to have sexualised power and control over their clients (Holland and Attwood, 2009); yet this same empowerment also breeds contempt and precludes any possibility of connection.

If this is widened out to a societal context and a consideration of the relations between men and women, Irigaray's notion of 'respect' becomes pertinent here. In *I Love to You*, and as a theme that characterises many of her other works, she suggests we need an understanding of humanity as 'at least two' (1996: 35), as the idea of a universal human being is a fallacy. This idea of relationality revisits the arguments of the last chapter and the need for a politics of difference, where this difference entails, in Irigaray's terms, mutual respect grounded in this difference. This relationship is not based on possession or the exchange of one by the other. Cixous (1997) also advocates this in *Rootprints*, with the need for a space in between. There is a key point of departure from their ideas of respect and those that are more widely used as they patronise women or reduce them to passive modes of femininity that need protecting. Koffman's discussion here is interesting as she highlights the ways in which patriarchy often praises and demonises femininity at the same time. She discusses respect as used by Kant as a way to protect ideas of modesty. Indeed, in Kofman (1982: 388), modesty is idealised in this version of respect as it 'prevents man from having... disgust for the sex of woman, to which the full and entire satisfaction of man's inclinations inevitably leads him'. To attain this kind of respect, women must censor their behaviour.

Although empowerment is invoked in terms of the individual, as has already been suggested, it can only ever be understood when the wider power structures and materialities are considered, within which these individual women's sense of themselves is situated. This structuring is always culturally specific, located in economic, social and cultural contexts. However, we remain critical of positions, often those arising from

Foucault, which over-assert the social construction of sex and gender. Instead, what we are arguing for is a way to understand difference, yet always in relation to the specificities of contexts. This is essential in order to understand the differential, gendered effects of power in operation, which are not merely a social construction. Foucault's argument in the *History of Sexuality* can be applied to the oppression of women in many societies which comes through disciplining their bodies, and he therefore highlights that there is nothing natural about sex, gender or sexuality. However, it is important to situate this in wider structures of inequality and gender difference. A key problem with Foucault's position is exemplified in his discussion of rape, which, he argues, is a crime to be punished for its violence, but not as a sexual crime (which he argues should never be condemned); in contrast, Plaza argues that it is sexual, as rape is 'an oppressive act by a (social) man against a (social) woman' (1996: 182). It is sexual as it involves 'men's brutal appropriation of female bodies' (1996: 182). However, Plaza is in favour of bringing down the idea of 'woman' (1996: 26). However, whilst we would agree with her desire to deconstruct essentialised and naturalised assumptions about women's bodies, woman is not just an idea or a construct (this will be explored more fully in the next chapter).

A more instructive position here is Irigaray's, who argues that Foucault's position 'eliminates the problem of respect for the female body' (2000: 31) and also importantly that women are vulnerable to these crimes as women, and should therefore be protected legally as women. She argues that getting rid of difference condones the appropriation of the other (by analogy to colonialism), whereas 'renouncing the desire to possess the other, in order to recognise him as other' is another possible stance (2000: 7).The suggestion therefore is that there is a need to retain these politics of difference: if women experience violence and exclusion in the world as women, then dismantling the category woman, as suggested in many poststructuralist accounts, is not instructive. Irigaray specifically highlights that we should not embrace postmodernism too uncritically as, like many other theories that have preceded it, it fails to acknowledge sexual difference. It is important not to displace the female/male binary 'before the female side has acceded to identity and subjectivity' (Whitford, 1991: 13). Women still do not have access to the imaginary as the 'dominant language is so powerful that women do not dare to speak (as) woman outside the context of non-integration' (Irigaray, in Whitford, 1991: 137). Indeed, as Delphy (1996) notes, difference and hierarchy are not the same, and so we can embrace a politics of difference that is not based on exploitation. Indeed, as this is the basis of much of women's exclusion from the imaginary, then this same domain of sexed difference is the means through which this exploitation can be challenged. Irigaray argues in *Je Tous Nous* ([1990] 2007) that the creation of a 'sexed culture' is necessary as this has been ignored. The next section outlines and explores what the current sexed culture is and the absences and invisibilities within it.

Context: situation

In advocating a politics of difference, we argue that this sexed difference always accords to a specific representational and linguistic context. Here we locate it in terms of the images that are presented of women in the western media and importantly what impact this has on young women and how they see themselves. The wider context of the contemporary UK and US has bee termed 'pornified' (Paul, 2005); that is, the images that would have once been categorised as top-shelf pornography are now part of the mainstream. This goes hand in hand with the rise of what has been termed 'lads' mags' in the UK, magazines targeted at men with images of semi-naked (in most cases topless) women, often in pornographic poses. This is widened through the spread of pornographic imagery on the internet, as these images are accessible in a way they were not previously, and images that are increasingly extreme and even found in the mainstream of fashion journalism. As Paul notes, a 2004 study found that pornographic sites are visited three times more often than the Google, Yahoo! and MSN search engines combined (2005: 60). Accessing pornography no longer involves the surreptitious buying of top-shelf magazines from a newsagent, nor sneaking into a back alley strip club in the hope of not being noticed. Now pornographic images are available at the click of a mouse and being sold in local high streets. As Paul notes, overexposure to such images only serves to desensitise: 'what initially thrills eventually titillates, what excites eventually pleases, what pleases eventually satisfies. And satisfaction sooner or later yields to boredom' (2005: 83). An aspect of this boredom means that images that perhaps would have once been seen as shocking are no longer even noticed, and have become part of the invisible landscape of television, magazines and the city itself. Therefore, as women are increasingly made visible in a sexualised way, they are also simultaneously made invisible, as the process of proliferation of images of semi-naked women is one which desensitises the viewer, such that many no longer notice or pay attention to them.

An aspect of this visibility is the attention accorded to the appearance of young women, as women are judged on the way they look, irrespective of what they have achieved (seen in the many comments on the appearance of female politicians or sportswomen). This is not to negate the increasing level of objectification of men's bodies, yet it is not occurring at the same level. No equivalent of a lads' mag for women has ever been successful in spite of several attempts to create this market. Glamour girls and footballers' wives are seen as a desirable identity for young women and girls, the latter being defined by who they are going out with and how they look. Another area of invisibility is those that are excluded from being represented in images of fashion and beauty, which remains dominated by the slim, usually white, able-bodied and young woman. Older women only attain visibility when they undergo a makeover in order to make themselves look significantly younger. Women of different body shapes, ethnicities and ages are made invisible through their absence. Black and Asian women, for example in fashion shoots, magazines and on the catwalk, are exoticised and sexualised through a similar prism of exaggerated body forms, which are mostly very tall, very young and very thin. In contrast, the semi-naked young women who adorn magazines and advertisements seemingly paradoxically become invisible through their very visibility, as images of them are so omnipresent that no longer seem to be noteworthy.

The complex relationship between the increasing visibility of women and the way their image is seen is explored in Sut Jhally's film *Dreamworlds* (1995, 2007). This is worthy of discussion here as it highlights the process through which the 'invisible' becomes visible, as young women who I-Sophie have shown this video to often start to realise how women's sexualised images are an ordinary part of daily life. The film is based on a range of clips from music videos shown on MTV; the earlier version of the video is one that I-Sophie showed my students, and here the majority of images are from the rock genre (interestingly not hip-hop, which arguably has some of the most objectified images there are, with artists such as Snoop Dog having a music video that contains actual pornography rather than its simulation). Jhally analyses it in terms of the 'stories' it tells about female sexuality; such as showing that 'women get depressed when men are not there' and women are shown to be bereft without men, or 'women like to get wet', with numerous clips of them being showered with water. As the film progresses, the images become gradually more extreme, culminating in images from music videos showing violent acts against women. This music is then silenced, whilst the images continue and the soundtrack from the film *The Accused*, from the scene where a woman is gang-raped, is played. It is striking how closely the sounds of a gang rape fit with the imagery from the music videos. Through changing the soundtrack of the videos, it changes the meanings that the images convey and the ways these same images are viewed. Visibility and invisibility occupy a complex relationship also to sound.

Issues of visibility relate to language, images, sounds and embodied feelings. The question of embodiment and its relationship to being seen was evident in the examples discussed earlier in this chapter when a young woman is looked at by someone in a way that she does not want, and she therefore feels uncomfortable and objectified. These same young women could often not articulate how they feel, but it is felt as an embodied sense of discomfort. These experiences raise several issues. First, there is a feeling of discomfort that is difficult to explain or even to locate which invokes that which cannot be spoken or that there is no language to explain or even say it. Second, it suggests that seeing is a corporeal practice in which all the senses are implicated. Vivien Sobchack argues, in the context of film spectatorship, that embodiment is central through the visibility of bodies on screen and the primacy of the visual through the medium of film, which demonstrates powerfully the 'embodied and radically material nature of human existence' (Sobchack, 2004: 1). This phenomenological focus on the whole experience of seeing and being seen and with sensation as part of being in the world differs from psychoanalytic accounts. Psychoanalytical discussions, instead, suggest the operation of an unconscious which can be accessed and works according to a set of laws that are distinct from those of the conscious mind and provides an alternative route to exploring what the feelings of discomfort might signify. Sobchack's account, although incorporating the whole sentient and sensate experience of spectatorship, also starts with what is visible and what is visual.

The issue of silence echoes with earlier feminist protests, one of which inverted the use of silence. Cinema has been the site of some dramatic attempts by feminists to address the problem of silence, none more so than the Dutch film *A Question of Silence* (Gorris, 1982) which portrays an incident of extreme violence committed in silence by three women, strangers who cross paths in a boutique, when a trivial act of shoplifting leads to the unleashing of suppressed frustrations. The film, which won the Golden Calf and Grand Prix prizes, was strongly criticised for its violence, which seemed all the more powerful because the women do not speak. The Dutch director used this device to protest against what she argued was the violence of patriarchy; an example of silence being deployed in protest in a reversal of the silencing of women in a male-dominated culture.

Sight and sound: the politics of visualisation

Visual images are central to the creation of sensation. Images are processed and reproduced through a variety of techniques and at different sites. Rosalind Petchesky's important contribution to the debate, using the example of foetal imagery in the anti-abortion film *The Silent Scream* ([1985] 1999), draws on semiotic theory and feminist political critiques. She deconstructs the presentation of medical truths and demonstrates that what appears to be a 'message without a code' is actually grounded in historical and cultural meanings. Petchesky analyses the visual images and the accompanying music as part of the whole embodied, sentient and sensate experience of the representational process. The impact of the film, which is aimed to create sensation, is carefully structured to produce affect and engages all the senses. Her work is located within the cultural studies tradition of a decoding exercise following Roland Barthes, but within a critical theoretical framework that raises issues about how women are made invisible; in this instance through the representation of the foetus *in utero* but apparently floating in space, without any image that reinstates a maternal embodied presence. She acknowledges that, by demystifying foetal images, she is re-embodying the foetus, which is, of course, the aim of the film: to embody the foetus and remove from visibility and thence personhood the mother. Petchesky's conclusion is that we have to 'image the pregnant women, not as an abstraction, but within her total framework of relationships, economic and health needs and desires. Once we have pictured the social conditions of her freedom, however, we have not dissolved the contradictions in how she might use it' ([1985] 1999: 188). The social conditions of freedom are the materialities through which women are made visible or invisible.

So far we have considered works which point to the links between sight, sound and embodied feeling; however, there is also a mirror side to this process that we shall consider: the potential disconnection between, in particular, embodied feeling and visibility. As Levy notes in *Female Chauvinist Pigs* (2005), in a currently pornified society, there are increasing numbers of images of sexiness, which have become so pervasive they are shorthand for everything, for being in the world. The emphasis is on the appearance of sexuality rather than the experience and enjoyment of actual sexual pleasure. 'Passion isn't the point. The glossy, overheated thumping of sexuality in our culture is less about connection than consumption. Hotness has become our cultural currency' (Levy, 2005: 31). This is clearly mirrored in pornography, where there is very little interest in what gives sexual pleasure to women; rather women are depicted moaning with pleasure at things which are unlikely to give them any pleasure at all. Despite more recent examples of pornography created for women (such as Anna Span) pornography is still predominantly produced by men for men, whether straight or gay (Levy, 2005; Paul, 2005). This same sense has been translated to the mainstream. As pornographic images increasingly seep across, so too, as Levy argues, there are images which show the appearance of sexiness but not real sexual pleasure. This is a particularly interesting phenomenon in light of third-wave feminism and the more popular versions of post-feminism, which emphasise sexuality and sexual pleasure as paramount and a key part of liberation and equality. The debates over whether pornography should be censored, which raged so strongly in earlier feminist debates, have all but closed down.

There is a very strong assumption in a great deal of writing, even within feminist works, that women have built on the battles won by second-wave feminism with regard to birth control, and are now liberated with regard to their sexual practices. The assumption is that women are now both more knowing and more confident to ask for what gives them pleasure. Henry discusses Koedt's article, which was revolutionary when it came out in emphasising the clitoral over the 'myth of the vaginal orgasm'. Henry notes that this is hardly shocking now as young women have grown up with the knowledge of the clitoral orgasm. However, this claim is questionable when we actually consider mainstream images. They invariably involve images of women pleasing men, with little consideration of female pleasure; the topic of female masturbation is still taboo, both at the level of representations (unless it is performed for male pleasure in pornography) and everyday discourses (see Storrs, 2003). The predominant imagery of sex in most films, and on television, is still that which does not connect with actual bodily pleasure. This is evidenced by one of I-Sophie's students who did a dissertation on female sexual pleasure. In discussions with this student and others, what was apparent is that she states she learnt more about sexuality and sexual pleasure from reading feminist texts than from anything else. Moreover, it was apparent that even in these supposedly liberated times there are still many subjects that are taboo.

The idea that we now live in an era of sexual liberation which was a key part of women's broader liberation is prevalent. However, as we argue, the wider prevalence of sexual imagery cannot be misread as liberation. Given the repetition of particular types of imagery, many ideas are still kept in their 'infancy or a state of animality' (Irigaray, [1990], 2007: 59) as the predominant imagery is based on the 'phallocratic sexual economy' (Irigaray [1977], 1985: 199). A useful way of understanding the position of female pleasure can be see in the notion of *jouissance*. Irigaray suggests there are two types: 'one is programmed in a male libidinal economy in accordance with a certain phallic order. Another is much more in harmony with what they are, with their sexual identity' (Irigaray, in Whitford, 1991: 45). The former can be seen in, for example, much pornography or in examples of women described in Paul's research, where women attempt to mimic the look and sexual behaviours shown in pornography, or women who lap dance and see this as empowering (analogous to Levy's female chauvinist pigs). The idea that this is liberation is based on the presumption that women's bodies are commodities to be used by men. Post-feminism in popular culture often defends the embracing of pornography or lap dancing in terms of an emphasis on pleasure, yet as Irigaray argued in *This Sex Which is Not One* (an argument that still holds weight), this justification does not signify pleasure, as 'those orgasms are necessary as the demonstration of masculine power. They signify the success – men think – of their sexual domination of women'. ([1977] 1985: 199). This is evident in the obsession in pornography with ejaculation and the 'money shot', the significance given to penis size and 'the reduction of the body to a mere surface to be broken through or punctured, violence and rape... all of these bring women forcibly to sexual pleasure... but what sort of pleasure is it? And if women stay mute about their pleasure, if they remain ignorant' (1985: 200), this is not surprising.

A trend running through more recent critiques of the pornification of society and Irigaray's earlier theoretical treatises is this sense of disconnection between women's sense of who they are and the bodies they inhabit. This disconnection in part arises from women adopting the path of mimicry, such as when they lap dance or engage in sexual acts by mimicking the pornographic. They are mimicking a model of woman that is created through the phallocentric sexual order, and in doing so, Irigaray argues, they 'also remain elsewhere; another case of the persistence of "matter", but also of "sexual pleasure" ' ([1977], 1985: 76). Female pleasure is 'elsewhere' as it is predominantly forbidden in discourse and language.

'Choice'?

The final section of this chapter considers the relationship between such imagery and how it is seen and interpreted by young women. As chapter 1 suggests, there is wide diversity within the view of young women, and this chapter is not comprehensive in its coverage of these views. In her research on the impact of the increasing availability of pornographic imagery, Paul (2005) does not point to any direct causal relationships between pornography and how people behave, but does discuss the links between questions of desensitisation and repeated exposure to images. The issue of pornography is not one that was raised often by the young women; instead, their discussions centred on lap dancing, being a glamour girl and lads' mags, all topics that elicited far more responses. The prevailing idea among many of the women was the issue of 'choice' (discussed in more depth in chapter 1). A classic example raised is the former model Jordan, with many of the young women expressing genuine admiration for her business acumen and ability to make so much money.

Jordan is an interesting example as someone who calls herself both 'Jordan' and also 'Katie Price', her original name – a clear separating off of the glamour girl persona from the mother of three. This dovetails interestingly with an example of one young woman I-Sophie spoke to who stated that she lap dances for one month a year in order to make money to pay off her debts. Whilst she is on one level full of the bravado of how much money she makes and how there is nothing wrong with it, she also talks about how she uses a different name when she lap dances. She goes on to describe how sad it is when you realise the situation of many of the women who lap dance who have no alternative or for whom this is not temporary employment. This raises questions over how much choice is actually exercised, as she realises that many women are desperate for money as a quick fix to a financial problem. There is a paradox in seeing it as acceptable to make money from objectifying one's own body yet calling oneself a name other than 'me', which reinforces the fact that it is dehumanising. Even if in some cases the name chosen can help a woman to play a role, it may also be done to make the self-objectification more manageable and also to mitigate against a sense of shame (very rarely when lap dancers are interviewed do they use their own name for fear of being identified by family or others). This reinforces the discussions in the previous section where women are seen as disconnecting their bodies from their sense of self. They put on this mask in the absence of a language or form of representation of their own. Hence the visibility is not of their own making.

This sense of self-objectification is exemplified in the case of the 'audience participation' area of the *Nuts* website (*Nuts* is a 'lads' mag'). The website has a section where women can send in pictures of themselves naked or in underwear, in simulated pornographic poses. Their name is not given, they are just a body, which is then rated by the readers and comments added, ranging from the positive ('nice boobs') through to the negative ('er how revolting is she?'). In some cases, young women justify their boyfriends looking at the magazine as 'he really gets it for the cars' or 'it's natural to want to look at the women'. Many of them say that they sneak a look at their boyfriend's copy, but only with their female or male gay friends – never with their boyfriend – and make comments about the women's bodies. This is mirrored in the site itself, where many of the comments come from women. None of the young women I spoke to said that they would send in a picture, with many stating that they weren't confident enough about their bodies. There was a consensus amongst them that it is a 'bit sad' when women send in images of themselves, yet at the same time they all like to look at them, as it allows them to compare themselves to other girls.

The young women's responses to the *Nuts* website is one that raises wider questions about the ways in which they are part of a cultural context in which women are accustomed to objectifying their bodies through implicit comparison to others. Moreover, this highlights that the competition between women is emphasised, primarily here in terms of appearance. There are numerous other examples which could be invoked to highlight this, one recent one being 'Miss Naked Beauty' (shown on Channel 4), which is supposed to be a beauty contest based on intelligence and personality, yet still involves the women in one scene being sprayed with water, as they stand shivering in their bikinis. The programme not only encourages the humiliation of women as they are judged for being 'too confident' or 'not confident enough', but also women's value is based on their appearance. This is an example of being reduced to the body and its visible appearance which is analogous to the ways in which male black athletes can be reduced to their body competences (Woodward, 2007). They are pitted against each other to create competition. Invariably, this results in feelings of inadequacy, mirrored in the example of young women I-Sophie spoke to who state they would not want to be a lap dancer as they don't have a good enough body, rather than for any other reason.

An interesting issue raised by this example is the relationship between being 'inside' and 'outside', that is as a viewer of an image or the object of that image, or actually lap dancing or having a general opinion about it. There are clear problems with the word 'choice' when there is a strong separation between the practice and the person employing the word. For example, when the young women discuss the topic of stripping and also prostitution, whilst they state they would not do it themselves they see nothing wrong with the job as a 'choice', especially as the women are paid for it. This may in part be due to wider representations where prostitution and being a 'glamour girl' are portrayed as positive jobs, seen for example in the television programme *Belle du Jour*, which is allegedly based on the real experiences of a female escort, which shows Belle in a series of sexy underwear, with little acknowledgement of any negative aspects of the job and the materialities of exploitation and harassment which may also be implicated. For the majority of young women there is a strong separation between 'others' and 'self', which allows them to talk with confidence about choice and empowerment. One young woman, who expressed such opinions, when pushed further stated that she would never want even to go to a strip club, not because of the women, but rather the threatening possibilities of the male audience. This example highlights the ways in which women may adopt a rhetoric of choice through which they can distance themselves from wider economic and social structures in which people are exploited.

Abjection and woman-ness

Running throughout the examples and the theoretical positions explained in this chapter are the ways in which the body, language and issues of representation can lead to disconnection. The two key issues that are raised are the ways in which women can be alienated from their own bodies and the underpinning relationship between the body, dominant modes of representation and language. When women connect to the dominant imagery of women in a normative sexualised way this involves a degree of alienation from their own bodies. In *Speculum of the Other Woman*, Irigaray (1985) argues that women's bodies are not absent *per se*, but are appropriated by male language, ideas and men themselves, instead of being the basis for their subjectivity. Irigaray posits a strong relationship between language and the body. Patriarchy and its Freudian articulation within psychoanalytic thought position male sexuality as the norm. As a result women are no longer in touch with their bodies; therefore, a pivotal issue for women is to regain this connection. For Irigaray this is through writing, as Cavallero surmises, through words which do not preclude the body but give it a voice (Cavallero, 2003: 119), by allowing the body to emerge from silence. Returning to the opening quote of this chapter, speech should be that of the body, rather than as a skin adopted from elsewhere, which betrays the body. Kristeva has argued that there is no sense of body before cultural inscription, as 'humans only endeavour to establish their corporeal boundaries at the point when they begin to develop a sense of themselves as subjects of the symbolic' (Cavallero, 2003: 126). However, this is not just as a product of culture; as Kristeva notes, there is 'another body' which cannot be grasped by language or society, as 'remnants' slip through from these cultural constructions, which are 'experienced as the body' (1988: 215), as the body is an 'excess which signs cannot capture' (Cavallero, 2003: 126). There is a need for words or language as expression goes beyond the dominant symbolic order, yet there is still an absence of the body.

Representational structures have to be altered; this resonates with McRobbie's (2008) discussion of the emphasis in representation and popular culture (and also in the behaviour expected of women), on girlishness. Even grown women adopt what McRobbie terms the postfeminist masquerade as the only viable alternative to being a phallic girl (the equivalent of Levy's female chauvinist pig). However, what is absent from this consideration, and indeed from representations in popular culture, is woman-ness. It goes beyond an absence and in fact leads to the stage of revulsion of that which is linked to womanhood, such as menstruation, bodily hair, cellulite or even understandings of childbirth. There is a fear and revulsion towards these things, which we theorise here through Kristeva's notion of the abject.

The sense of the abject develops as the child grows up, enters the symbolic and comes to define the boundaries of the body, through shedding material that threatens the body being self-contained. The threat that spills over is experienced as the abject, and feelings of horror:

> abjection is something that disgusts you, for example, you see something rotting and you want to vomit – it is an extremely strong feeling that is at once somatic and symbolic, which is above all a revolt against an external menace from which one wants to distance oneself, but of which one has the impression that it may menace from the inside.
>
> (Kristeva, 1996: 118)

For Kristeva this is a constant threat throughout our lives and the fear of anything that threatens the body's definition and boundaries. In some instances, she argues, this can lead to an internal form of alienation and estrangement through ambiguous states of the body. For example, childbirth or menstruation can be considered in terms of abjection, which has a long history in western culture and in monotheistic religions, as manifest in the biblical claims that the curse of Eve is to suffer pain in childbirth in retribution for her tasting the forbidden fruit of knowledge. These ideas can be used to relate to the ways in which woman-ness is made abject within culture through the revulsion that is experienced towards menstruation and the actualities of childbirth. This for women can lead to alienation within themselves as they feel revulsion for their own body.

Conclusion

The problems of silence and invisibility have been expressed in different ways in feminist histories. Much of the debate with which feminism has engaged has been concerned with how to speak and be seen, as well as about how women might gain some control over how they are seen.

At one level it seems as if women, and women's bodies in particular, are too present and too visible. There is a volubility about women's bodies akin to the modern explosion of sexuality, which, as Foucault (1981) argued, failed to offer any liberatory possibilities and more powerfully generated a new regime of restraint. Critiques of the objectification and sexualisation of women have presented the problem as one that disempowers women by reducing us to particular aspects of our lives and to present women as objects who are looked at but who do not look. Such approaches have been contrasted with more recent, mostly postfeminist, versions of the story in which those who are present in the dominant forms of visualisation are either adopting parodic poses or are taking control. Either way the venture is read as empowering rather than disempowering.

In this chapter we have suggested that these ideas of empowerment and disempowerment demand further analysis and that theoretical approaches that address not only the mechanisms but also the source of power are vital to a critical political analysis of the apparatuses of contemporary culture and to feminism as a political project which addresses inequalities and exploitation. There is more to what is taking place than healthy exercise around a pole or even ironic subversion.

The stages through which we suggest a more substantial argument can be developed involves exploring some of the ways in which women are silenced and made invisible and the relationship between feminist critical analyses and lived experience, including the mechanism and regimes of popular culture. This involves thinking through some of the intersections between feminist knowledge and theory and feminist activism as co-producers of feminism as a political project that has relevance for women, especially in addressing questions of inequality and silencing. The recirculation of regimes of truth about the sexualisation of women leaves little scope for resistance, except within the terms of the dominant sets of meanings and practices. It is this theoretical framework that lacks any sense of where power is located, which may lead women to deploy the highly sexualised practices that were initially construed as objectifying, as an ironic or parodic source of resistance. The resultant discomfort and sense that something is wrong is a reconfigured aspect of the problem with no name; difficult to name without the language to do so and hard to eliminate without an understanding of its materiality.

It is only through a reinstatement of a speaking subject who speaks as a woman and a deconstruction of the material power that the problem with no name might be named. This is not to deny the multiple locations of power, but rather to bring its materiality into the discussion. Patriarchy, although far from the only materiality in play, remains a significant factor in understanding how gendered selves are made visible or invisible and of who is allowed to speak, as well as what it is possible to say.

Much of the discussion of visibility and invisibility in this chapter has highlighted the place of embodied selves in popular culture and as constitutive of lived experience. The next chapter takes up bodies and embodiment as another of the materialities that are crucial to an understanding of feminism in the twenty-first century and of the usefulness of recovering some seemingly lost feminist critiques.

6
Material Bodies: Bodies as Situations

Bodies are material and bodies matter, especially when things go wrong, but they also matter when things go right. As chapter 5 demonstrates, much of the debate about visibility, invisibility and silence involves bodies and corporeality. Bodies invoke the senses and sensation and, in explaining the status of the category woman and a politics of difference, embodiment carries specific meanings as well as generating problems and questions. The body seems to offer the boundaries of the self (Price and Shildrick, 1999), a tangible manifestation of the person (Bourdieu, 1984) and are important sites of difference among women and between women and men. Body practices are the source of success and human achievement as well as the body being the site of pain and the limit to what we are each able to do. Bodies are particular to each of us, no more so than in the experience of physical breakdown, yet bodies are also social. Gender is one of the categories universally applied, as Butler (1993) argues, at the moment a human being arrives in the world; the newborn is labelled by the equivalent of the pink or blue blanket as signifiers of sex which, she argues, starts the series of iterative, ritualised norms that create sex itself. Gender difference and the classification of humans into one of the two universally used categories have traditionally been made on grounds of visible, physical difference. However, social constructivist arguments that emphasise the discursive formation of the body through processes of inscription marginalise the materiality of the body.

One of the manifestations of the interrelationship between the social and the personal, the natural and the social, is apparent when we consider that this body is always a dressed body. It is subject to the social conventions of clothing, which are culturally and gender-specific, yet as these items of clothing are worn on the body it is also through this clothing, how it allows us to move, and the cultural competences (Mauss, 1973) that pertain to this, that we experience this. Feminist thinking has been enormously influential in demonstrating the ways in which differences among and between people have been created through the meanings that are given to the bodies we have. Women have always been more closely associated with the body, its frailties and contingencies, than men in western culture; nature is itself called 'mother nature', as noted by scholars commenting on western culture (Spelman, 1982; Sulieman, 1986, Schiebinger, 2000) and anthropologists (MacCormack and Strathern, 1980). The history of bodies is significant because 'gender differences are not fixed in the character of the genes but arise from specific histories and from specific divisions of labour and power between the sexes' (Schiebinger, 2000: 1). Feminists, along with other critics like Michel Foucault and Norbert Elias, although not always from the same perspective, argue that bodies are cultural and political as well as biological. As Grosz argued in *Volatile Bodies*, 'the stability of the unified body image, even the so-called normal subject, is always precarious. It cannot simply be taken for granted as an accomplished fact, for it must be continually renewed' (1994: 43–4). This reflects an intellectual movement towards the disappearing body and raises some of the important contemporary questions about the extent of mobility on embodiment and the implications this has for the further destabilisation of the category woman.

Bodies and embodiment have emerged as important aspects of feminist concerns with difference, which have often been framed by the question of essentialism. Feminist critiques have made significant contributions to the corporeal turn in the social sciences and humanities. However, the materiality of bodies has led to an elision with biology, in an equation of body and fixity or reductionism. This has the unfortunate consequences that an emphasis on social constructionism and a disregard for the specificities of embodied experience have sometimes ensued as the only possible and positive route into political activism. The debates that we have raised in previous chapters, such as those that focus on the tensions between equality and difference and the contradictions and tensions of visibility and invisibility, highlight the relevance of embodiment to feminist politics and the generation of feminist theories. Most notably, the matter of bodies raises questions about how to configure feminist political projects that relate to lived experience. This chapter focuses on the problem of bodies and embodied difference. Bodies also present particular problems in relation to the category woman. The body may be fighting back (Griggers, 2005) and the corporeal turn has been particularly powerful in feminist theorising, especially from the 1980s, in a diverse range of contexts, including technoscience (discussed in chapter 3), but bodies are still troubling.

Bodies, like the material culture that we live our lives through, are theoretically and intellectually problematic; these problems are analogous to the issues posed by a study of material culture. Material culture is a pivotal aspect of human culture and daily existence, yet its very thingness and solidity are precisely what makes it so difficult to theorise. It seems so obvious, routine and separate from metaphysical questions of ontology. However, as has been argued for material culture, it is precisely through its materiality that these questions are articulated (Miller, 1987). The objects that surround us, that are made, used and consumed by people, are central to our experience in this social world. So too for bodies. Embodiment is central to being in the world, yet in many instances and situations this embodiment is routine and therefore becomes taken for granted. As has been argued, technoscience and the march of technological and scientific progress might appear to offer freedom from the constraints of corporeality and a transgression of the boundaries of the enfleshed self. The equality and difference debate highlighted some of the difficulties of a politics of difference that focuses on a universalised category 'woman' and underestimates differences among women. Feminist engagements with the policies and practices of governance suggested that gendered democratisation could be achieved through recognition of difference and diversity. Chapter 5 pointed to ways in which visibility, silence and invisibility can restrict women to a category which constrains and limits the possibilities through processes of objectification and sexualisation and argued for alternative conceptualisations and practices of difference that acknowledge the materialities of power. Even in the twenty-first century women are called sluts and slappers and run the gamut of sexualised insults in many of their routine encounters. Each of these chapters signposted problems with understanding difference and reconfiguring a politics of difference with embodied implications.

Body problems

A major problem which recurs in relation to embodiment and a focus on bodies is Butler's (1990) argument in *Gender Trouble* that the concept 'women' becomes a coercive category, which normalises femininity in restrictive and exclusionary ways. This is because the only common thread that could be maintained, binding women into any common political project that could attempt to encompass all the diversity of race, ethnicity, class, sexuality, disability and generation, to mention but a few aspects of diversity, would be some shared corporeal or anatomical characteristics – the bare bones of anatomical sex which might carry little of relevance. More recent research indicates that bones too carry information about gender and race and are constituted through the life experience of individuals in particular economic and political regimes (Fausto-Sterling, 2005, 2006), which is partly consonant with Butler's argument for the fluidity and contingency of sex as a category that cannot be disassociated from repeated social practices and inscriptions. Butler suggests that to retain the category of women would be to limit women and the projects of feminist politics to the very classificatory systems which are the target of feminist critiques. Butler extends her argument for the dismantling of the category to Spivak's strategic essentialist account, which proposes a pragmatic use of the generic category in order to advance political claims and to promote feminist political agenda. These are strong but worrying arguments, especially in the wake of developments, or largely lack of developments, in the progress of feminist politics through intellectual work which could make sense of social, political and cultural transformations in the world since Butler first put forward these arguments.

This chapter works through some of the relationships between the changes taking place in the academy and feminist theorising, popular culture and practices and embodied, lived experience, and argues for alternative ways of thinking that retain the subject and category women through a politics of difference which does not underestimate the limitations to which Butler has drawn our attention. In order to address these debates, the chapter starts with an evaluation of the feminist phenomenological contributions that have been made to an understanding of embodiment and the status of a politics of difference. Phenomenology is important here because of its focus on lived experience and the interrelationship between the embodied self and the social worlds so constituted and which reproduce those selves. Phenomenological approaches are considered as a route into exploring the wider social structures in which individual experience is positioned, and what implications this has for a wider politics of difference. In drawing on phenomenology, we are not suggesting that there is a transparency in experience that is unmediated, but in order to focus on the possibilities of examining the specificities of social life in the feminist tradition of arguing that embodied selves are made and remade in particular spaces and times and through particular relationships and materialities.

Another useful dimension of phenomenology is the concept of embodiment as embracing both mind and body as inseparably combined in being in the world. This chapter takes up recent attempts to revisit de Beauvoir's conceptualisation of the body as situation as a route out of the problems identified in earlier chapters. In a sense, as Haraway has argued, all twentieth-century feminism could be seen as arising from and in conversation with de Beauvoir's *Second Sex*, a conversation which remains relevant in the twenty-first century.

This discussion engages with the ways in which feminists have been in dialogue with de Beauvoir's work and, in particular, in this chapter we examine the points of contact and, especially, dissonance between Butler and Beauvoir and Irigaray. Indeed, Butler quotes them both at the opening of *Gender Trouble*: 'one is not born a woman, but rather becomes one' (de Beauvoir) along with 'Strictly speaking "women" cannot be said to exist' (Kristeva) and Irigaray's 'Woman does not have a sex' (although she omits the context of this one, in that Irigaray suggests two not one, rather than no sex at all) (1990: 1). Butler includes Wittig's emphasis on sex as a political category and also a quotation from Foucault which contextualises the discussion in her book in relation to his argument that sex is established through its deployment. These are powerful arguments which relate to our discussion of the sexualisation of women's bodies in chapter 5. The problem for feminism is where this critique takes the possibilities of transformation and, crucially, where it takes feminist politics. The discussion in *Gender Trouble* and *Bodies That Matter* is cited as constitutive of more recent developments within feminist thought, which Butler to some extent anticipated and feared in her recognition of the dangers of dismantling 'woman', 'as if the indeterminacy of gender as eventually culminate in the failure of feminism' (1990: vii).

We draw on the debate triggered by the work of Irigaray, Kristeva and Cixous and French materialists such as Delphy and Wittig to explain how these critical voices speak to contemporary concerns. Thus it seems pertinent at this point in the twenty-first century to think about what these conversations can contribute to the debate about what feminisms mean and how relevant a feminism that requires active and activist women as subjects and political agents remains. In seeking to deconstruct the category woman and to destabilise its universalism, feminist theorising may have opened a gap between its explanation and routine experience and representation and could be complicit in the distancing of the academy from the everyday lives of many contemporary women and from popular culture. The word 'woman' carries connotations of a classless, raceless, universal category, and is one from which academic feminists are keen to distance themselves. Whilst Butler's critique of the heterosexual and universalising assumptions of some of the second-wave feminism are important, they do not have to be relegated to a naïve and best-forgotten past. Butler has offered some direct engagement with so-called French feminisms which have been recognised as having the diversity and depth that warrants reconsideration (e.g. Irigaray's politics of difference).

Toril Moi's (2001) work has also led to a reconfiguration of interest in de Beauvoir and raises the importance of considering these seminal texts as offering crucial insights into the present. Moi's work is a particularly interesting version of this approach which has been developed by other feminist phenomenological conceptualisations (e.g. Young, 2005). We argue that revisiting texts like de Beauvoir's through the lens of more recent theoretical approaches can be undertaken in light of, and in conversation with, subsequent critiques that are largely framed by postmodernist and poststructuralist thinking and current social contexts. Yet in rediscovering and rethinking these ideas that are no longer the 'past', but revitalised as a powerful critique of the ever-more discursive intellectual present, it is possible to encompass the differentiations of bodies and selves within a critical feminist perspective that includes analysis of power relations as lived and experienced.

The material turn

One of the major problems for feminists in thinking about bodies has been to negotiate and counter the historically negative associations of women with the body and that women are subject to and limited by their 'nature', which is devalued in relation to men's links with culture and rationality. It is thus not surprising that there has been considerable stress on the processes through which women and women's bodies are socially constructed. Although the social constructionist, discursive turn has been useful for feminists, it has, as we have argued, been problematic for its marginalisation of enfleshed bodies and the materiality of experience. Butler has not been alone in attempting to reinstate the material into theories of the body. She engages with materiality in *Bodies That Matter* because she is concerned to establish the relation between the material and the representational. Her arguments, however, remain firmly weighted on the side of signification, following a well-worn feminist path of stressing the safety of social constructionism (Alaimo and Hekman, 2008).

De Beauvoir has been criticised for her retreat from materiality and overemphasis on social construction, which we argue (following Moi, 2001) is an overstatement and a distortion of the material, embodied experience of both situated bodies and bodies as situations. Feminist science studies have taken up strong, materialist-based positions, even standpoints, that assert the importance of the material world and the actual body each of us inhabits in a variety of ways, most recently by focusing on the interrelationship between the material and the symbolic, rather than in positivist, empiricist ways that present representation as separate from the material or 'real' world. Haraway has refused to embrace a separation between the discursive and the material and presented a universe in which it is impossible to separate nature and culture, or the body from its representations, as illustrated in the example of cyborg thinking in chapter 3.

Difference remains core to material feminism, although it is taking many different forms. Braidotti uses Deleuzian notions of becoming woman in an affirmative conceptualisation of the multiplicities that are afforded by Deleuze and Guattari's (1987) flows of affect, but deploys Irigaray to focus on difference as she is aware that Deleuzian assemblages and challenges to the subject offer more limited scope for feminist activism and certainly a politics of difference (Braidotti, 1994, 2002). For this reason, we find Irigaray more useful, but wish to include the Deleuzian argument that symbolic systems are inseparable from materiality and to include materialities in our account.

Other feminist takes on the material turn have engaged with biology as well as bodies, showing how the natural world is imbricated with the social and cultural; gender is in our bones (Fausto-Sterling, 2006) and in our hair (Bordo, 2008) so that difference is constituted by and constitutive of the interrelationship between the natural and the social and, as Bordo (2008) argues, the personal, the political and the material are braided together.

We start from the position that nature is not a blank sheet, a *tabula rasa* on which culture inscribes. Our focus in this chapter is on how these connections are lived through their representations.

The right way forward or an essentialist backwater?

Feminist dilemmas have often been characterised by two alternatives, however complex and muddied the waters of postmodernist thinking have become. Liz Stanley, back in 1984, described the argument as being one between biological essentialism which prioritises embodied sex as the determinant of femininity or masculinity and social constructionism which focuses on gender as a social, cultural category. Sex and gender have been combined, but there is still an assumption, which is maintained in many routine practices and cultural and social fields today, that sex is privileged over gender as covering social attributes in terms of the objectivity and certainty it affords in relation of the constitution of the self. Where the two concepts have been explicitly disentangled the influence of sex on gender has been awarded priority and higher status than any influence gender as a social construct might have over sex. There is a normative claim in this hierarchy that sex should determine gender.

Although the dangers of polarisation and oversimplification are widely acknowledged (Segal, 1994; Gillis, Howie and Mumford, 2007), attempts to reconstitute a feminist voice that speaks as a woman are often treated with suspicion and charged with essentialism. Even Kristeva is accused of leaving her readers and feminist followers lost between the Scylla of essentialism and the Charybdis of postmodernist social constructionism. This is recognised as a problem and one that leaves feminism as a political movement with limited options. As Fraser and Bartky put it, Kristeva 'leaves us oscillating between a repressive version of gynocentric-maternalist essentialism, on the one hand, and a profeminist anti-essentialism on the other' (1992: 190). Fraser acknowledges that this is not a useful or desirable position because, in

> Denise Riley's terms, the first over-feminizes women by defining us maternally. The second, by contrast, under-feminizes us, by insisting that 'women' do not exist and by dismissing the feminist movement as a proto-totalitarian fiction.
>
> (1992: 190)

This 'over-feminization' is often associated with a focus, or even a celebration, of maternity and women's ability to bear a child with all its embodied dimensions, including women's capacity to be more than one body. There is to some extent a fear of venturing into the 'dark continent' which Irigaray (1991) calls motherhood in western culture, because of the dangers it presents of reducing women to a single function, an essence that is rooted in biology, which is another source of alarm to those who fear the limitations of essentialist accounts of difference, especially when applied to embodiment. Biology and bodies have been entangled within essentialist frameworks, with an understanding of the centrality of bodies in the making of selves being confused for a reduction of the self to biological make up (Rose, 1985).

The problems that have been posed here are, first, those of essentialism, which is construed as invoking naturalist explanations or those that necessarily involve fixity and some version of reductionism. The possibilities of political action and change are threatened by an oversimplified essentialism, which might also prioritise embodied similarities at the expense of the massive social, economic and political differences that are constitutive of social life and experience. This is particularly powerful threat in relation to women's experience, where women have been reduced to their bodies and excluded from participation in paid work and public life on the grounds of their embodied, essentialised characteristics. Women have been seen as governed by their bodily cycle, biology and hormones. Aristotle's 'wandering womb' has been translated into a psy-discourse of gendered emotional disturbances. Men are less likely to be seen as subject to the vagaries of their emotions but, for example in athletics, African American and other black men have been seen as essentially more suited to sport than to intellectual pursuits in a similarly essentialising discourse. A second and related problem is that of maternalism, which is understood as troubling because its dramatic corporeality and the intensity of the embodied experience, combined with its gendered aspects, have led to a somewhat celebratory positioning of those who argue for its centrality in the configuration of gendered identities and notably the argument for a distinct category woman.

Some areas of experience are more corporeal than others, where we are reminded of the flesh at every turn. Corporeality is central to all areas of experience, whether we are reminded of this or not. For example, in the case of the relationship we have to clothing, as this is something that we wear on the body, it would appear to be a very embodied relationship. However, as I-Sophie have discussed elsewhere, getting dressed is something that is done routinely; we do not think about our bodies at every moment. Even though we constantly feel the clothing on our skins, and it allows certain movements and not others, we become so accustomed to it that it is not felt as a limit to ourselves, but as a part of ourselves. It is often only when this routinised relationship is disrupted that we become aware of the body, seen for example when a new item of clothing is bought or we gain or lose weight. On such occasions as the body bulges out of the top of a new pair of jeans, we are conscious of the body and its limits, or when the bulging body causes a garment to split at the seams, the previously unproblematic boundary between body and clothing is tested. The purchasing of a new item of clothing or pair of shoes means that the body cannot move in the same way and this involves a relearning of the cultural competences of walking and sitting. Considerations of clothing are always fundamentally about the body, yet this is not necessarily something we are aware of. Similarly in the case of sport, there is a routinised competence of doing it, yet this is different in that it often involves pushing the body to its limits. Maybe too it is the very centrality of body practices to sport that creates the danger, especially for those on the margins, who engage in sport as a route out of poverty and the constraints of racism and social exclusion, as has so often been the case in the history of boxing. Sporting bodies too are marked by differences and the inequalities that are part of 'being in the world'. Embodied selves are engaged in routine practices of training and bodies are deeply and widely implicated in the representations and discourses of sport. Sport, especially one situated within a genealogy of disadvantage and deprivation like boxing, raises questions about how can we acknowledge and address the materiality of embodiment without reducing the self to the flesh.

It is not by chance that Joyce Carol Oates (1987), in writing about boxing, argues that this sport is to men and masculinity what childbirth is to women and femininity. The analogy is not as simplistic or as absurd as might at first appear. Bodies have been associated with constraints and the opposition of mind and culture. Similarly, boxing, which involves an investment of physical capital by largely disadvantaged, working-class, racialised, ethnicised men, can be read deterministically, through the familiar tropes of the route out of the ghetto and 'rags to riches' narratives implicated in a reductionist version of gender identity (Woodward, 2007). There are, of course, significant areas in which there are no points of contact in this analysis between sport, motherhood and indeed the previous example of clothing, but the comparison raises two important issues: first, the social dangers of being reduced to the body and its practices and processes, and second, the political dimensions of focusing on embodiment and the cultural meanings associated with some aspects of embodiment, which invoke particular gendered polarities. The problem is how to acknowledge the experience of the embodied subject and, indeed, to recognise that subject without being implicated in the process of reducing the subject to the body – a Foucauldian problem in a sense, which Foucault describes but does not resolve (nor does Butler in *Bodies That Matter*).

Motherhood, especially in pregnancy and childbirth, is an embodied experience in the life-course which has generated a massive literature which aims to provide critical analyses that could locate and explain its significance within a wider field of theorising embodiment (Kitzinger, 1978, 1979; Oakley, 1979, 1980; Ferguson, 1989). The problem here, however, is how to provide a means of explaining an area of experience that has a dramatic and powerful impact, as well as being central to the cultural field in which gender identities are forged, that accommodates the sensation and force of lived experience and the constraining limitations of social and cultural constraint. One starting point is phenomenology, at least in relation to acknowledging lived experience that is embodied and in which there is no distinction between mind and body or concomitantly what is natural and what is cultural.

Phenomenological accounts

Phenomenology is attractive because of its focus on lived experience; Being in the world is inextricably bound up with the constitution and extension of the body. In phenomenology, the structure of the self is indivisible from its corporeal capacities. Different strands of phenomenology and of Mauss's work on body techniques have drawn on Bourdieu's work, especially on habitus.

Bourdieu's extension of habitus from class to gender remains deeply suspicious of claims to roots in biology and argues for a social and cultural construction of sexual difference. To produce a gender habitus requires a complex process of social education, in which the body is a key aspect of the process of social inscription (Bourdieu, 2000). Bourdieu's discovery that men occupy the more privileged position in the sexual division of labour was not news when *Masculine Domination* was published in 2000. He fails to acknowledge his feminist predecessors, notably de Beauvoir and subsequently French feminists like Michelle le Doeuff and Christine Delphy. However, his concept of habitus, especially with its focus on the body, does have its uses for feminist critiques (e.g. Skeggs). A gendered habitus, Bourdieu argues, can be best critiqued by those who lack its legitimacy; the 'masculine illusion' of self-importance is difficult to deconstruct for those who are within its illusory powers.

Merleau-Ponty's (1962) work has informed much of the more recent explanation of corporeal schemata that have been developed to challenge the binary logic of mind and body and its associated problem of how to accommodate agency. For Merleau-Ponty, the body has to be understood outside the dualisms that separate nature from culture and mind from body because of the unique status of the body for each person as both an external object and a subjective condition through which it is possible to have relations with the object that is the body. Making the case against a purely objective view of the body, he argues:

I am not the outcome of the meeting point of numerous causal agencies which determine my bodily or psychological make-up. I cannot conceive of myself as nothing but a bit of the world... All my knowledge of the world, is gained from my own particular point of view, or from some experience of the world... Scientific points of view, according to which my existence is a moment of the world's... take for granted, without explicitly mentioning it, the other point of view, namely that of consciousness, through which from the outset a world forms itself round me and begins to exist for me.

(Merleau-Ponty, 1962: viii–ix)

Rather than taking this position as an expression of a somewhat naïve understanding of the complexities of consciousness, it can be seen to have particular advantages that benefit a reconceptualisation of embodied subjectivity and of the relationship between body and mind. It permits both a focus on the lived experience of material bodies and the possibility of resistance and subversion of norms. Perceived as part of lived experience, the body is a way of being present in the world; the body as a situation encompasses both the subjective and the objective aspects of experience. Merleau-Ponty's theory of perception most effectively challenges the machinic mind/body distinction of Cartesian dualism by demonstrating that perception is formed by the interrelationship between the lived body and its environment; acts of perception are what create perceived objects and perceiving subjects. This has benefits in a study of embodied practices in diverse fields because it shifts the emphasis from women's experience being concerned only with corporeality that can be separated from intellectual achievements and from intentionality which can be applied to political action. Merleau-Ponty's corporeal schema also offers an alternative to the notion of an isolated self/body located within, but separate from, an external world and presents a means of comprehending how embodied experience works and can thus be seen as embedded in a dynamic relationship with social and cultural practices.

One important aspect of the corporeal schema which is developed is that it is possible to live in the body without constant reflection about the relationship between the subject and the object. Thus it is suggested that we experience our bodies and the external environment in a pre-reflective way that does not require thought at every moment. However, this lack of reflection is not simply pre-reflective, as it is through a subject-object relationship becoming routine that it ceases to be a cause for reflection. This point emerged from the ethnography I-Sophie carried out into women's wardrobes. Even though this research was on women, the issues are more widely applicable, given that clothing is worn by everyone, from the moment they are born to the end of their life. As my work has demonstrated (Woodward, 2005, 2007), the most significant dynamic in understanding everyday clothing choices is that between what I have termed the habitual and non-habitual relationship to clothing. Habitual clothing is items that women put on routinely and do not require any thought as they just 'know' how it looks and what it will go through. These routine practices are not reflected on everyday, yet through continued practice they have become routine and unreflective. In contrast, non-habitual clothing is that which requires self-conscious engagement in terms of how it looks, what it goes with and the effect it has on the body. When it is worn, such clothing is something we are conscious of; a woman accustomed to wearing low-rise jeans and decides to wear high-waisted jeans is conscious of them gripping her waist. Every time she bends over or sits down, she is aware of the style of jeans she is wearing. As I have argued, if clothing is an externalisation of aspects of the self, then the wearing of habitual or non-habitual clothing also has implications for the self. Habitual clothing involves a routine and un-thought-out sense of who I am through clothing, yet in the case of non-habitual clothing this involves an interrogation of the self and a consideration of who I could be (Woodward, 2007). A corporeal schema is achieved through the acquisition and development of habits, where ways of being in the world become habitual, whether through observation and learning or innovation and creativity. Embodied subjects acquire new habits through dynamic processes of interaction. These interactions and the interrogation of the self also involve testing the boundaries of the body and the self, as it is not a free and unconstrained act but involves an interaction between the self, the body and the clothing.

A consideration of clothing raises important questions about the category woman. Clothing and concerns over appearance are something which has historically and socially been encoded as female (Berger, 1972; Wilson, 1985; de Grazia and Furlough, 1996). In the contemporary world, fashion still carries these feminised connotations. This is part of a longer historical association of femininity with appearance and therefore with artificiality (Tseelon, 1995), which raises an interesting paradox, as through the issue of motherhood and maternity, women are associated with nature and the body yet through considerations of clothing, women and femininity are associated with artifice and superficiality. When these two aspects – artificiality and the surface in opposition to nature and biology – are taken together it is clear that cultural associations of womanhood are contradictory. Concerns with the surface of the body, whether through clothing or make-up, are still concerns of the body, and as such, although they appear contradictory, each involves associating women with the body. In both cases, there is an assumption that the body is separate from the self, whether this is bodily concerns from the inside, in the ability to bear a child (and also in the other bodily changes that accompany pregnancy), or through external concealment and modification through wearing clothing. In each case, we would argue that it is a question of being in the world, of selfhood. Clothing is central in the everyday enactment of gender differences, yet would also seem to offer possibilities and potentials for rupture and change. It would seem to fit easily within a cultural or social constructionist understanding where clothing is part of what constructs gender. However, we wish to argue for a material and embodied understanding of womanhood, which does not negate the cultural norms and associations of clothing, but suggests that these acquire significance over time as they are worn next to the body. Gender is not a socialisation into values that already exist and are fixed; as a young woman, or indeed a young man, negotiates the changes in their body through puberty and then later in the life-course, clothing is part of how embodied change and experience are negotiated. This process involves changes in the body, in clothing, selfhood from which none of these aspects can be separated. These changes also depend on the individual life-course and the aims that a person has. As Moi notes, a woman may experience her body as clumsy in relationship to her desire to be a dancer. This is not an inherent bodily condition. The example of clothing leads on to and raises questions about the body as situation and the situated body (de Beauvoir).

Situated bodies: bodies as situations

The meanings of bodies are not written on the surface, nor will the experience be the same for everyone. De Beauvoir suggests that the human body is ambiguous, subject to natural laws and to the human production of meaning:

> It is not merely as a body, but rather as a body subject to taboos, to laws, that the subject becomes conscious of himself and attains fulfilment-it is with reference to certain values that he valorizes

himself. To repeat once more: physiology cannot ground any values; rather, the facts of biology take on the values that the existent bestows upon them.

(1989: 76)

Bodies as represented, for example, as marginalised also experience themselves and are crucial to an understanding of selfhood and the processes through which people position themselves and are positioned within the social world: 'the body is not a thing, it is a *situation*...it is the instrument of our grasp upon the world, a limiting factor for projects' (de Beauvoir, 1989: 66).

This approach provides a way of bringing together the natural, material body, the experiences of embodied selves and the situations, which include representations, practices and policies, which re-create the lived body. Bodies are not 'just' in a situation, nor are they just objects of empirical inquiry; they are more than this. De Beauvoir's analysis of the 'lived body' provides a means of enabling 'a situated way of seeing the subject based on the understanding that the most important location or situation is the roots of the subject in the spatial frame of the body' (Braidotti, 1994: 161).

Bodies are situated on the margins through structural factors such as economic inequalities, racialisation, ethnicicisation, discrimination on the grounds of gender and of physical or mental impairment, but bodies are also themselves situations through which people experience themselves, both negatively and positively. As Moi argues: 'To claim that the body *is* a situation is not the same as to say that it is placed *within* some other situation. The body is both a situation and is placed within other situations' (2001: 65).

Embodied selves, understood through the trope of lived bodies, accords greater agency and possibility for transformation and avoids the reduction of the self to the body by acknowledging both the situations which bodies inhabit and the interrelationship between bodies and situations. De Beauvoir argues that to claim that the body is a situation is to acknowledge that having a woman's body is bound up with the exercise of freedom. The body-in-the-world is in an intentional relationship with the world, although, as Young (2005) argues, women do often end up living their bodies as things. Living the body as a thing in part arises from an internalisation of how it is seen by other people. Young argues that this process is more marked for young women, as they internalise how they are supposed to appear to others. This is seen most markedly in women in professions such as lap-dancing, where the entire presentation of the body in terms of what is worn, and how women move their bodies, is performed through an internalisation of what is seen as sexy to men. This example is also a powerful reminder that the exercise of freedom is often very limited, no matter how often words such as 'choice' are employed. Lived embodiment disrupts dichotomies of mind and body, nature and culture, public and private, and foregrounds experience (Young, 2005).

Young's feminist phenomenological approach, which deploys the concept of embodiment, attempts to redress the imbalance in Merleau-Ponty's work by focusing on gender and, in particular, the specificities of women's embodiment. Young challenges the universal account of the gender-neutral body implied by Merleau-Ponty and claims that the female body is experienced not simply as a direct communication with the active self, but is also as an object. She suggests that there are distinctive manners of comportment and movement that are associated with women. Young attributes these different modalities first, to the social spaces in which women learn to comport themselves. This is manifest in all aspects of being in the world, which are present in representations of public life as well as routine encounters. Sport offers a particularly powerful example of gendered comportment which is used to marginalise and diminish women's body practices (Woodward, 2009). For example, sporting practices involve constraints of space and, for women, repeatedly acting in less assertive and less aggressive ways than men. Conversely, from this it might be deduced that men acquire those embodied practices, which are competitive and even aggressive. Second, Young suggests that women are encouraged to see themselves through the gaze of others, including the 'male gaze', as developed in the work of Laura Mulvey (1975) and, as the previous chapter highlighted, to become more aware of themselves as objects of the scrutiny of others. Whereas young women practise the comportment of femininity, young men engage in the techniques of masculinity, which can be embodied in the 'hard man' image or, less dramatically, at least involve working up a sweat and performing the actions required by the sport, rather than being concerned with appearance, which often accompanies sporting practices. In each case the embodied expectations are limiting in the cases of masculinity and femininity. It also raises questions about the extent to which femininity and femaleness, and masculinity and maleness, can be equated. As Young (2005) notes, there is a clear distinction between being female and being feminine. Many women do not have a problematic relationship with their everyday embodied identity as women, yet have a far more unclear or problematic relationship with femininity (Woodward, S., 2007). For many this is not something they 'do' habitually, such that when they, on a particular social occasion, are called on to wear a dress by social convention, they are faced with the issue that they have to stand in a certain way, and feel compelled to adopt a corresponding feminine manner. These hegemonic forms of masculinity and femininity need to be problematised, yet this same act of problematisation does not have to involve abandoning the category woman or the category man. Social space is constituted by body practices which make up the social world and demonstrate how embodiment is constitutive of social differences, especially gender differences.

There is no simple, linear trajectory of progress and change, but a series of disruptions and realignments, which do, however, suggest that there is fluidity and transformation in lived experience. It is only possible to theorise change if there is an acknowledgement of the possibility of creativity and collective action. Whilst dominant hierarchies persist, as de Beauvoir argues, constraints can be not only structural, as in the operation of patriarchal and colonialist discourses of exclusion, but also corporeal, in terms of the impairment and disease that flesh is heir to and the specificities of embodied experience which can indeed be gendered. This does not mean that gendered characteristics determine who we are, but that they are part of the body as situation. However, an understanding of embodiment that challenges distinctions between body and mind and takes on the political project of transformation has to incorporate the dynamic of an embodied being-in the-the-world. Feminist phenomenology offers an entry point to linking the structural constraints of the wider social and cultural arena with the body as situation with which they are inextricably linked in a version of 'we are our bodies' that permits the politics of action and activism.

Category woman

Butler's work in the early 1990s was part of a bigger movement which was concerned with deconstructing and scrutinising categories of person; within feminism this meant the category woman. The task for feminists, as Butler argues, is 'redefining and expanding the category of women itself to become more inclusive [or] to challenge he place of the category as part of a feminist normative discourse' (1990a: 325). Just as Louis Althusser was criticised for assuming a subject already existing who is summoned into place by the process of interpellation, so Butler argued that feminists have assumed that gender was grafted onto

Material Bodies: Bodies as Situations 153

sex, and that the sexed subject was natural and pre-given. She argued, against this, that sex is not natural but performative and that sex and gender are both constituted through iterative acts. This challenges a stable unitary concept of woman which could be the basis of any sort of politics, let alone feminist ones. Thus the subject cannot exist prior to its representations because it – she – is generated by them. Feminism, Butler argues, reifies what it means to be female in collusion with the forces that regulate and discipline women in Foucauldian terms, in a manner which is anti-democratic. Butler cites the example of the clothes we wear as part of this disciplinary regime; indeed, clothing is one of the areas in which difference between men and women is most marked, not just for children (items in pink of blue) yet also for adults as almost all retail outlets are divided into men's and women's sections: very few shops are genuinely unisex. Throughout the life-course, then, it could be argued, in Butler's terms, that women are regulated through the connection between clothes and the anatomical body which mirrors the constraints of the sex-gender links. Clothes are one of the strongest markers of visible difference and also how we experience our embodied gendered subjectivity. In her argument, the very concept of femaleness is coercive and thus prevents a meaningful category that could unite women in a definition that could be inclusive of the disparate axes of identity. However, whilst there is a strong sense that femininity can be coercive, to suggest that femaleness is always coercive is problematic.

Clothes are an important dimension of the performance and performativity of gender, although this is not acknowledged as explicitly as it might be in Butler's writing. In her discussion of drag, in particular, which was central to Butler's illustrations of performativity, this could do with more attention, given that clothing, make-up and the subsequent bodily postures that are adopted are so central to how this is performed. Moya Lloyd (2007) cites the moment at which Butler describes thinking that men in drag performed femininity better than she did and the realisation that this provided that one never is one's gender but only in a condition of doing it. By imitating women, or at least imitating gender, drag reveals the structure of gender. This is rather like Erving Goffman's claim that we can understand social rules through their subversion. What we take for granted is revealed when we act in a contrary or unexpected way. However, what is missing in the explanation of drag is the social circumstances in which it is enacted, including the misogyny that can accompany parody and the history of embodiment and specificity of the situated body, as well as the body as situation. There is something deeply offensive about the suggestion that a man wearing excessive make-up, in a pantomime version of femininity, in any way comes close to an embodiment of femaleness. It may make explicit the ways in which gender is performed, yet it negates any question of the body and of difference.

In *Bodies That Matter* Butler suggests that, in order to recognise the materiality of women's lives without taking a foundational line; a more acceptable approach is to see the category woman as a 'permanent site of contest, or as feminist agonistic struggle' (1993: 221). When the connection between sex and the body is subverted, there is a danger of failing to engage with the materiality of difference, which can only be attributed to a set of iterative practices.

It is doubtful, however, whether denying the importance of gendered embodiment and insisting on woman as a contested space does anything to address the problems of real women and their experience of violence, torture, deprivation and marginalisation. The problem here is the lack of a means of understanding victimisation or exploitation (Nussbaum, 1999) and of bridging the divide between feminist political action based on an understanding of that directed at redressing social inequalities.

Some of the criticisms that have been targeted at this dismantling of the category woman, including some of Butler's (2004) later reflections, have focused on the problems it creates for political activism. Others, which are linked to this, include the claim that to deny the possibility of a category woman that can embrace all the contradictions and differences within the purported category, does relate to lived experience. As we stated at the outset, most women have no problem calling themselves women and identifying moments when this aspect of their subjectivity is relevant. The fact that women have been invisible is no justification for rendering the place from which they speak fragmented and meaningless.

Phenomenological accounts which focus on lived experience, although problematic, offer some redress to the incompatibility and disconnections between lived experience and postmodernist, even queer, theorising which bears no resemblance to that experience. Butler was aware of the force of de Beauvoir's arguments in *The Second Sex*, but makes the case that lived experience is always mediated through historical specificity; all we know as everyday life and experience is the historical body (Butler, 1989). This would seem to accord with the idea that the body is situated and a site of becoming, but also limited by historical, contingent circumstances. However, in making this claim, which draws heavily on Foucauldian arguments about the inscribed body, there is some slippage between the biological body, and especially biological sex, which Butler denies, and the embodied experience of the body as situation in de Beauvoir's account. Butler still fails to address the problem of what it is to embody an historical idea; she accommodates the situated body, but less so the body as situation, which is also reconstituted and lived through the everyday experience of sex and gender.

Sex/gender

Sex/gender has a long history in feminist debates. Earlier arguments which pointed to the distinction between sex as a biological category and gender as dependent on social practices and cultural mores, although seeming to state the obvious, had a considerable impact on feminist political projects and continues to do so. By making this distinction they threw into question all the taken-for-granted assumptions about what is natural or normal (Oakley, 1980). It became apparent that there was nothing natural or biological about earning less than a man doing the same job; it was just statistically normal. However, Butler's argument was particularly radical in taking the debate a stage further by actually denouncing the distinction and even the existence of a category of sex that was outside the social and cultural processes through which it was produced and reproduced. Butler also subverts the phenomenological claim that there is an autonomous agent behind actions; even if essences are constituted through being in the world and through actions, which may be significantly socially constrained and shaped, there is conceptually someone who performs those actions and has experiences. For Butler, gender is not linked to something called sex, which is part of the body you inhabit; sex is gender and gender is sex. Thus gender does not describe a thing or an essence; it is a process. This claim accords with social constructionist, especially Foucauldian, branches of feminism which have stressed the social inscriptions on the body which are what constitute gender and sexuality. Butler appears to go further, though, in following Nietzsche to argue that gender is an activity made through and by the activity; there is nothing behind the doing of gender; 'the doer is merely the fiction added to the deed- the deed is everything' (1990: 33). The sexed body is an effect rather than a cause. Both sex and gender, Butler argues, are produced within a heteronormative matrix. Butler goes on to use the example of drag to illustrate the moment of realisation that men in drag could 'do' femininity exceptionally well and maybe even better than someone who classified female at birth. As we have suggested, it is important to note that there is a clear difference between femininity and being female. There may be some confusion of stereotypical behaviour and masquerade, but there is some injustice in the criticism that Butler has experienced because of her use of the example of drag, which is illustrative rather than presented as a political solution. There is little cognisance of lived experience through the life-course of having a sexed identity; even if sex is a process, this argument raises questions about the extent of the iterative practices that constitute sex and whether a few iterations would be sufficient. There is no indication of the genealogy or history of sexed identity or whether being a woman could be effected with a single performance. There seems to be limited mileage in men masquerading as women in the most exaggerated and stereotypical manner, but it does point to the performative dimensions of gender and the processes through which sex and gender are one and the same.

Butler's focus was on sexual differences, of which she noted many, but not on the hierarchies of those differences. She acknowledges, but does not explain, the 'continuing cultural and political reality of patriarchal domination (2004: 210). This is one of the big problems that have been generated in the wake of her earlier work.

Second-wave feminism had already subjected the category woman to considerable scrutiny before Butler took the more drastic step of challenging the very notion. As she writes in *Gender Trouble*, the task facing feminism at this point was to redefine and expand the category woman to become more inclusive or 'to challenge the place of the category as part of a feminist normative discourse' (1990: 325). Thus Butler contests the assumptions of many if not most feminists that gender is based on sex. If sex, gender and desire are all effects and none has its roots or basis in anything natural and gender is performative through the iteration of particular acts, there can be no self prior to representations. Thus feminism is responsible for reifying the category woman which regulates women so that this is not an inclusive category but one that is in effect undemocratic and coercive; to speak of or as a woman is to normalise femininity and femaleness in a restrictive way. In order to promote greater inclusion and democracy, Butler argued, woman has to be dismantled.

Although Butler's critique was greeted with some excitement at its democratic possibilities for opening up who could be included and as offering a new starting point for feminist politics, this being – what is wrong and what can be done about it rather than asking where women are in this situation – also caused alarm (Segal, 1994). Butler has created some innovative strategies for deconstructing the sex/gender binary and for interrogating our understanding of biology and embodiment, but the extent of her dismantling of the subject position of women has had a significant impact on the political project of feminism rather than opening up the category. Her focus on sexuality and the potential liberatory possibilities of drag and diverse sexual identities marginalises more important material inequalities, an aspect of her earlier work which she has later recognised when taking up her own position in relation to global political conflicts.

A post too far?

Whatever the excesses of some postmodernist, poststructuralist critiques which have so dematerialised the body that it appears to have disappeared, the deconstruction of distinctions between sex and gender have also been productive. Butler's arguments focusing on how sex too is constructed and on the discursive elements of sex are crucial to contemporary reworkings of feminist theories. She has demonstrated that the sex/gender distinction is somewhat spurious in its separation of what is biological and natural and what is cultural; indeed, the distinction itself serves to obscure the social inscriptions that create the sexed body as well as the elision of bodies and biology that might also have been implicated in the binary logic of sex/gender. The unravelling of what constitutes nature, of course, has a longer history and pre-dates the 1990s, for example in the argument that nature elides with ethics so that frequently, especially when women are agents of particular actions, what they have done is deemed 'unnatural' if subject to moral or social censure or 'only natural', if approved (Brown and Jordanova, 1981). It has also been pointed out that distinctions that have been made between what is natural in a biological sense and what is statistically normal have also merged so that what most people do, that is what is usual, is normal and hence natural – an easy slippage, which earlier feminism had questioned, although Butler's arguments are more radical and less empiricist.

Butler's careful discussion of the processes through which people are sexed and cannot be a sex until they are situated within those social/biological categories is also useful in creating spaces for the deconstruction of sex/gender. However, what these arguments do not deliver is what the something or, more importantly, someone, is before birth to whom a gender, or sex, is attributed. This problem immediately raises the questions about the status of the pre-birth being as merely a collection of cells.

The major problem, however, involves the extent to which the dismantling of the category woman and especially the embodied subjects, women, does for feminist political projects and engagements with the materialities of experience. The over-socialising of sex renders embodied experience redundant or meaningless, except as determined by social inscriptions, in a paradigm which may be as reductionist as the dualistic sex/gender logic it seeks to subvert. It is not only binaries that are dislodged; it is the embodied subjects that recognise, rather than misrecognise, themselves as women.

Phenomenological accounts, although in danger of overemphasising the agentic subject and the individual's perceptions, offer some redress to the over-socialisation that destabilises women as subjects to the extent that there can be no meaningful political action generated and effected, however diverse and fragmented, that brings together a gendered alliance. This raises two issues: an excessive emphasis on the individual and concomitant freedoms to act and speak as an individual, and the homogeneity of the category woman which distorts other aspects of difference which, at different times and places, far outweigh any shared interests arsing from or linked to sex. In answer to the first point, political agents cannot act only as individuals. As de Beauvoir argued in the context of philosophical writing, 'It is impossible to shed light on one's own life without at some point illuminating the life of others' (1988: 10). This is not to say that there is not enormous diversity which can be overlooked by universalising categories including those of sex.

Feminist activists/agents

Feminist activism in the 1970s can be seen to have reinserted the body into history by arguing for serious scholarly engagement with matters that had hitherto been seen as trivial or vulgar (Schiebinger, 2000); they also focused on activism that drew attention to the political importance and relevance of embodied experience. Feminist activism has brought together the enfleshed body and the body politic by demanding and achieving recognition of women's rights over their own bodies. Such campaigns and protests have been central to what can be seen as constituting feminism, from whatever theoretical stance. Campaigns have ranged across a wide political arena in which women have drawn attention to the exploitation and destruction of war, in South America with the Mothers of the Disappeared, against the wars in Iraq and Afghanistan, and in the Middle East against the Israeli invasion of Gaza and against acts of terrorism worldwide. Violence and aggression on the local or global stage have often been the focus of activism, especially since women have so often been the targets of particular acts of violence. Sexual violence against women, whether domestic violence in the home or on the streets, triggered campaigns like Reclaim the Night, and feminist activism and politics combined to provide explanatory frameworks for the ways in which rape has been used as an act of aggression and means of control (Kappeler, 1981; Radford and Russell, 1992).

Women have been politicised through their support of male partners and colleagues, as in the miners' wives campaigns against pit closures in the 1980s. They may have been called 'wives', but their collective actions were spontaneous and independent of patriarchal control.

Other activism has incorporated demands for greater control of bodily states that are associated with women, such as reproductive rights over how and where to give birth and under what conditions, or the rights to terminate pregnancy or to benefit from reproductive technologies that can make childbearing possible. Women have fought to have conditions such as premenstrual tension and postnatal depression recognised and achieved considerable success in putting women's embodied experience, marked as different from men's, on the medical agenda. Such experience is not always linked to reproductive capacities, but these are the areas which have attracted the most activist attention. There has been less political action over issues such as women's different experience of cardiovascular disease, including heart attack, and osteoarthritic illness. Medical practices which have involved treating women in the same ways as men, for example, by assuming that men experience a higher incidence of myocardial infarction in all groups than women and that women's symptoms are the same as men's, results from a long tradition in which women are seen as deficient men (Schiebinger, 2000). Sports medicine offers a particularly striking example as it has developed almost entirely premised on the male body (Socolove, 2008). However, feminists have been anxious about venturing into this arena and arguing for the recognition of physiological differences in a field in which they seek to minimise difference in order to open up the possibilities of participation and competition. It is hardly surprising that feminist campaigns have concentrated on those aspects of corporeality that do not involve men.

Conclusion

The discussion of bodies in this chapter, which builds on earlier chapters in the book, has demonstrated several distances. First, between the academy and its search for yet more complex explanatory frameworks, which may be validated within the academy but have little to do with a feminist politics of engagement with lived inequalities. Second, this discussion suggests a distance between popular cultural representations as part of lived experience and feminism as a set of ideas and practices that have politics at their heart. There is a marked shift from the politics of *Our Bodies Ourselves* and feminist activism which aims to create knowledge that enables women to control their bodies and themselves. This is not a temporal or chronological transformation, since such activism is still a key part of global feminism, but rather one that illustrates the distances that have opened up between feminist theorising and the possibilities of a politics of difference.

The focus on bodies and embodiment in this chapter arises from the problem with which we started and reflects some of the major concerns of feminism in the twenty-first century. Thinking about bodies has always been an important strand in feminist thinking, albeit a troubling one, which always carries the threat of essentialism and reducing women to their bodies and to nature within traditional dualistic thinking. The corporeal turn in feminist thinking has been enormously productive in providing new ways of explaining embodied experience as well as providing links between lived experience and women's concerns and feminist activism and feminist theory. Bodies have long been the focus of feminist activism, but the corporeal turn has also taken some more worrying routes into approaches that seem disembodied. Notably, the discursive turn, whilst usefully presenting critiques of the processes through which gendered bodies are constructed, has emphasised the social construction of bodies to the extent that the category woman might have disappeared.

Butler's contributions to the debate have been very productive, especially in her arguments about the discursive production of sex. However, the trends which it has set in motion could be constitutive of the dismantling, not only of sexed bodies and the category woman, but of feminism as a political project.

One way of addressing the excesses of the discursive and even the combined psychoanalytic and discursive turn is to reinstate an analysis of the body as situation, which is also a materialist critique and one which acknowledges and engages with the situation of feminists in the production of knowledge. As Howson argues, 'feminist philosophies of the body have masked their own situatedness as story tellers by the artifice of story telling' (2005: 151).

7
Conclusion

To address the question why feminism matters involves understanding the issues that face women in the twenty-first century. However, to talk about feminism for the twenty-first century suggests that this is somehow different from the twentieth century; it implies a newness offered by a new millennium, which requires a concomitant feminism that is similarly novel and exciting. Baumgarder and Richards claim that what has been defined as the third wave of feminism is a 'media-savvy, culturally driven generation' (2000: 77), capturing the supposed knowingness and awareness of young feminists today. It also posits feminist activism as a question of generations and implies that feminist commonality is primarily shared between contemporaries and is a product of the time you grew up in. In this formulation, feminism is something to be discovered; it cannot be passed down by others. We would agree that this sense of ownership and self-identification with feminism is an important one, and equally that this excitement is crucial to feminist activism and to mobilising young women. Moreover, feminism has to engage with social change for there are different challenges facing feminism today and different possibilities for a new generation. A generational binary also distances not only time-scales but also women's experiences, by suggesting that young is now and old was then, *passé* and something to be rejected. The challenge that we have taken up in this book is how to hold on to this sense of excitement, social change, the articulation of new ideas and activism, yet at the same time acknowledge areas of continuity with what has gone before. Gender inequalities still persist in terms of unequal pay, childcare responsibilities and the abuse of women's bodies, violence directed against women because they are women as well as for racialised and ethnicised motives, and there is persistent misogynistic representation. Beauty pageants are still held, although now sometimes framed by irony; yet ironic misogyny is still misogyny. In order to understand and address these persisting concerns, we have argued that it is important to establish connections and continuities in feminist thought. Indeed, many of the possibilities that women face today were opened up by the campaigns of the second-wave feminists.

One of the biggest challenges that feminism faces today is encapsulated in Baumgardner and Richard's description of their generation as 'savvy'. This highlights an area of knowingness they suggest their generation possesses, the implication being that the older generation do not have the same knowledge. This is part of a wider concern within academia and also within what has been termed post-feminism and wider media representations and contemporary culture. Within academic circles there is an implicit assumption in much writing that the second wave of feminism was important in its day; but when seen through the lens of postmodernism and poststructuralism, it appears to many as naïve. This is seen in particular through the establishment of poststructuralism as a widely adopted theoretical approach in feminist thinking, which presents many important critiques and challenges, yet in doing so has set in motion the dismantling of the category woman. In such a climate, it is as if using the word woman suggests a naivety, as shown in the example that we gave in our introduction when I-Sophie stated she was doing research into women. There is a reluctance to use the term, out of a sense that it is irrelevant or not interesting, yet, like the crowd watching the emperor in his new clothes, there is also a fear of looking stupid. Indeed, perhaps what is most problematic about poststructuralist feminism is that it has become its own dogma. What was once incredibly radical with the publication of Butler's *Gender Trouble* (1990), which challenged binaries and existing orthodoxies, now runs the risk of becoming its own orthodoxy. In such a climate, perhaps rather than the word woman being seen as naïve, according to how it is used, this in fact constitutes a new form of radicalism, in academic circles certainly, where putting woman in scare quotes seems to have become the current orthodoxy.

This same assumed sense of knowingness is not just a concern for the academy as it mitigates against both academic work which engages with the concerns of everyday life, and also as a position of knowingness, one that is adopted, albeit in a different stance, within forms of popular culture. One protective strategy against accusations of lack of knowing that pervades popular culture, and even the academy on occasion, is irony. This is in keeping with wider discussions of postmodernism, where irony is seen to be a key feature of the adoption of images of the past. For example, adopting some of the imagery or clothing of a traditional 1950s housewife is not seen as re-enacting this, but rather assumes that the wearer is aware of the connotations and is subverting and challenging them by wearing the garments ironically. A reading of the parodic performativity of drag may have set in train less subversive outcomes than queer theory might have hoped. Irony and masquerade might be constitutive of a new silencing and marginalisation of the women's voices. Thus, rather than simply break with the past, the past is seen as something to play with, a new form of masquerade. These aspects of subversion may have been radical when they were first adopted; however, such practices are so widespread, they have in most instances been emptied of meaning and critique. This is particularly pertinent in a climate where popular culture attempts to sell images back to young women as liberation, as with the Spice Girls and girl power, or groups such as the Pussycat Dolls, who started as a burlesque troupe and are supposedly liberated in their tendency to perform semi-naked as they writhe around the stage. This is part of the wider sense in which many of the ideas of feminism, such as equality or choice, have been co-opted by popular culture and more widely so that it appears to negate the need for feminism. When something is positioned as 'knowing', it makes it very difficult to present a challenge to it or offer a critique of it, when the implication is that as it is 'knowing' you are already aware of the potential critique. Furthermore, the claims for irony and the assumption that anything called irony is subversive have become so well established it is no longer critical and has lost connection to what it was once trying to make a stance against. It has become increasingly hard to differentiate between the subversion of popular culture and the way in which the rhetoric of liberation is adopted to try to sell things to young women. We argue that a critical stance is necessary.

Dialogue/dialectic: lost and found

Feminism not only needs to accommodate change, it also needs the investment and involvement of the young; however, the emphasis on youth should not be at the expense of eradicating the past or dismantling feminist politics as they have been reworked in the past. Without laying claim to the authenticity of sources or romanticising the past through myths of origin, we argue that feminist ideas at different moments are constitutive of the present, as part of the stratified deposits that make up the common sense of contemporary feminism with which it is in dialogue. Baumgardner and Richard's (2000) discussion of what characterises their generation is characteristic of much writing within what has been termed the third wave. In this book we have attempted to deal with the terrain between change and continuity, the past and the present, by establishing a cross-generational dialogue. In this conclusion, we reflect on the nature of this particular dialogue and dialectic to consider what this has highlighted. Most importantly, the emphasis is on how we can reclaim ideas that have been lost in the generational model of feminism and counter some recent trends towards the disarticulation of feminist politics as they have become not only more complex, but also more obtuse and less directly engaged with inequalities and differences. Our story is complex too, but through relational dialogic thinking we have sought to argue for a feminist politics of difference.

This book is based on a series of dialogues between the two of us, which began as a series of informal conversations then became a set of more focused verbal discussions that informed the decision to write the book. These conversations have been a continuing part of the process of writing, where the series of written exchanges and processes of revision and editing mean that writing itself is an interchange and a dialogue. The book itself is therefore a dialogue: between two individuals, I-Sophie and I-Kath, between different periods of feminism and everyday experiences, and between opposing or complementary feminist theorists. The aim was to see how constructing a series of dialogues, and different feminist ideas, could highlight shared points of agreement and challenge the ideas of historical boundaries by using our own historical situatedness.

This dialogue has also been informed by dialectical thinking, given that it is a dialogue between opposing and multifaceted views. Yet between these oppositions, tensions and ambiguities there are still common points which allow for the building of connections. The dialectic comes from differences between the two of us and also multiple feminist perspectives. The dialectic presented in this book does not fall directly within any one tradition of the dialectic – Hegelian, Socratic or Marxist among other possibilities – although it has strong resonance with the Bahktinian notion of a dialogic through which change takes place and meanings are reconfigured. We have held on to the idea of the dialectic throughout as it constructs a sense that feminist ideas can move forward and across intersecting fields in a process that challenges linearity so that we are also not stuck in an oppositional impasse. However, our book also marks an important departure from dialectical thinking which emphasises linear historical progression, albeit through oppositional syntheses. For us, moving forward in our argument also involves looking backwards; in the case of feminism, we argue that the feminist past is a resource in understanding the present and in the development of ideas. Using the past is not always regressive: instead, a synthesis can be created utilising a thesis and antithesis from different historical moments (e.g. between what has been termed 'third'- and 'second'-wave thinkers). Waves may be fluid but, through the process of writing this book, we have realised that, although the wave metaphor has some practical application, feminist thinking crosses temporal boundaries and the present has a tendency to reconstruct the past through a contemporary, distancing reification of what has gone before.

The way we have used the idea of the dialectic in many ways characterises the nature of the book: it is not informed by any specific school of thought, just as our dialectic itself is not formulated in any one tradition, except perhaps the feminist tradition of trans- and interdisciplinarity. As such, the range of perspectives may appear to some readers somewhat eclectic; we have drawn on phenomenology, psychoanalytic theory, critical theory, empirical research, sociology, cultural studies and material culture theories. We remain critical of aspects of all of these, yet see them as offering something useful. Drawing together these theories (whilst not always outlining, for example, psychoanalysis explicitly as a particular perspective) was a deliberate strategy as it allowed this dialectic and dialogue. We wanted to see what was relevant to feminism and women today in order to develop the ideas that are important for contemporary feminist theory to address. However, it is our argument, in the spirit of the dialogue, that there are commonalities and useful strands of connection between earlier moments in feminism and today. We could only start to illuminate these by challenging the boundaries of particular theoretical schools or disciplines.

The dialogue presented between the two of us is a particular one: that between a mother and daughter. We did not want to prioritise this relationship as individuals but to use it to think about questions of change. By writing as a mother and daughter we can redress the absence of positive images of the mother–daughter relationship, something Irigaray highlights. We speak differently and are differently situated, but we are also related, in a mother–daughter relationship, which we aim to make visible. Second, we could consider the crucial question of change and also of continuity. What emerged from the dialogues between us is that, although we are differently situated, there was often agreement about which arguments to make or what were the most important things to write about. We have, however, arrived at these points in different ways, and as such the arguments we have come to are through convergence;

we have travelled different routes. Although there are obvious similarities between us, especially of class and ethnicity, there are also points we have made separately when discussing our empirical research, as we both remain committed to what matters in ordinary life. No matter how much the category woman is disputed or disbanded in academic circles, it remains a very powerful means through which women live their lives, whether this is experienced as exclusion or inequality. The category woman is one of several other things to be addressed in this conclusion and is crucial to moving forward in the feminist present.

Apart from the similarities between us, there are also key differences: our lives, the world we grew up in and our generational position among others. Whilst there are, of course, individuals who are much more clearly differentiated, the similarities between us, and the differences, allowed us to address the issues of change and continuity as we look towards what the issues are that face feminism and feminism itself; our focus has been on generation. In this book we have challenged the idea that feminist history is either a teleological development where the past once built upon is no longer useful in the present, or that there has been a linear narrative of transformation so that there is a clear rupture between periods of feminism (seen in the wave metaphor). There are others who have highlighted the problem with the wave metaphor for feminism (Gillis and Munford, 2007) and the problems of the generational metaphor (Henry, 2004). We have built on these suggestions by working through our own situatedness and commonalities. Through this dialogue we aim to recover what has been lost, as the past is a resource in the present, as we reconfigure former ideas to make them relevant to today.

Finding and making links – feminist thinkers

A useful tool in exploring the possibilities of dialogue has been the discussions we have had about particular feminist thinkers, around whom we have both mobilised ideas. Many of these feminist thinkers do not belong in any kind of wave. One such writer is Luce Irigaray. I-Sophie was familiar with Irigaray and had read about her, but had not read any of her original work until late in 2008. On several occasions, when we had conversations about the book, I-Kath suggested that I read Irigaray – on one occasion as we were discussing the need for the category woman, and in turn a politics of difference, and the other in a discussion about who is silenced and who has the right to speak. After being loaned a copy of *I Love to You*, I-Sophie then went on to read several

Conclusion 167

of Irigaray's works. I was inspired by her writing; most striking of all to me was how even works that she wrote in the 1970s were so contemporary and so relevant, in particular in relationship to some of the issues discussed in chapter 5 about how young women feel about their bodies and being objectified. Much earlier than this, I-Kath had used Irigaray in her work on motherhood to provide a means of framing the discussion within a politics of difference, by using a psychoanalytic set of explanations critical of the Lacanian a space for a female imaginary and of redressing some of the circularity of a discursive critique was presented. Whilst a discourse analysis yielded insights into the processes through which new figures of motherhood emerge, they provide no explanation of why such identities should be taken up and what meanings they have in the experience of the embodied selves who appropriate them. Both of us have found her to be particularly useful in formulating why a politics of difference is important. Irigaray's writing does, of course, stretch over a long period of time, yet this does not explain how she is interesting or useful. Moreover, in line with the dialectic and bringing into dialogue, this was not only something that as writers we both engaged with; it was also something we could bring into dialogue with other feminist texts. For example, in considering her in relation to contemporary writers on pornification, Irigaray adds useful theoretical weight to writers such as Levy (2005).

Another writer who was useful in establishing this dialectic was Simone de Beauvoir. Perhaps symptomatic of the way the second wave has been characterised, I-Sophie had previously seen her as part of the feminist past, crucial for opening up debate, but one from which more recent texts had evolved and even taken as their pivotal moment and point of reference. I-Kath first read the *Second Sex* in the reference library at university in 1967. As the book was restricted, perhaps because it was considered too subversive and could not be taken out by an undergraduate, it may have seemed even more exciting. (This was a time when there was still the notion that women needed to be protected. The swinging sixties were not all licence.) At a time when studying politics and philosophy meant studying men's lives and thoughts, in texts mostly written by men, it was a revelation that women could be the subject of serious critical analysis. Sartre's existentialism was troubling, misogynistic and in the longer philosophical texts quite boring, but de Beauvoir's was gripping. We have come a long way, but such feminist thought put the politics of difference into ways of thinking and being in the world.

I-Sophie had always felt a certain frustration about the disconnect between some poststructuralist writing and the relations this had with everyday experiences. In particular, this often crystallised over the use of the word woman. Having been pointed to Toril Moi by I-Kath, this was a route through which I was able to discover de Beauvoir (in turn going on to read the original). Moi played a pivotal role in making de Beauvoir relevant to today. In many ways this gave voice to many of the concerns that I-Sophie had had, and discussions we both had around the both writers helped to navigate our own arguments.

Another such instance of these dialectics and dialogues is Betty Friedan: her writing on the problem with no name was something that I-Sophie was guilty, once again, of seeing as part of a feminist past. However, on reading it, was inspired to think about how relevant this was to young women I taught today, that their verbal accounts claiming they are liberated cannot help but leave them with feelings of dissatisfaction. In conversation with I-Kath, she commented how similar in its application this in fact was to Cixous (and also Irigaray) in terms of the feelings of dissatisfaction and silence. Writers such as Irigaray and Cixous are rarely considered in the same vein as Friedan – as one is psychoanalytical and the other seen as empirical, one a French feminist the other American. Whilst it is always important to consider a writer in context, it is equally important not to be bound by dualities of discipline or academic traditions. There are, of course, key differences between the writers, but they can usefully be placed in a dialogue together in order to understand the issues facing women today. In this book we have used them together to help explicate the key theme of silence and absence.

Remaking what is lost

These key thinkers were the pivotal ones we used to create the dialogue between ourselves and also to place texts in dialogue with each other in order to reclaim what has been relegated to a less knowing feminist past. Here we outline the key questions and debates that we wish to highlight as being central to why feminism matters in the twenty-first century. These issues are: the feminist polemic and writing with a political agenda; an understanding of patriarchy; repoliticising the personal; and bringing back a politics of difference, through an understanding of both woman and embodiment. In each area there are key thinkers who are engaging with these issues, and as such we are not suggesting that we are alone in making these claims. Yet we wish to bring all these key themes together, with a particular focus: seeing how ideas and theories from previous feminist moments can be brought together with more recent ones in order to establish a contemporary feminism that draws on a feminist past.

First, one of the concerns that we have had throughout this book is for a feminism that is theoretically and academically rigorous, yet does not create and reinforce the division between academia and lived experience. Much is made of the perceived divide between the two in many of the third-wave writers, as academic writing is seen as overly academic and exclusionary. Whilst we would not agree with this as there are many writers who write in an accessible manner, it is a concern of ours that the recent turn in academic feminism is characterised by opacity of language. There are examples of current writers who not only write lucidly but introduce a strong polemic (e.g. Ariel Levy and Angela McRobbie). We wish to suggest that the polemic is an important part of many feminist projects and in particular for us as we have a strong political aim. If feminism is to address key areas of inequalities in the world, it needs to critique and challenge mainstream ideas. This equally accords with a rejection of current academic fashions and attempts to engage with the issues that really matter. One of the problems with the multiplicities of becoming, for example, which Braidotti argues are among the most useful and affirmative elements in Deleuzian thinking, is the claim that it is animals and women who are in a state of becoming.

Second, we wish to reintroduce and reconsider the question of power in feminist analyses. In earlier feminist writing there was a strong tradition of understanding how wider power structures operate, whether from a materialist or psychoanalytical framework. In many works on contemporary feminism an understanding of power is not foregrounded. One such example is McRobbie's recent book on the state of contemporary feminism, in which she presents a strong polemic and raises many important issues about the ways in which aspects and the language of feminism have been co-opted in a neoliberal state in order that feminism is not seen as necessary. We would argue that as a result of many of the features that McRobbie highlights a stronger understanding of patriarchy is needed than she herself offers. One of the ways in which feminism is, in McRobbie's sense, dismantled, is through the use of terms such as empowerment, which have come through the young women's voices very strongly. When the word empowerment is used to justify individuals' choices, it does not acknowledge the wider power structures that operate (indeed these are obfuscated and made unclear). In many third-wave texts, and in more popular feminism, an emphasis on inequality and power structures is seen as old-fashioned and irrelevant (as part of the construction of the second wave as 'boring'). Indeed, much of the emphasis in writings on the third wave (and this is mirrored in the adoption of the post-feminist in popular culture) is on being sexy and pleasure-seeking. The materialities of patriarchy and inequality may not be sexy, but they are operating in pernicious ways and feminism needs to get to grips with these. One route which we have suggested in our approach is a re-versioned standpoint epistemology which focuses on the specificities of gendered situations. Whereas standpoint theory initially put women on the agenda, sometimes at the expense of other aspects of inequality, postmodernism seems to have removed women from all agendas. We suggest a review of social worlds through the lens of gendered inequalities and to seek a source of the power through which knowledge is produced. This is not a return to oversimplification but a focus on situation and situatedness. Butler's hopes that destabilising the category woman would open up a more inclusive politics have not been fully realised. Feminists have turned to more materialist approaches in order to reinstate the body and difference, but many of these theoretical frameworks are still problematic in their insistence, for example, in Deleuzian theories of becoming that it is women who are 'becoming women' and it is possible for men to be. Braidotti has turned to Irigaray to insert a politics of difference into Deleuzian theories of becoming, which raises question about the limitations of Deleuze's theoretical position, whatever its strengths, in explaining change. The turn to materialities has, in some instances, involved a somewhat dematerialised set of explanations, rather like some theories of the body have seemed very disembodied. Our suggestion is that a politics of difference has to accommodate situation and situatedness and be attentive to the sources as well as the circulation of power. The theories of postmodernism may conceal the stories of those about whom the stories are told (Howson, 2005) and deconstruction obscures the sources of power.

Third, we have addressed the slogan 'the personal is political'. This has become a key feminist slogan, from the 1970s through to the current day. It was crucial in early feminist writings in order to show the ways in which patriarchy operated in everyday life, and also for women to recognise the emphases of feminism as their own struggles. However, what was once significant, liberatory and a key tool for mobilisation has lost its way. The current emphasis is on an in-depth discussion of personal issues, and often sexual desires and pleasure. Yet what is lacking is the political critique and discussion of this. This can only be allowed by an understanding of patriarchy. In part this is a symptom of the wider factors in popular culture, where there is an emphasis on the confessional, where what would have once been considered to be the private is now expected of public figures. In such a context the personal is no longer political, but a source of voyeurism. We are arguing not for the abolition of the personal, but instead that it needs re-politicising. There is much to be learnt from the earlier politicisations of the personal in the 1970s.

Finally, a core issue that has run throughout the book is the need for a politics of difference. We have explored this by looking at bodies and have attempted to navigate the difficult terrain between essentialism and social constructionism. We have argued that bodies matter, and when we consider de Beauvoir's theory of the body as situation, it is necessary to talk about women. The category woman still matters on an everyday level, as women live their lives as women, they experience things as women, and they are excluded and experience inequality often as women. We therefore cannot simply deconstruct the category or place it within the reassurance of scare quotes, it matters to contemporary feminism too much and any sense of feminism as a political project. We are not being reductionist in focusing solely on, for example, women's childrearing capacity. Instead, according to how a woman is socialised and her subsequent interaction in the world, experience is constituted through an interaction between the body, the world and experience. As such, the body is a situation and placed in various situations. Women are not all the same, yet there are enough important common grounds to use the category woman. Oppression and marginalisation take diverse forms and are experienced in different ways, for example through racism and ethnicisation, sexuality, disability and generation. Women do not share experience in any kind of essentialist way but nonetheless experience is gendered. Women's knowledge has been subordinated to men's in ways which render the category woman a meaningful position from which to speak and to effect change. We have also argued that feminist theories generate new ideas through which social relations can be understood and do not have to rely on the work of the founding fathers of social philosophy. Post-feminism may have been accused of being complicit with malestream thought and introducing a new silencing of women, but by reinstating a politics of difference, it is possible to reclaim some of the critical edge of earlier feminist ideas, without losing the responsiveness and dynamism of new articulations of feminism.

The body as a subject is in vogue, and we are not alone in suggesting that bodies matter; however, focusing throughout on bodies, embodiment and also disembodiment has proved a useful route into the core ideas this book presents. Bodies are material and their effects are experienced materially, as even images of the body which abound in the contemporary world are implicated in women's embodiment. This connection between images of the bodies of others and how women live their bodies on an everyday level can, we have argued, paradoxically lead to a lack of connection between women and their own bodies. Pornification encourages women to see their body as an image, at a distance, as women do not know their own bodies. *Our Bodies Ourselves* is needed as much today as it was when it was first written. There is a clear analogy between this example and the supposedly liberating effects of the web, where the body is technically not present (although, as we have suggested, this links in important and powerful ways to the everyday material world). Liberation is not just about being separated from the body, it is also about being reconnected.

We have addressed these four themes throughout the book through a range of aspects of contemporary life: the internet, technologies, motherhood, clothed bodies, neoliberal regimes of governance, the interrelationship between representation and materialities among many others. These are issues that we think are important to feminist attempts to engage with life in the twenty-first century.

Conclusion

We are not suggesting that we are the first to try to reinvigorate the ideas of the past; we draw on important precedents. Our aim has been to challenge the boundaries set by generational models of feminism and to combine feminist projects through a particular type of dialogue. We have used our own cross-generational dialogue to set up a dialogue between and among feminist texts that perhaps would not have been understood together. We have looked at how the past can be reconfigured in a positive feminism that engages with specific concerns of the twenty-first century. We have aimed to challenge binary oppositions in our dialogue; between theory and practice, academic and activist or popular culture, between essentialism and social constructionism, and between the second and third waves of feminism within an analysis that does not separate out materialities and representations and symbolic systems. This book offers a theoretical approach that we have outlined in the conclusion, yet, more than anything, it is about opening more possibilities for ways of thinking and future conversations. Our agenda is also to give rise to future conversations and dialogues and we hope that this is the first dialogue amongst many.

Let the conversations begin.

Appendix

This appendix outlines the process of obtaining the comments and quotations from young women that are interspersed throughout this book. When we initially conceived the ideas for this book, there was no explicit plan to interview young women. However, as we discussed how we would write the book and what it would include, we realised that this was an important component of understanding feminism for the twenty-first century. Through the routine course of teaching, in discussions in seminars, a number of comments were made, which speak to the concerns of this book.

The students were all taking degree progammes at a college of fashion and design and studying a range of fashion courses, from design to promotion. The majority of the 100 students included were aged between 18 and 22 (a tiny minority were mature students). A wide range of ethnicities were included in this group, as is at the college that represents the new diasporic student communities that attend HE in London, and in all major centres in the UK.

Over the course of a year, I-Sophie set about asking particular questions in seminars (What is feminism? What does it mean to you?) and discussing issues that arose organically from their concerns. The data that have been accrued are not systematic in methodology; our concern is to get a sense of what matters to young women who do not define themselves as feminists. This material does not constitute an ethnography on which the book is based, but rather provides ethnographic material which we use to substantiate and problematise some of our thoughts and discussions about feminism in the twent- first century. While over 100 young women were included, as they were in groups and seminars, often not every single one of them spoke individually. At no point were the young women recorded, and the data are based on notes I-Sophie made routinely in the process of conducting a seminar. The process of gathering these young women's opinions was one that arose organically as we had not decided in advance that we could include such data in the book. It was more a question that we realised it was relevant to include this. We also utilised the data as I-Sophie realised how important the ideas of feminism were to students like these. The comments that are gathered arose from seminar discussions on topics such as femininity, or media representations, for example. The nature of these seminars is that they either are led by students or centre on questions posed by the tutor. If the seminar is effective a discussion among the students ensues in which the tutor offers questions or comments at particular points. Although not all seminars run as effectively as this in practice, there is little doubt that these students do have strong opinions, and on occasion do debate at best, or at the very least, discuss.

References

Adam, A. (1998) *Artificial Knowing: Gender and the Thinking Machine* (London: Routledge).
Adam, A. (2002) 'The ethical dimension of cyberfeminism', in M. Flanagan and A. Booth (eds) *Reload: Rethinking Women + Cyberculture* (Cambridge, MA: MIT Press), 158–74.
Akrich, M. and B. Pasveer (2004) 'Embodiment and disembodiment in childbirth narratives', *Body and Society*, 10 (92–3), pp. 63–84.
Alaimo, S. and S. Hekman (2008) (eds.) *Material Feminisms* (Bloomington and Indianapolis, IN: Indiana University Press).
Alexa (online) 2009 www.alexa.com/data/details/traffic_details/feministing.com/. Accessed 1 March 2009.
Althusser, L. (1971) *Lenin and Philosophy and Other Essays* (London, New Left Books).
American Society for Aesthetic Plastic Surgery (2008) http://www.surgery.org/. Accessed 20 March 2009.
Angryblackbitch (online) 2009. http://angryblackbitch.blogspot.com/. Accessed 25 March 2009.
Anthias, F. and N. Yuval Davis (1989) 'Contextualizing feminism: gender, ethnic and class divisions', *Feminist Review*, 15, pp. 103–16.
Arnot, M. (1986) 'State education policy and girls' educational experiences', in V. Beechey and E. Whitelegg (eds.) *Women in Britain Today* (Milton Keynes: Open University Press), pp. 132–72.
Arnot, M., M. David and G. Weiner (1999) *Closing the Gender Gap* (Polity Press. Cambridge).
Balsamo, A. (1997) *Technologies of the Gendered Body* (Durham, NC and London: Duke University Press).
Barrett, M. (1992) *The Politics of Truth: from Marx to Foucault* (Cambridge: Polity Press).
Barrett, M. and A. Phillips (1992) *Destabilizing Theory: Contemporary Feminist Debates* (Stanford, CA: Stanford University Press).
Barton, L. http://www.guardian.co.uk/lifeandstyle/2009/mar/04/grrrl-power-music. Accessed 12 May 2009.
Battersby, C. (1998) *The Phenomenal Woman* (Cambridge: Polity Press/New York: Routledge).
Baumbardner, J. and A. Richards (2000) *Manifesta: Young Women, Feminism and the Future* (New York: Farrar, Straus & Giroux).
Beattie, G. (1997) *On the Ropes: Boxing as a Way of Life* (London: Indigo, Cassell).
Beechey V. (1979) 'On patriarchy', *Feminist Review*, No. 3, pp. 66–82.
Berger, J. (1972) *Ways of Seeing* (London: Penguin).
Bindel, J. (2004) 'It's more like a strip club than a restaurant'. Guardian online,; www.guardian.co.uk/lifeandstyle/2008/apr/11/women.business www.guardian.co.uk/lifeandstyle/2008/apr/11/women.business, 11 April 2008. Accessed 11 May 2009.

References

Birke, L. (1999) *Feminism and the Biological Body* (Edinburgh: Edinburgh University Press).
BitchPhD (online) (2009) http://bitchphd.blogspot.com/. Accessed 13 March 2009.
Bordo, S. (1989) 'The body and the reproduction of femininity: a feminist appropriation of Foucault', in S. Bordo and A. S. Jaggar (eds.) *Gender/Body/Knowledge* (New Brunswick, NJ: Rutgers University Press).
Bordo, S. (1993) *Unbearable Weight: Feminism, Western Culture and the Body* (Berkeley, CA: University of California Press).
Bordo, S. (1998) 'Bringing body to theory', in D. Whelton (ed.) *Body and Flesh: A Philosophical Reader* (Oxford: Blackwell).
Bordo, S. (2003) *Unbearable Weight: Feminism, Western Culture and the Body* (Berkeley, CA: University of California Press).
Bordo, S. (2008) Cassie's hair', in S. Alaimo and S.Hekman, *Material Feminisms* (Bloomington and Indianapolis, IN: Indiana University Press), pp. 400–24.
Boston Women's Health Collective (1969[1970]) *Our Bodies Ourselves*. British edition (Harmondsworth: Penguin).
Bourdieu, P. (1984) *Distinction: A Social Critique of the Judgement of Taste*, trans. R. Nice (Cambridge, MA: Harvard University Press).
Bourdieu, P. (1992) The Logic of Practice (Cambridge: Polity Press).
Brah, A. and A. Phoenix (2004) 'Ain't I a woman? Revisiting intersectionality', *Journal of International Women's Studies*, 53, pp. 73–86.
Braidotti, R. (1991) *Patterns of Dissonance: A Study of Women in Contemporary Philosophy* (Cambridge: Polity Press).
Braidotti, R. (1994) *Nomadic Subjects: Embodiment and Sexual Difference in Contemporary Feminist Theory* (New York: Columbia University Press).
Braidotti, R. (1996) 'Signs of wonder and traces of doubt: on teratology and embodied differences', in N. Lykke and R. Braidotti (eds.) *Between Monsters, Goddesses and Cyborgs* (London: Zed Books).
Braidotti, R. (2002) *Metamorphoses: Towards a Materialist Theory of Becoming* (Cambridge: Polity Press).
Brown, P. and L. J. Jordanova (1981) *Oppressive Dichotomies: the Nature Culture Debate* (London: Virago).
Brown, W. (2003) 'Neo-liberalism and the end of liberal democracy', *Theory and Event*, 7(1), pp. 4–25.
Bunting, M. (2009) http://www.guardian.co.uk/lifeandstyle/2009/jan/09/womenmaternitypaternityrights. Accessed 20 February 2009.
Butler, J. (1993) *Bodies That Matter: On the Discursive Limits of Sex* (New York: Routledge).
Butler, J. (1990) *Gender Trouble: Feminism and the Subversion of Identity* (New York: Routledge).
Butler, J. (1990a) 'Gender trouble, feminist theory, and psychoanalytic discourses', in L. Nicholson (ed.) *Feminism and Postmodernism* (London: Routledge), pp. 324–40.
Butler, J. (1992) 'Contingent foundations: feminism and the question of "postmodernism" ', in J. Butler and J. W. Scott (eds.) *Feminists Theorize the Political* (London: Routledge).
Butler, J. (1997) *Excitable Speech: A Politics of the Performative* (New York: Routledge).

Butler, J. (2000) *Antigone's Claim* (New York: Columbia University Press).
Butler, J. (2004) *Undoing Gender* (New York: Routledge).
Cameron, D. (1992) *Feminism and Linguistic Theory* (London: Macmillan).
Cameron, D. (ed.) (1998) *The Feminist Critique of Language: A Reader* (London: Routledge).
Cameron, D. (2006) *On Language and Sexual Politics* (London: Routledge).
Campbell, A. (2007) *The Blair Years: Extracts from the Alistair Campbell Diaries* (London: Random House).
Castells, M. (1996) *The Rise of the Network Society* (Oxford: Blackwell).
Cavallero, D. (2003) *French Feminist Theory* (London: Continuum).
Cerwonka, A. (2008) 'Travelling feminist thought: difference and transculturation in Central and Eastern European feminism', *Signs: A Journal of Women in Culture and Society*, 33(4), pp. 809–32.
Chakraborty, M. N. (2007) 'Wa(i)ving it all away: producing subject and knowledge in feminisms of colours', pp. 101–13, in S. Gillis, R. Howie and R. Munford (eds.) *Third Wave Feminism: A Critical Exploration*. Expanded second edition (Basingstoke: Palgrave Macmillan).
Cixous, H. ([1975] 1980) 'Sorties', in *La Jeune Née* (Paris: Union Générale d'Éditions), pp. 10–12, cited in E. Marks and I. Courtviron (eds.) (1980) *New French Feminisms: An Anthology* (Amherst, MA: University of Massachusetts Press).
Cixous, H. (1997) *Rootprints: Memory and Life Writing*, trans. M. Calle Gruber (London, Routledge, 1997).
Cixous, H. and C. Clement (1986) *The Newly Born Woman* (Minneapolis, MN: Minnesota University Press).
Coles, R. (2005) *Beyond Gated Politics: reflections for the Possibility of Democracy* (Minneapolis, MN: University of Minnesota Press).
Cooke, R. (2009) 'Should lap dancing be run out of town?' *The Observer*. 8 March.
Daly, M. (1979) *Gynecology: the Metaethics of Radical Feminism* (Boston, MA: Beacon Press).
Danowitz Sagaria, M. A. (ed.) (2007) *Women, Universities and Change. Gender Equality in the European Union and the United States* (Basingstoke: Palgrave Macmillan).
Davidoff, L. and C. Hall (1986) *Family Fortunes: Men and Women of the English Middle Class, 1780–1850* (London: Routledge).
Davis, K. (2007) *The Making of Our Bodies, Ourselves: How Feminism Travels across Borders* (Durham, NC: Duke University Press).
de Beauvoir, S. 1989 *The Second Sex*, trans. H. Parshley (New York: Vintage Books).
de Grazia, V. and E. Furlough (eds.) (1996) *The Sex of Things: Gender and Consumption in Historical Perspective* (London: University of California Press).
Deleuze, G. and F. A. Guttari (1987) *Thousand Plateaus: Capitalism and Schizophrenia* (Dublin: Athlone Press).
Delphy, C. (1996) 'Rethinking sex and gender', trans. D. Leonard, in L. Adkins and D. Leonard (eds.) *Sex in Question: French Materialist Feminism* (London: Taylor & Francis).
Denfeld, R. (1995) *The New Victorians: A Young Woman's Challenge to the Old Feminist Order* (New York: Warner Books).
Dent, G. (1995) 'Missionary position', in R. Walker (ed.) *To Be Real: Telling the Truth and Changing the Face of Feminism* (New York: Anchor), pp. 61–75.

Devine, F., M. Savage, R. Crompton and J. Scott (eds.) (2004) *Rethinking Class, Identities, Cultures and Lifestyles* (Basingstoke: Palgrave Macmillan).
Di Stefano, C. (1990) 'Dilemmas of difference: feminism, modernity and postmodernism', in L. J. Nicholson (ed.) *Feminism/Postmodernism* (London: Routledge).
Dicker, R. and A. Piepmeier (eds.) (2003) *Catching a Wave. Reclaiming Feminism of the 21st Century* (Boston, MA: Northeastern University Press).
Dinesen, I. (1975) *Last Tales* (New York: Vintage).
Diprose, R. (1994) *The Bodies of Women: Ethics, Embodiment and Sexual Difference* (London: Routledge).
Doane, M. A. (1990) 'Technophilia, technology, representation and the feminine', in M. Jacobus, E. Fox Keller and S. Shuttleworth (eds.) *Body/Politics: Women, Literature and the Discourse of Science* (London: Routledge, Chapman and Hall).
Donnison, J. (1985) *Midwives and Medical Men: a History of Interprofessional Rivalries and Women's Rights* (London: Heinemann).
Douglas, M. (1966) *Purity and Danger: An Analysis of the Concepts of Pollution and Taboo* (London: Routledge).
Duggan, L. (2003) *The Twilight of Equality? Neoliberalism, Cultural Politics, and the Attack on Democracy* (Boston, MA: Beacon Press).
Dworkin, A. (1981) *Pornography: Men Possessing Women* (London: Women's Press/New York: Perigree).
Dworkin, A. and C. MacKinnon (1988) *Pornography, Sexual Violence: Evidence of the Links* (London: Everywoman Publications).
Eagleton, T. (1990) *The Ideology of the Aesthetic* (Oxford: Blackwell).
Ensler, E. (2001) *The Vagina Monologues* (London: Virago).
Earle, S. and G. Letherby (2003) *Gender, Identity and Reproduction: Social Perspectives* (Basingstoke: Palgrave Macmillan).
Epstein, D., J. Elwood, V. Hey and J. Maw (eds.) (1998) *Failing Boys? Issues in Gender and Achievement* (Buckingham: Open University Press).
F Word (2009) http://www.thefword.org.uk/. Accessed 14 February 2009.
Faludi, S. (1991) *Backlash: The Undeclared War against Women* (London: Virago).
Fausto-Sterling, A. (1992) *Myths of Gender; Biological Theories about Women and Men*. Second edition (New York: Basic Books).
Fausto-Sterling, A. (2000) *Sexing the Body: Gender Politics in the Constructions of Sexuality* (New York: Basic Books).
Fausto-Sterling, A. (2005) 'Bare bones of sex: Part II', *Signs*, 30(2), pp. 1491–528.
Fausto-Sterling, A. (2006) 'Bare bones of sex: Part II, Race and Bones', *Social Studies of Science*, 38(5), pp. 657–94.
Felski, R. (1997) 'The doxa of difference', *Signs* 23(1), pp. 23–40.
Feministing (online), 2009 http://www.feministing.com/. Accessed 1 March 2009.
Ferguson, A. (1989) *Blood at the Roots: Motherhood, Sexuality and Male Dominance* (London: Pandora).
Findlen, B. (1995) 'Introduction', pp. xi–xvi in *Listen up: Voices from the Next Feminist Generation*, (Seattle, WA: Seal Press).
Firestone, S. (1970) *The Dialectic of Sex. The Case for Feminist Revolution* (London: Jonathan Cape).
Foucault, M. (1981) *The History of Sexuality*. Volume 1: *An Introduction* (Harmondsworth: Penguin).

Franklin, S. (1997) *Embodied Progress: A Cultural Account of Assisted Conception* (New York: Routledge).
Franklin, S. (2007) *Dolly Mixtures: The Remaking of Genealogy* (Durham, NC: Duke University Press).
Fraser, M. and Greco, M. (2005) (eds.) *The Body: A Reader* (London: Routledge).
Fraser. N. and S. L. Bartky (eds) (1992) *Revaluing French Feminism: Critical Essays on Difference, Agency and Culture* (Bloomington, IN: Indiana University Press).
Friedan, B. ([1963] 2001) *The Feminine Mystique* (New York: Norton).
Friedan, B. (1981) *The Second Stage* (New York: Summit Books).
Gangoli, G. (2006) 'Engendering genocide: gender conflict and violence', *Women's Studies International Forum*, 5(29), pp. 534–8.
Gangoli, G. (2007) *Indian Feminisms – Law, Patriarchies and Violence in India* (Farnham: Ashgate).
Gatens, M. (1991) *Feminism and Philosophy: Perspectives on Difference and Equality* (Cambridge: Polity Press).
Gatens, M. (1992) 'Powers, bodies and difference', in M. Barrett and A. Phillips (eds.) *Destabilising Theory: Contemporary feminist debates* (Cambridge: Cambridge University Press).
Gatens, M. (1996) *Imaginary Bodies: Ethics Power and Corporeality* (London: Routledge).
Geetanjali, G. (2006) 'Engendering genocide: gender, conflict and violence', *Women's Studies International Forum*, 5(29), pp. 534–8.
Geetanjali, G. (2007) *Indian Feminism: Patriarchies, Violence in India* (London: Ashgate).
Genz, S. (2006) 'Third way/ve: the politics of postfeminism', *Feminist Theory*, 7(3), pp. 333–53.
Giddens, A. (1990) *The Consequences of Modernity* (Cambridge: Cambridge Polity).
Giddens, A. (1998) *The Third Way: Renewal of Social Democracy* (Cambridge: Polity Press).
Giddens, A. (1999) *Runaway World* (London: Profile Books).
Gillis, S. and R. Munford (2004) 'Genealogies and generations: the politics and praxis of third wave feminism', *Women's History Review*, 13(2), pp. 165–78.
Gillis, S., R. Howie and R. Munford (eds.) (2007) *Third Wave Feminism: A Critical Exploration*. Expanded second edition (Basingstoke: Palgrave Macmillan).
Gledhill, C. (1984) 'Recent developments in feminist film criticism', in M. A. Doane, P. Mellencamp and J. Williams (eds.) *Re-Vision: Essays in Feminist Film Criticism* (Frederick, MD: University Publications of America in association with the American Film Institute).
Goldberg, T. and A. Quayson (eds.) (2002) *Relocating Postcolonialism* (Oxford: Blackwell).
Gorris, M. (1982) *A Question of Silence*, Quartet Films.
Gorton, K. (2007) '(Un)fashionable feminists: the media and Ally McBeal', pp. 212–23, in S. Gillis, G. Howie and R. Munford (eds.) *Third Wave Feminism: A Critical Exploration* (Basingstoke: Palgrave Macmillan).
Greene, G. and C. Kahn (eds.) (1985) *Making a Difference. Feminist Literary Criticism* (London: Routledge).
Greer, G. (1971) *The Female Eunuch* (London: MacGibbon & Kee).
Greer, G. (1985) *Sex and Destiny* (London: Picador).

180 References

Greer, G. (2003) 'This V-word is no victory for women', www.telegraph.co.uk, 5 March.
Griggers, C. (2005) *Becoming Woman* (Minneapolis, MN: University of Minnesota Press).
Grimshaw, J. (1986) *Feminist Philosophers: Women's Perspectives on Philosophical Traditions* (Brighton: Harvester Wheatsheaf).
Grosz, E. (1994) *Volatile Bodies: Towards a Corporeal Feminism* (Bloomington, IN: Indiana University Press).
Grosz, E. (1995) *Space, Time and Perversion. Essays on the Politics of Bodies* (New York: Routledge).
Grosz, E. (1999) *Becomings: Explorations in Time, Memory and Futures* (Ithaca. NY: York Cornell University Press).
Grosz, E. (2008) 'Darwin and feminism', in S. Alaimo and S. Hekman, *Material Feminisms* (Bloomington and Indianapolis, IN: Indiana University Press), pp. 23–51.
Gubar, S. (2007) *Rooms of Our Own* (Urbana, IL: University of Illinois Press).
Gurley Brown, H. (2003) *Sex and the Single Girl* (Fort Lee, NJ: Barricade Books).
Hall, S. (1982) 'The rediscovery of "ideology": return of the repressed in media studies', in M. B. Gurevitch, T. Curran and J. Woollacott (London: Methuen), pp. 56–90.
Hall, S. (1992) Introduction, in S. Hall and B. Gieben (eds) *Formations of Modernity* (Cambridge: Polity Press).
Haraway, D. (1985) 'A manifesto for cyborgs: science, technology and socialist feminism in the 1980s', *Socialist Review*, 80, pp. 65–107.
Haraway, D. (1988) 'The biopolitics of postmodern bodies: determinations of self in immune system discourse', *Differences: A Journal of Cultural Studies*, 1(1), pp. 3–44.
Haraway, D. (1989) 'The biopolitics of postmodern bodies: determination of self in the immune system discourse', *Differences: A Journal of fFeminist Cultural Studies*, 1, pp. 34–43.
Haraway, D. (1991) *Symians, Cyborgs and Women: the Re-invention of Nature* (London: Free Association Books).
Haraway, D. J. (1997) 'The virtual speculum in the new world order', *Feminist Review*, 55, Spring.
Harding, S. (1986) *The Science Question in Feminism* (Milton Keynes: Open University Press).
Harding, S. (ed.) (1987) *Feminism and Methodology: Social Science Issues* (Milton Keynes: Open University Press).
Harding, S. (1993) 'Rethinking feminist standpoint epistemologies; what is "strong-objectivity"?' in L. Alcoff and E. Potter (eds.) *Feminist Epistemologies* (London: Routledge).
Hargreaves, J., P. Vertinsky and I. McDonald (eds.) (2007) *Physical Culture: Power and the Body* (London: Taylor & Francis).
Harris, A. (2001) 'Not waving or drowning: young women, feminism, and the limits of the next wave debate', pp. 1–9, in *Outskirts, Feminisms along the Edge*, 8, http://www.chloe.uwa.edu.au/outskirts/archive/volume8/harris.
Hartman, H. (1981) The unhappy marriage of Marxism and feminism: towards a more progressive union', in L. Sargent (ed.) *Women and Revolution* (London: Pluto).

Heater, D. (1999) *What is Citizenship?* (Cambridge: Polity Press).
Heilbrun, C. (1989) *Writing a Woman's Life* (London: Women's Press).
Heilbrun, C. (1991a), 'Margaret Mead and the question of woman's biography', in *Hamlet's Mother and Other Women* (London: Women's Press).
Heilbrun, C. (1991b), *Hamlet's Mother and Other Women* (London: Women's Press).
Held, D., A. McGrew, D. Goldblatt and J. Perraton (1999) *Global Transformations: Politics, Economics and Culture* (Cambridge: Polity Press).
Henry, A. (2004) *Not My Mother's Sister: Generational Conflict and Third Wave Feminism* (Bloomington, IN: Indiana University Press).
Hernandez, D. and B. Rehman (eds.) (2002) *Colonize This! Young Women of Color on Today's Feminism* (New York: Seal Press).
Hester, M., L. Kelly and J. Radford (eds) (1996) *Women, Violence and Male Power* (Buckingham: Open University Press).
Heywood, L. (ed.) (2006) *The Women's Movement Today: An Encyclopaedia of Third-wave Feminism*. Volume 2: *Primary Documents* (London: Greenwood Press).
Heywood, L. and J. Drake (1997) 'Introduction', pp. 1–20, in L. Heywood and J. Drake (eds.) *Third Wave Agenda: Being Feminist, Doing Feminism* (Minneapolis, MN: University of Minnesota Press).
Holland, S. and F. Attwood (2009) 'Keeping fit in 6" heels: the mainstreaming of pole dancing classes', in F. Attwood, *Mainstreaming Sex: The Sexualization of Culture* (London. I. B. Tauris).
hooks, b. (1984) *Feminist Theory from Margins to Center* (Boston, MA: South End Press).
hooks, b. (1992) *Black Looks: Race and Representation* (Cambridge, MA: South End Press).
hooks, b. (2000) *Feminism is for Everybody: Passionate Politics* (London: Pluto Press).
hooks, b. (2003) *Teaching Community: A Pedagogy of Hope* (London: Routledge).
Howson, A. (2005) *Embodying Gender* (London: Sage).
Hurdis, R. (2002) 'Heartbroken: women of color, feminism and the third wave', pp. 279–92, in D. Hernandez and B. Rehman (eds.) *Colonize This: Young Women of Color on Today's Feminism* (New York: Seal Press).
Independent (2008) http://www.independent.co.uk/news/education/education-news/farewell-to-predictable-tiresome-and-dreary-womens-studies-799631.html. Accessed 28 July 2008.
Irigaray, L. [1977] (1985) *This Sex Which is Not One* (New York: Cornell University Press).
Irigaray, L. (1991) 'The bodily encounter with the mother', trans. David Macey, in M. Whitford (ed.) *The Irigaray Reader* (Oxford: Blackwell).
Irigaray, L. (1992) 'When our lips speak together', in M. Humm, *Feminisms: A Reader* (Hemel Hempstead: Harvester Wheatsheaf); first published as 'When our lips speak together', *Signs* 6(1), 1980.
Irigaray, L. [1983] (1999) *The Forgetting of Air* (Austin, TX: University of Texas Press).
Irigaray, L. [1990] (2007) *Je Tous Nous* (London: Routledge).
Irigaray, L. (1996) *I Love to You. Sketch of a Possible Felicity in History*, trans. Alison Martin (London: Routledge).
Jackson, S. and S. Scott (2001) *Gender: A Sociological Reader* (London: Routledge).
Janmohamed, S. Z. (2009a) http://www.spirit21.co.uk/

Janmohamed, S. Z. (2009b) *Love in a Headscarf* (London, Aurun Press).
Jhally, S. (1995) *Dreamworlds 2 Desire, Sex & Power in Music Video* (Northampton, MA: Media Education Foundation).
Jhally, S. (2007) *Dreamworlds 3 Desire, Sex & Power in Music Video* (Northampton, MA: Media Education Foundation).
Johnson, M. (2002) 'Jane Hocus, Jane Focus: an introduction', pp. 1–11, in M. Johnson (ed.) *Jane Sexes it up: True Confessions of Feminist Desire* (New York: Nation Books).
Jouve, N. W. (1991) *White Woman Speaks with Forked Tongue: Criticism as Autobiography* (London: Routledge).
Kaplan, E. A. (1992) *Motherhood and Representation: the Mother in Popular Culture and Melodrama* (London: Routledge).
Kappeler, S. (1986) *The Pornography of Representation* (Cambridge: Polity Press).
Kaw, E (1994) ' "Opening" faces: the politics of cosmetic surgery and Asian American women', pp. 241–65 in N. Sault (ed.) *Many Mirrors: Body Image and Social Relations* (New Brunswick, NJ: Rutgers University Press).
Kitch, S. (2000) *Higher Ground: From Utopianism to Realism in Feminist Thought and Theory* (Chicago: Chicago University Press).
Kitzinger, S. (1978) *Women as Mothers* (Glasgow: Fontana Collins).
Kitzinger, S. (1979) *The Experience of Childbirth* (Harmondsworth: Penguin).
Kofman, S. (1982) 'The economy of respect: Kant and respect for women', trans. N. Fisher, *Social Research*, 49(2), pp. 383–404.
Kristeva, J. (1977) *About Chinese Women*, trans. A. Barrows (London: Marion Boyars).
Kristeva, J. (1982) *Powers of Horror*, trans. Leon S. Roudiez (New York: Columbia University Press).
Kristeva, J. (1988) 'The speaking subject', pp. 210–21, in M. Blonsky (ed.) *On Signs* (Baltimore, MD: Johns Hopkins University Press).
Kristeva, J. (1996) 'Feminism and psychoanalysis', pp. 113–21 in R. Guberman, *Julia Kristeva Interviews* (New York: Columbia University Press).
Lacan, J. (1977) *Ecrits: A Selection* (London: Tavistock).
Lacqueur, T. (2000) 'Amor veneris, vel dulcedo appeletur', pp. 58–86 in L. Schiebinger (ed.) *Feminism and the Body* (Oxford: Oxford University Press).
Lakhani, N. (2008) 'Farewell to "predictable, tiresome and dreary" women's studies', www.independent.co.uk/news/education/education-news, 23 March. Accessed 25 March 2009.
Leadbeater, C. (1998) 'Welcome to the knowledge economy', in I. Hargreaves and I. Christie (eds.) *Tomorrow's Politics: The Third Way and Beyond* (London: Demos).
Lee, A. (2004) http://girlwithaonetrackmind.blogspot.com/
Letherby, G. and J. Marchbank (2007) *Introduction to Gender: Social Science Perspectives* (London: Pearson Education).
Levy, A. (2006) *Female Chauvinist Pigs: Women and the Rise of Raunch Culture* (New York: Free Press).
Lewis, J. (1992) *Women in Britain since 1945* (Oxford: Blackwell).
Lloyd, M. (2007) *Judith Butler* (Cambridge: Polity).
London Feminist Network (2009) http://www.ldnfeministnetwork.ik.com/home.ikml/. Accessed 5 January 2009.

Lorde, A. (1978) *Uses of the Erotic: The Erotic as Power* (Berkeley, CA: University of California, Out & Out Books).
Lorde, A. (1984) *Sister Outsider: Essays and Speeches* (Freedom, CA: Crossing Press),
Lykke, N. (1996) 'Between monsters, goddesses and cyborgs: feminist confrontations with science', in Nina Lykke and Rosi Braidotti (eds.) *Between Monsters, Goddesses and Cyborgs: Feminist Confrontations with Science Medicine and Cyberspace* (London: Zed Books).
MacCormack, C. and M. Strathern (1980) *Nature, Culture and Gender* (Cambridge: Cambridge University Press).
MacKinnon, C. (1994), *Only Words* (London: HarperCollins).
Maguire, A. (1985) 'Power: now you see it, now you don't', cited in L. Steiner-Scott (ed.) *Personally Speaking; Women's Thought on Women's Issues* (Dublin: Attic Press).
Mailer, N. (1975) *The Fight* (Harmondsworth: Penguin).
Margolis, Z. (2006) *Imagine*, BBC 1, 5 December.
Martin, E. (1989) *The Woman in the Body: A Cultural Analysis of Reproduction* (Milton Keynes: Open University Press).
Mauss, M. (1973) 'Techniques of the body', *Economy and Society*, 2(1), pp. 70–89.
McCracken, E. (1989) *Decoding Women's Magazines: From Mademoiselle to Ms* (Basingstoke: Macmillan).
McNay, L. (2000) *Gender and Agency* (Cambridge: Polity Press).
McRobbie, A. (2008) *The Aftermath of Feminism: Gender, Culture and Social Change* (London: Sage).
Merleau-Ponty, M. (1962) *Phenomenology of Perception* (New York: Routledge).
Mikhailova, A. (2006) 'By day she worked on Harry Potter. But by night... Revealed: identity of erotic diarist behind summer's hottest book', *Sunday Times*, 6 August.
Miller, D. (1987) *Material Culture and Mass Consumption* (Oxford: Basil Blackwell).
Minogue, S. (1990) *Problems for Feminist Criticism* (London: Routledge).
Mitchell, J. (1974) *Psychoanalysis and Feminism* (London, Pantheon Books).
Mitchell, J. (1985) *Sexuality. Jacques Lacan and the école freudienne* (New York: W. W. Norton).
Mitchell, J. and S. K. Mishra (2000) *Psychoanalysis and Feminism: A Radical Reassessment of Freudian Psychoanalysis* (London: Basic Books).
Moi, T. (2001) *What is a Woman: And Other Essays* (Oxford, Oxford University Press).
Morgan, D. (1992) *Discovering Men* (London: Routledge).
Morgan, J. (1999) *When Chickenheads Come Home to Roost: My Life as a Hip Hop Feminist* (New York: Simon & Schuster).
Morgan, J. ([1999] 2004) 'My life as hip-hop feminist', pp. 277–83, in M. Dyson, M. Foreman and M. Neal (eds.) *That's the Joint! The Hip-Hop Studies Reader* (New York: Routledge).
Morrison, T. (1989) 'Unspeakable things unspoken: the Afro-American presence in American literature', *The Michigan Quarterly Review*, 38(1), Winter.
Mulvey, L. (1975) 'Visual pleasure and narrative cinema', *Screen*, 16(3), pp. 6–18.
Mulvey, L. (1989) *Visual and Other Pleasures* (Bloomington, IN: Indiana University Press).

Nicholson, L. J. (1984) 'Feminist theory: the private and the public', in C. C. Gould (ed.) *Beyond Domination: New Perspectives on Women and Philosophy* (Lanham, MD: Rowman & Littlefield).
Nicholson, L. J. (1994) 'Interpreting gender', *Signs*, 20(1), pp. 79–103.
Nussbaum, A. (1999) http://www.akad.se/Nussbaum.pdf. Accessed 12 May 2009.
Oakley, A. (1979) *From Here to Maternity* (Harmondsworth: Penguin).
Oakley, A. (1980) *Women Confined: Towards a Sociology of Motherhood* (Oxford: Martin Robertson).
Oakley, A. (1984) *Taking it Like a Woman* (London: Jonathan Cape).
Oakley, A. (2007) *Fracture: Adventures of a Broken Body* (Bristol: Policy Press).
Oates, J. C. (1987) *On Boxing* (London: Bloomsbury).
Octuplets (2009) http://www.timesonline.co.uk/tol/life_and_style/health/article 5600866.ece/.
Paechter, C. (1998) *Educating the Other: Gender, Power and Schooling* (London: Falmer Press).
Pateman, C. (1988) *The Sexual Contract* (Cambridge: Polity Press).
Pateman, C. and E. Grosz (eds.) (1987) *Feminist Challenges: Social and Political Theory* (Boston, MA: Northeastern University Press).
Paul, P. (2005) *Pornified: How Pornography is Transforming Our Lives, Our Relationships, and Our Families* (New York: Times Books).
Penley, C. E., Lyon, L. Spigel and J. Bergstrom (eds) (1991) *Close Encounters: Film, Feminism and Science Fiction* (Minneapolis, MN: University of Minnesota Press).
Philips, A. (1987) *Divided Loyalties: Dilemmas of Sex and Class* (London: Virago).
Philips, A. (1992) 'Universal pretensions in political thought', in M. Barrett and A. Phillips (eds.) *Destabilizing Theory: Contemporary Feminist Debates* (Cambridge: Polity Press), pp. 10–30.
Plant, S. (1995) 'On the matrix: cyberfeminist simulations', R. Shields (ed.) *Cultures of the Internet: Vitrual Spaces, Real Histories, Living Bodies* (London: Sage).
Plant, S. (2000) 'Coming across the future', in D. Bell and B. M. Kennedy (eds) *The Cyber Cultures Reader* (London: Routledge), pp. 460–7.
Plaza, M. (1996) 'Our costs and their benefits', trans. D. Leonard, in L. Adkins and D. Leonard (eds.) *Sex in Question: French Materialist Feminism* (London: Taylor & Francis).
Poirier, A. (2009) www.guardian.co.uk/commentisfree/2009/jan/08/france-rachida-dati/. Accessed 30 January 2009.
Price, M. and J. Shildrick (1999) *Feminist Theory and the Body* (Edinburgh: Edinburgh University Press).
Radford, M., M. Friedberg and L. Harne (2000), *Women, Violence and Strategies for Action* (Milton Keynes: Open University Press).
Radford, J. and D. Russell (eds) (1992) *Femicide: The Politics of Woman Killing* (Buckingham: Open University Press).
Ramazanoğlu, C. (1989) *Feminism and the Contradictions of Oppression* (London: Routledge).
Ramazanoğlu, C. (1995) 'Back to basics: heterosexuality, biology and why men stay on top', in M. Maynard and J. Purvis (eds.) *Hetero/sexual Politics* (London: Taylor & Francis).
Ramazanoğlu, C. and J. Holland (2002) *Feminist Methodology Challenges and Choices* (London: Sage).

Rawls, J. (1972) *A Theory of Justice* (Cambridge, MA: Belknap Press of Harvard University Press).
Readings, B. (1996) *The University in Ruins* (Cambridge, MA: Harvard University Press).
Rees, T. (2002) 'The politics of "mainstreaming" ', in E. Breitenbach et al. (eds.) *The Changing Politics of Gender Equality in Britain* (Basingstoke, Palgrave).
Rich, A. (1977) *Of Woman Born. Motherhood as Experience and Institution* (London: Virago).
Richardson, D. and V. Robinson (2008) *Introducing Gender Studies* (Basingstoke: Palgrave Macmillan).
Riley, D. (1988) *Am I that Name? Feminism and the Category of Women in History* (London: Macmillan).
Riley D. (2005) *Impersonal Passion Language as Affect* (Durham, NC: Duke University Press).
Roiphe, K. (1993) *The Morning After: Sex, Fear and Feminism on Campus* (Boston, MA: Little, Brown).
Rose, N. ([1989] 1999) *Governing the Soul. The Shaping of the Private Self* (London: Free Association Books)
Rose, N. (1996) *Inventing Ourselves* (Cambridge: Cambridge University Press).
Rose, S. (1998) *Lifelines: Biology, Freedom, Determination* (Harmondsworth, Penguin).
Rowbotham, S. (1973) *Woman's Consciousness, Man's World* (Harmondsworth: Penguin).
Rowbotham, S. (1974) *Hidden from History: 300 years of Women's Oppression and the Fight against it* (London: Pluto Press).
Said, E. (1978) *Orientalism* (London: Routledge & Kegan Paul).
Sassatelli, R. (2007) *Consumer Culture. History, Theory and Politics* (London: Sage).
Schiebinger, L. (ed.) (2000) *Feminism and the Body* (Oxford: Oxford University Press).
Scott J. W. (1988) 'Deconstructing equality-versus difference: or, the uses of post-structuralist theory for feminism', *Feminist Studies*, 14(1), pp. 33–48.
Scott, J. W. (1998) *Gender and the Politics of History* (Columbia, Columbia University Press).
Searle, J. R. (1995) 'The mystery of consciousness: Part II', *The New York Review of Books*, 42(18), 16 November, pp. 4–61.
Segal, L. (1994) *Straight Sex: the Politics of Pleasure* (London: Virago).
Segal, L. (2007) *Making Trouble: Life and Politics* (London: Serpent's Tail Press).
Shapiro Sanders, L. (2007) 'Feminists love a utopia', collaboration, conflict and the futures of feminism', pp. 3–15. in S. Gillis, G. Howie and R. Munford (eds.) *Third Wave Feminism: A Critical Exploration* (Basingstoke: Palgrave Macmillan).
Sheffield Fems (online) (2009) http://sheffieldfems.wordpress.com/. Accessed 1 March 2009.
Shilling, C. (1993) *The Body and Social Theory* (London: Sage).
Siegal, D. (1997) 'Reading between the waves: feminist historiography in a "post-feminist" moment', pp. 55–77, in L. Heywood and J. Drake (eds.) *Third Wave Agenda: Being Feminist, Doing Feminism* (Minneapolis, MN: University of Minnesota Press).
Siegel, D. (2007) *Sisterhood Interrupted: From Radical Women to Girls Gone Wild* (Basingstoke: Palgrave Macmillan).

Skeggs, B. (1997) *Formations of Class and Gender: Becoming Respectable* (London: Sage).
Smith, D. E. (1997) 'Comment on Hekman's Truth and Method: Feminist Standpoint Theory Re-visited', *Signs*, 22(21), pp. 392-7.
Smith, D. E. (1998) *Writing the Social: Critique, Theory and Investigations* (Toronto: University of Toronto Press).
Sobchack, V. (2004) *Carnal Thoughts: Embodiment and Moving Image Culture* (Berkeley, CA: University of California Press).
Social Trends (2009) (London: HMSO).
Socolove, M. (2008) *Protecting Our Daughters against the Injury Epidemic in Women's Sports* (London: Simon & Schuster).
Spelman, E. V. (1982) 'Woman as body: ancient and contemporary views', *Feminist Studies*, 8(1), pp. 109-31.
Spivak, G. C. (1987) *In Other Worlds: Essays in Cultural Politics* (London: Methuen).
Spivak, G. C. (1998) 'Foucault and Najibullah', in K.L. Komar and R. Shideler (eds.) *Lyrical Symbols and Narrative Transformations. Essays in Honor of Ralph Freedman*, (Columbia, SC: Camden House), pp. 218-35.
Spivak, G. C. (2000) 'Thinking cultural questions in "pure" literary terms', in P. Gilroy, L. Grossberg and A. McRobbie (eds.) *Without Guarantees: In Honour of Stuart Hall* (London: Verso), pp. 335-58.
Springer, K. (2002) 'Third wave black feminism?' *Signs: A Journal of Women in Culture and Society*, 27(4), pp. 1059-82.
Stallabrass, J. (1995)' Empowering technology: the exploration of cyberspace', *New Left Review*, 211, pp. 3-32.
Stallybrass, P. and A. White (1986) *The Politics and Poetics of Transgression* (London: Methuen).
Stanley L. (ed.) (1990) *Feminist Praxis. Research Theory and Epistemology in Feminist Sociology* (London: Routledge).
Stanley L. (ed.) (1997) *Knowing Feminisms: On Academic Borders, Territories and Tribes* (London: Sage).
Stanley, L. and S. Wise (1993) *Breaking Out Again: Feminist Ontology and Epistemology* (London: Routledge).
Stanworth, M. (1987) *Reproductive Technologies: Gender, Motherhood and Medicine* (Cambridge: Polity Press).
Steinberg, D. L. (1997) *Bodies in Glass* (Manchester: Manchester University Press).
Stone, A. R. (1991) 'Will the real body stand up?' in M. Benedikt (ed.) *Cyberspace: First Steps* (Cambridge, MA and London: MIT Press).
Stone, A. (2007) 'On the genealogy of women: a defence of anti-essentialism', pp. 16-29, in S. Gillis, R. Howie and R. Munford (eds.) *Third Wave Feminism: A Critical Exploration.* Expanded second edition (Basingstoke: Palgrave Macmillan).
Storr, M. (2003) *Latex and Lingerie: Shopping for Pleasure at Ann Summers Parties* (Oxford: Berg).
Sugden, J. (1996) *Boxing and Society: An International Analysis* (Manchester: Manchester University Press).
Suleiman, S. R. (1986) *The Female Body in Western Culture Contemporary Perspectives* (Lafayette, LA: Holmes & Meier).
Tasker, Y. and D. Negra (eds.) (2007) *Interrogating Postfeminism: Gender and the Politics of Popular Culture* (Durham, NC: Duke University Press).

Taylor, C. (1992) *Multiculturalism and 'The Politics of Recognition'* (Princeton, NJ: Princeton University Press).
Thiele, B. ([1987] 1992) 'Vanishing acts in social and political thought: tricks of the trade', in L. McDowell and R. Pringle, *Defining Women. Social Institutions and Gender Divisions* (Cambridge: Polity), pp. 26–33.
Tseelon, E. (1995) *The Masque Of Femininity* (London: Sage).
Turner, B. (1984) *The Body and Society* (Oxford: Basil Blackwell).
Turner, B. (1992) *Regulating Bodies: Essays in Medical Sociology* (London: Routledge).
Tzintzun, C. (2002) 'Colonize this!', pp. 17–28, in D. Hernandez and B. Rehman (eds.) *Colonize This! Young Women of Color on Today's Feminism* (New York: Avalon).
USA today (online) (2008) http://www.usatoday.com/life/people/2008-03-06-kelly-rowland_N.htm/.
Wacjman, J. (1991) *Feminism Confronts Technology* (Cambridge: Polity Press)
Wacquant, L. (1995a) 'Pugs at work: bodily capital and bodily labour among professional boxers', *Body and Society*, 1(1), pp. 65–93.
Wacquant, L. (1995b) The pugilistic point of view: how boxers think about their trade', *Theory and Society*, 24(4), pp. 489–535.
Wacquant, L. (2001) 'Whores, slaves and stallions: languages of exploitation and accommodation among professional fighters', *Body and Society*, 7, pp. 181–94.
Wacquant, L. (2004) *Body and Soul. Notebooks of an Apprentice Boxer* (Oxford: Oxford University Press).
Wakeford, N. (1998) 'Gender and the landscapes of computing in an internet café', in M. Crang, P. Crang and J. May (eds) *Virtual Geographies: Bodies, Space and Relations* (London: Routledge).
Walby, S. (1990) *Theorizing Patriarchy* (Oxford: Basil Blackwell).
Walby, S. (2002) 'Feminism in a global age', *Economy and Society*, 31(4), pp. 533–57.
Walker, A. (1982) *The Colour Purple* (New York: Harcourt Brace Jovanovich).
Walker, R. (1992) 'Becoming the third wave', in *Ms Magazine*, 39, January/February.
Walker, R. (ed.) (1995) *To Be Real: Telling the Truth and Changing the Face of Feminism* (London: Anchor Books).
Webster, F. (2002) *Theories of the Information Society*. Second edition (London: Routledge).
Webster, W. (1992) 'Our life: working-class women's autobiography in Britain', in F. Bonner, L. Goodman, R. Allen, L. Janes and C. King (eds) *Knowing Women: Cultural Representations of Gender* (Cambridge: Polity Press), pp. 116–27.
Wells, S. (2008) Our Bodies Ourselves: reading the written body', *Signs: Journal of Women in Culture and Society*, 33(3).
Wheaton, B. (2004) *Understanding Lifestyle Sport: Consumption, Identity and Difference* (London: Routledge).
Whitford, M. (ed.) (1991) *The Irigaray Reader* (Oxford: Blackwell).
Wilson, E. (1985) *Adorned in Dreams* (London: Virago).
Winship, J. (1987) *Inside Women's Magazines* (London: Pandora).
Witz, A. (2000) 'Whose body matters? Feminism sociology and the corporeal turn in sociology and feminism', *Body and Society*, 6, pp. 1–24.

Wolf, N. (1991) *The Beauty Myth: How Images of Beauty are Used against Women* (London: Vintage/New York: William Morrow).

Wolf, N. (1993) *Fire with Fire: The New Female Power and How it Will Change the 21st Century* (London: Chatto and Windus/Random House).

Women's Studies (2008) 'Last women's studies course to end', http://www.bbc.co.uk/worldservice/learningenglish/newsenglish/witn/2008/03/080326_womens_studies.shtml/. Accessed 28 July 2008.

Woodward, K. (1997a) 'Concepts of identity and difference', in K. Woodward (ed.) *Identity and Difference* (London: Sage), pp. 6–62.

Woodward, K. (1997b) 'Motherhood: identities, meanings and myths', in K. Woodward (ed.) *Identity and Difference* (London: Sage), pp. 239–98.

Woodward, K. (2002) *Understanding Identity* (London: Arnold).

Woodward, K. (2003) 'Representations of motherhood', in S. Earle and G. Letherby (eds.) *Gender, Identity and Reproduction* (London: Palgrave), pp. 18–32.

Woodward, K. (2004) 'Rumbles in the jungle: boxing, racialization and the performance of masculinity', *Leisure Studies*, 23(1), pp. 1–13.

Woodward, K. (2008) 'Hanging out and hanging about: insider/outsider research in the sport of boxing', *Ethnography*, 9(4), pp. 536–60.

Woodward, K., D. Goldblatt and E. McFall (2004) 'Changing times, changing knowledge', in D. Goldblatt (ed.) *Knowledge and the Social Sciences: Theory, Method Practice* (London: Routledge), pp. 149–53.

Woodward, S. (2005) 'Looking good, feeling right: aesthetics of the self', in S. Kuechler and D. Miller (eds.) *Clothing as Material Culture* (Oxford: Berg), pp. 21–40.

Woodward, S. (2007) *Why Women Wear What They Wear* (London: Berg).

Woodward, S. (2008) 'Digital photography and research relationships: capturing the fashion moment', *Sociology*, 42(5), pp. 857–72.

Young, I. M. (1990) 'Throwing like a girl and other essays', in *Feminist Philosophy and Social Theory* (Bloomington, IN: University of Indiana Press).

Young, I. M. (2005) *Female Body Experiences. Throwing Like a Girl and other Essays on Feminist Philosophy and Social Theory* (Oxford: Oxford University Press).

Yuval Davis, N. (2003) 'Intersectionality and feminist politics', *European Journal of Women's Studies*, 13(3), pp. 193–209.

Index

abject/abjection 132
  Kristeva 133–4
academy 53
  academic feminism and everyday 3, 36–7, 140
  feminism 5
Alien/s 75

blogs 80–1
  Girl with a One Track Mind 80–1
body/bodies
  category woman 137–8
  cosmetic surgery 77–9
  cyber- 60
  disappearing 82
  dressed 136–7, 144
  embodied 49
  Kristeva 74
  language 67–8
  material 11, 171
  Our Bodies Ourselves 63
  projects 78
  reductionism 131, 141
  reproductive technologies 62, 71–3, 75–6
  self 63, 136
  situated 150–1, 160
  situations 11, 149–50
  social constructionism 64
  speaking 66–7
Brown, W. 101–2
Butler, J. 2, 64, 108, 138, 145
  bodies 64, 140–1, 151–3
  discursive 160
  drag 153
  feminism 154
  Gender Trouble 138–40
  sex/gender 155–7

choice 25–6, 129–32
  pornography 130
  power 117–19
  psy-discourse 118

Cixous, H. 43, 59
  power dualisms 90–1, 122
  spaces 122
clothing 37–8, 59, 66, 113–15, 136–7, 144–5, 148–9, 153–4
conversations 1, 5
  cross-generational 6, 172
  dialogues 1, 163–4, 168
  second- and third-wave feminism 6–8, 22
corporeal turn 42
  Howson 64, 65, 68
cosmetic surgery 77–9
  Haraway 74, 76–7
cultural change 82–4, 160–3, 166, 58–62
cyberspace 58–64

de Beauvoir, S. 140–1, 149–50, 154, 167
Deleuze, G. and Guttari, F. 142, 170
  luminosity 119
dialogue 1, 5–7, 37–57, 140, 163–8
  empirical and theoretical 54–5, 56
  Gubar 52–4
  liberation and constraint 84
  second- and third-wave 6–8
  Segal 51–2
différance, Derrida 86
difference 10, 25, 76, 85–110
  bodies 107–8
  equality 102–7
  politics of 9, 10, 89, 92, 167–8, 171–2
  problems 90
  sameness 86, 99
  sexed 85–9, 93, 124, 156
Dreamworlds 22–24, 125–6
Duggan, L. 96, 100

education 12–13, 15
  see also women's studies
Engels, F. 99

190 *Index*

equality 15
 of gender 106
 inequality 99
 see also equality and difference
equality and difference 10, 102–7
 Felski 107
 Scott 104
Enlightenment 101
 subject critiques 41–2
ethnocentrism 23–4, 41–2

Fausto-Sterling, A. 66, 71, 139
feminism
 essentialist vs. postmodernist 143–4
 generations 20–1
 irony 33
 knowledge 91
 label 21
 liberalism 97–8
 poststructuralism 50
 second-wave 43
 voice 26–7
 websites 30–1
 young women 12, 19–23, 30
feminist activism 29–32, 34, 158–9
 Butler 154
 magazines 54
 politics 54–6
 standpoint theory 6, 8, 170
 websites 30–1
Findlen, B. 27
Firestone, S. 60, 75
first-person pronoun 42–44, 56–7
 Sojourner Truth 44
Foucault, M. 134, 145, 153
 post-Foucauldian 112, 123
 power 117
Freidan B. 8
 Feminine Mystique 27
 problem with no name 27–8
 revisionism 17, 93

gaze 24, 112–14, 112, 151
gender mainstreaming 93–4
Genz, S. 95
 critique of unstable category woman 108
 Third way/Third wave 95–6

Greer, G.
 critique of *Vagina Monologues* 67–8
 Female Eunuch 23
 revisionism 93
Grosz, E. 40, 88, 105, 137
Gubar, S. 51–4

Harding, S. 6, 8, 48
Haraway, D. 44, 65, 76–7, 79, 142
 cyborgs 76–7, 79
 Hegel's dilemma 103
Henry, A. 49–50
heterosexuality 69
housewife
 image of 27–9
 women's magazines 28–9

inequality 18–19, 89–90
Internet 79–82
interpellation 3
Irigaray, L. 47, 72–3, 101, 111–12, 129, 143, 166–7
 difference 87–9
 essentialism 70
 imaginary 123–4
 Lacan critique 115
 language 115–17
 phallocentric sexual economy 129
 respect 123–4
 speaking through body 66–7

Kristeva, J. 133–4, 143
 maternal space 74

Lacan, J. 115, 116, 167
lack 11
lap dancing critiques 114, 130
 Levy 105–7
Levy, A. 19, 24, 81
 visibility 127–8
liberalism 97–102

Mackinnon, C. 98
malestream 4, 105
masculinity 39–40
 hegemonic 95
 material turn 141–2

McRobbie, A. 18, 28–9, 91–2, 119, 169
  disarticulation 91
  feminist politics 55, 169
  post-feminist masquerade 28
  young women 18
men
  boxing 145
  racialised 145
  in sport 144
Merleau-Ponty, M. 63, 146–7
methodologies
  feminist 43–5
  insider/outsider 37–40
  objectivity 41–2, 46
  research relationship 38
  situated researcher 37–40
  writing 45–7, 51–4
Mill, J. S. 98
Moi, T. 141, 150, 168
Morrison, T. 43–4
motherhood 36, 39, 51, 70–3, 92–3, 145–6
  absent presence 72
  bodies 145
  difference 92
  mothers and daughters 37, 70
  science fiction 73–5
Mulvey, L. 112, 151

neoliberalism 93–7, 101

patriarchy 9
  false masks 67
pedagogy 3–5, 12–16, 22
Paul, P. 124–5
  pornification 124, 128
personal is political 3, 44, 54, 119, 170–1
phenomenology 139–41, 146–52, 154, 158
  Bourdieu 63
  feminist 150–2
  Merleau-Ponty 146
Plant, S. 66, 79
popular culture 18–19, 102–3
pornification 124, 129–32
  lads' mags 124
postcolonialism 89

postfeminism 14, 20–1, 28, 129
  irony 28–9, 162–3
poststructuralism 64, 86, 119, 162, 167
  French 53
power 2, 15, 25–6, 112, 113–24, 169–70
  empowerment critique 113–14
  Marxist view 117, 119
  patriarchal 120–1
  sexualised 114–17

queer theory 89

race 53
  race equality 100
  Internet 58
Ramazanoğlu, C. 87
  feminist solidarity 48
  and Holland 45
Rawls, J. 102
Reclaim the Night 31
Rich, A. 70
Riotgrrrls 79–82

Said, E., Orientalism 20
second wave 6, 43, 48, 89
Segal, L. 26, 51–2, 54
sex/gender 143–4, 155–7
sexuality 69, 127–9
silence/invisibility 8, 26, 67–8, 70, 78–9, 111, 114, 120–1, 124–9
  Cavallero 116
  Deleuzian luminosity 119
  Question of Silence 126–7
Skeggs, B. 41
Spivak, G. C., strategic essentialism 48, 139
sport 39–40, 145, 159
Stanley, L. 38, 44, 45, 46, 142
Steinberg, D. L. 76

technoscience 10
  bodies 62–4
  promise of monsters 60
Thiele, B. 117
  and Lukes 117–18
Third Way 95–7
  Giddens 95

Index

third wave 5, 14, 109
difference 87
post-feminism 17
post-feminist problems 95
vs. second wave 14
twenty-first century 161

Vagina Monologues 67–70
violence against women 68, 100, 159

Walby, S. 119
Walker, R. 50–1
Wakeford, N. 50, 80
whiteness 23, 39, 41
Wolf, N. 25, 118
woman/women
  racialised 48
  rights 35
woman
  category 2–3, 7, 8, 9, 31–3, 35–74–5, 48, 53, 71, 85–7, 132–4, 138–41, 152–6, 171–2
  destabilised 9
  racialised 48, 149–152, 171
  reinstatement 92
  social constructionism 64–5, 141–2
women's magazines 20, 27–8, 54, 63
women's studies 3, 4, 52, 88
  demise of 13
  role of 16
Wollstonecraft, M. 97
writing
  academic 2–3
  dialogic 37
  vs. everyday 35–6, 41, 53–4, 169
writing
  I-Sophie, I-Kath 1, 7, 37–8, 53
  we 1–2, 48–51

Young, I. M. 150–1

Žižek, S. 52